The Complete
Vegetable
Cookbook

A Guide to Cooking
Vegetables in Over 300 Ways

Vasantha Moorthy

📖 UBSPD

UBS Publishers' Distributors Ltd.

New Delhi • Bombay • Bangalore • Madras •
Calcutta • Patna • Kanpur • London

UBS Publishers' Distributors Ltd.
5 Ansari Road, New Delhi-110 002
Bombay Bangalore Madras Calcutta Patna Kanpur London

First Published **1995**

Cover Design : UBS Art Studio

Lasertypeset in 12/14 pt. Times New Roman by
Typin, J-115, 10th Cross, L.N. Puram, Bangalore 560 021
Printed at Nutech Photolithographers, New Delhi-110 002

In loving memory of

Akka

my mother-in-law

Mother Nature, in her bounty, has stored enormous nutritive health in various parts of the vegetable kingdom **– seeds, roots, stems, leaves, flowers, fruits, nuts and seeds."**

– MRN

Foreword

THE urge to eat is a basic instinct of all living beings from time immemorial. Except Man, all living creatures eat a particular type of natural food for their survival and reproduction. With the advance of civilisation, Man experimented and innovated, producing over the centuries, different kinds and combinations of food.

The desire to cater to the pleasure of taste is strong in Man. Eating tasty food is one of the greatest pleasures of life. When this is combined with a natural desire for health and longevity, what emerges is a vast variety of healthy and tasty food.

"The Vegetable Cookbook", a sequel to her earlier book "The Vegetarian Menu Book" (UBSPD - 1993) by Vasantha Moorthy, is unique in its presentation, using a single leafy or non-leafy vegetable, for preparation of varied fare of many a mouth watering dish. Her keen interest in cooking and in the subject of the art and science of cooking are backed by years of study and practice in her kitchen. Her food specialities have delighted many invitees to her 'home' — all over India and abroad.

This book is a valuable addition to the number of cookery books already in circulation. Confined to vegetarian cooking, the large number of recipes in this book and her earlier one contribute greatly to the store of expertise in producing vegetarian dishes. She has also detailed the nutritional and medicinal properties of the vegetables and the ingredients used in cooking.

The discerning reader will find the dishes prepared, as per her recipes, both tasty and nourishing. I wish Vasantha Moorthy all success in her continuing endeavours. May God bless her for producing such eating delights.

Sir Oscar Prof. Dr. AMAN
Director: **Indo-American Hospital**, Mysore-Bangalore.

Acknowledgments

The inspiration for incorporating the nutritional and medicinal properties of the various vegetables, in what is mainly a cookbook, came by chance through Dr. Aman's monumental treatise "Medicinal Secrets of Your Food" Also, Dr. Aman readily agreed to write the foreword. I am greatly indebted to him and to his valuable research in this field.

I deem it a great honour that Mr. T. S. Satyan, the photo-journalist of international fame, spared his time to shoot these excellent photographs for this book. I am equally indebted to him.

Mr. S. V. Gopal of "Typin", Bangalore worked closely with me, for hours on end, both in my home and at his office. The 'print-out' is a testimony to his sense of dedication. I thank him profusely.

I thank my sisters Sabita, Prema and Gowra who assisted me in this project. My heartfelt thanks to my husband, M. R. N. Moorthy, for his contribution to the processing of this book.

A Word from the Author

THIS book is unique in its presentation of recipes of vegetables in their alphabetical order – A to Z (Amaranthus to Zucchini). Those of you who used my earlier book, *The Vegetarian Menu Book*, would, I hope have been pleased with the large number and variety of recipes contained there. I also hope that you, your family and your guests would have enjoyed the dishes you chose to cook and serve.

The diversity of the recipes dealing with some of the vegetables reflects the great diversity of our country, and perhaps in its own small way, serves to integrate it. You will be surprised to discover the large number of ways in which you can cook a vegetable. Some vegetables have over ten entries, and a few even twenty! When preparing an elaborate menu, you thus have a choice of different preparations of the same vegetable, or similar preparations of different vegetables.

In order to assist (and perhaps educate) the reader, the recipes mention the region to which they belong, and also the names by which they are known in that region. For example, *Keerai Kuzhambu* of Tamil Nadu (amaranthus gravy) is as tongue-teasing a delicacy as it is a tongue-twister. Wherever no specific region is mentioned against the recipe, it is a blend of different recipes, or recipes common to two or more regions, and is classified as South or North.

Each chapter begins with a short paragraph bringing out the general medicinal and food value of the vegetable concerned. Then the sundry recipes for that vegetable are listed. I have tried to provide a mix of traditional recipes from yesteryear and modern favourites. Each recipe has been tried, tested and appreciated by discerning tasters, and range from the simple but appetising, to the delectably exotic. It has been a formidable task to cover the entire gamut of vegetable cooking. Almost all the recipes cater to four persons except in the chapter on ''Vegetables'' (page 317); they are for 6-8 persons.

I urge you to go ahead and try them out for yourself, and am confident you will not be disappointed.

Vasantha Moorthy

Bangalore

A Word on Indian Vegetarian Food

A nation's cuisine is shaped by its history, climate, religion and many other factors. The flavours and textures that abound in Indian cooking have been enriched by the influence of foreigners who came in large numbers to India over the centuries.

Broadly categorising, Indian cooking falls into 20 major regions and if one were to take the border states where there is a blend of 2 or more regions, the variety is mind-boggling. Indian cuisine is as diverse at its peoples.

It has evolved over 5000 years and is perhaps the most balanced and varied of vegetarian cuisines in the world, with its distinctive flavours and character. It is the SPICES that have added variety to the Indian food. The right blend of spices with other ingredients is what makes Indian cooking different from any other cuisine in the world. Even in India, it is the spicing that determines the cooking of various regions. In the South, it is a blend of coriander, cumin, fenugreek, mustard and pepper as well as chilli and turmeric powders and coconut, providing the distinctive taste. In the North, it is the *garam masala* (a blend of cloves, cinnamon, cardamom and pepper) along with nuts and saffron. Besides, it is the addition of onion, ginger and garlic which add a distinctive flavour to their food. In the Eastern region, there is another blend of spices called "panchforon" (5 spices – aniseeds, nigella, fenugreek seeds, mustard seeds and cumin seeds) which is specific to these regions.

In the olden days, recipes were specific to one region, with conservative tastes and habits. Today, it is a happy blend of various cooking styles. Thus the contemporary Indian vegetarian cooking covered in this book is a blend of traditional recipes – a heritage of the past and an innovation of the present.

Vegetables & Their Values

VEGETABLES play an important part in our daily intake of food. They are a cheap source of vitamins, minerals, proteins, fats, carbohydrates and fibres. Vegetables are appetising and help in easy digestion.

Vegetables are of two types – green, leafy vegetables such as green leaves of plants and non-leafy vegetables. The latter is obtained from various parts of plants like stems, roots, flowers and fruits. Some of these are cooked, some are eaten raw. Both leafy and non-leafy vegetables contain **carbohydrates** which are superior to those present in pulses and nuts as they get easily assimilated in the system. **Carbohydrates** are essential as they supply the body with the necessary energy. **Proteins** in vegetables are as good as animal proteins. **Proteins** help in building and nourishing the body. **Vegetable fats** are unsaturated unlike animal fats. The latter build up cholesterol levels which cause heart problems. **Fats** are essential as they not only supply energy to the body but also protect delicate tissues from injury. Vegetables contain **minerals** which are highly soluble like calcium, phosphorous, iron, magnesium, copper and potassium. Minerals help absorption of vitamins, proteins, fats and carbohydrates present in food. They also help in the process of elimination of excess liquids and salts in the system.

Vitamins are accessory food factors and are essential for good health. They are found abundantly in a soluble form in various parts of plants. Vitamins are a **must** for the proper building and maintenance of the body. Lack of vitamins leads to several diseases. Vitamin A is found in the dark green leaves. Vitamin B in the yellow stem of plants, Vitamin C in the tender tips of leaves, Vitamin D is stored in leaves which are exposed to sun-rays. Folic acid is found in spinach and tomatoes.

Fibres are important in our diet as they help in elimination of waste matter. They prevent constipation. But a certain amount of caution is to be exercised in the consumption of leafy vegetables as excess consumption leads to formation of gas. Fibrous vegetables such as beet root, carrot, cabbage, cucumber, tomatoes, peas, beans, etc. should form a daily part of our diet.

Food Values and Their Sources

Constituents	Source
Carbohydrates	Dried fruits, Honey, Maize, Millets, Potatoes, Rice, Sago, Sugar, Sweet Potatoes, Tapioca, Wheat.
Fats	Butter, Cheese, Cream, Ghee, Nuts, Soyabeans, Oils, Dried fruits.
Calcium/Minerals	Cheese, Curds, Eggs, Milk, Nuts, Green Vegetables, Wood Apple.
Iron	Celery, Cucumber, Eggs, Lettuce, Oatmeal, Onions, Pulses, Spinach, Tomatoes.
Iodine	Common Salt, Salt water.
Phosphorus	Beans, Cheese, Dals, Eggs, Milk, Nuts.
Proteins	Amaranth Leaves, Beans, Cheese, Dals, Eggs, Fenugreek Leaves, Maize, Milk, Millets, Nuts, Oats, Peas, Wheat.

Vitamins

Constituents	Source
Vitamin A	Apricots (dried), Bitter Gourd, Cabbage, Carrots, Cheese, Oil, Eggs, Ghee, Green Leaves including Drumsticks, Green Peas, Lettuce, Mango (ripe), Milk, Papaya (ripe), Red Palm Oil, Spinach, Tomatoes and Mango.
Vitamin B	Cabbage, Cheese, Celery, Eggs, Grams, Lettuce, Maize, Meat, Milk, Nuts, Oatmeal, Pulses, Pumpkin, Ragi, Spinach, Tomatoes, Unpolished Rice, Whole Wheat, Yeast, Raisins, Apples, Red Plums, Dates, Pomegranate.
Vitamin C	Nellikai, Cabbage, Cashew Fruit, Citrus Fruits like Oranges, Lime, Grape Fruit, Drumsticks, Green Walnuts, Guavas, Onions, Papaya, Potatoes, Spinach, Sprouted Pulses, Strawberry, Tomatoes, Unboiled Milk.
Vitamin D	Butter, Ghee, Milk, Eggs.

– *Extract from **"Vegetable Delights"** by Malini Bisen*

Table of Contents

Amaranthus	...	*1*
Banana (Raw)	...	*7*
Beans	...	*17*
Beet root	...	*35*
Brinjal	...	*43*
Cabbage	...	*61*
Capsicum	...	*77*
Carrot	...	*89*
Cauliflower	...	*103*
Colocasia	...	*117*
Cucumber	...	*123*
Drumstick	...	*131*
Fenugreek Leaves	...	*137*
Garlic, Ginger & Green Chillies	...	*147*
Gourds	...	*157*
Greens	...	*191*
Herbs	...	*201*
Jack fruit	...	*209*
Knol-khol	...	*215*
Lady's Finger	...	*219*

Mango (Raw)	...	*225*
Onion	...	*231*
Peas	...	*245*
Pineapple	...	*255*
Potato	...	*259*
Radish	...	*279*
Spinach	...	*285*
Sweet Potato	...	*295*
Tomato	...	*299*
Vegetables	...	*317*
Yam	...	*341*
Zucchini	...	*347*
Glossary	...	*350*
Index	...	*356*

Amaranthus

This is a variety of greens, available in plenty all over India. There are two types – ordinary and spiked. Other varieties of greens are dealt with in different chapters – greens, herbs, spinach.

Nutrition value is high in amaranthus. They are rich in protein, calcium, minerals and have plenty of iron. More details of nutrition of amaranthus can be found under 'Greens'. Here are six ways of cooking amaranthus.

Preparations

1. **Keerai Kuzhambu** (Tamil Nadu)
2. **Keerai Kootu** (Tamil Nadu)
3. **Keerai Masiyal** (Tamil Nadu)
4. **Keerai Thoran** (Kerala)
5. **Keerai Pachadi** (Kerala)
6. **Chawlai ka sag** (Punjab)

Keerai Kuzhambu

(Amaranthus Gravy)

Ingredients

4 cups chopped amaranthus
1 large onion, chopped
½ tsp turmeric powder
Salt to taste

Seasoning

2 tbsp sesame seed oil
½ tsp mustard
1 tsp urad dal
2 sprigs curry leaves

Fry in 2 tsp oil and grind to paste

2 tbsp tuvar dal
1 tbsp coriander seeds
1 tsp cumin seeds
3-4 red chillies
3 tbsp coconut gratings

Method

1. Clean, wash and cook greens with turmeric powder and salt.
2. Heat oil, add seasonings and, when done, add onion and curry leaves; fry till onions are browned.
3. Add ground masala and some water if too thick. Simmer 1-2 min.; add cooked greens; simmer for 3-5 min. more or till gravy is well blended.

Serve hot with rice.

Keerai Kootu

(Amaranthus with Moong Dal)

Ingredients

3 cups chopped amaranthus
½ cup moong dal
½ tsp turmeric powder
Salt to taste

Seasoning

2 tsp oil
½ tsp mustard
1 tsp urad dal
1 sprig curry leaf

Grind to paste

3 tbsp coconut gratings
3 green chillies
1 tsp cumin seeds

Method

1. Cook dal with turmeric powder; set aside.
2. Cook greens separately, adding salt.
3. Mix together cooked dal, greens and ground masala, adding some water if too thick.
4. Season in oil the ingredients given, add to kootu mix.

Serve with rice or chapathis.

Note

This can be prepared with spinach also.

Keerai Masiyal
(Amaranthus Puree)

Ingredients

4 cups chopped amaranthus
2 sprigs curry leaves
A pinch of turmeric powder
Salt to taste
A few urad dal vadams
   (*vadis* – optional)

Seasoning
  2 tsp oil
  $\frac{1}{2}$ tsp mustard seeds
  1 tsp urad dal
  1 big pinch of asafoetida
  1-2 red chillies
    (broken into 2-3 pieces)

Method

1. Boil amaranthus with turmeric powder, salt and enough water so that when it is cooked, water gets fully absorbed.
2. Remove from fire and, while still hot, mash thoroughly with a wooden ladle to a very soft puree (alternatively, you could pass the cooked amaranthus through a liquidiser).
3. Season in oil the ingredients given, adding curry leaves when dal is browned; pour into mashed greens, mix thoroughly.
4. Fry in 1 tbsp oil separately the 'vadams' and add to 'masiyal' – gives additional nutrition.

Serve with 'puli kuzhambu' – refer to Cucumber, Page No. 129.

Keerai Thoran

(Amaranthus with Coconut)

Ingredients

4 cups chopped amaranthus
½ tbsp oil
A pinch of mustard
½ tsp urad dal
1 sprig curry leaf
Salt to taste

Grind to a very rough paste

3 tbsp grated coconut
1 tsp cumin seeds
3 green chillies
3 cloves garlic (optional)

Method

1. Boil amaranthus with some salt, set aside.

2. Heat oil, add mustard, dal and curry leaf; when done, add ground paste. Then fry for 2-3 min.

3. Add cooked amaranthus, simmer 1-2 min. till well blended, mixing thoroughly.

Serve with rice as a side dish.

Keerai Pachadi

(Amaranthus in Curds)

Ingredients

4 cups chopped amaranthus
1 medium chopped onion
3 green chillies
2 tbsp grated coconut
2-2½ cups curd
Salt to taste

Seasoning

1½ tbsp oil
½ tsp mustard
½ tsp cumin seeds
1 red chilly, broken
1 sprig curry leaf

Method

1. Cook amaranthus with 2 cups of water along with salt. When cooked, mash thoroughly with a wooden spatula; set aside.

2. Grind green chillies and coconut to a rough paste.

3. Heat oil, add seasonings in the order given and, when done, add onion, fry till browned.

4. Add ground paste, stir fry 1-2 min. Add mashed greens, cook till dry. Cool.
5. Beat curds smooth, add to greens, mix.

Serve with rice or chapathis.

Chawlai ka sag

Ingredients

3 cups chopped sag
$\frac{1}{2}$ tsp turmeric powder
$\frac{1}{2}$ tsp chilli powder
1 tsp cumin powder
Salt to taste

Mince fine
1 large onion
$\frac{1}{2}$ piece ginger
3 green chillies
1 large tomato
1 tbsp oil or ghee

Method

1. Heat oil, add minced onion, ginger and chillies. Fry till onions are browned. Add chopped tomatoes, continue to fry till they turn soft.
2. Add chopped sag along with turmeric powder, chilli powder and salt. Stir fry for 1-3 min.
3. When sag has cooked, add cumin powder, fry for 1 more min. Remove from fire.

Serve hot with chapathis.

Note

$\frac{1}{2}$ cup cooked moong dal can be added after the greens are cooked. This gives additional nutrition and taste.

Do's & Don'ts
in Cooking Vegetables

1. As far as possible, use fresh vegetables as most vegetables lose their food value on storage.

2. Before cooking, wash vegetables thoroughly in running water two or three times to remove any pesticides or insects.

3. Avoid peeling of vegetables as most vegetables, specially potatoes, have all their nutrients just below the skin; preferably cook them with their jackets on.

4. Do not cut vegetables too small as this causes a loss of nutrients, specially minerals and water soluble nutrients.

5. Do not leave vegetables in water for too long as the nutrients get drained away.

6. Cook with minimum water and *do not* discard water left over after cooking – use it in soups and gravies.

7. Avoid over-cooking of vegetables to prevent loss of nutrients. The best way to cook is steam cooking, pressure cooking or cooking with just enough water.

8. In cooking vegetables, avoid use of baking soda as this also causes loss of nutrients.

9. Try to mix a number of vegetables together in cooking – a combination of vegetables is a good source of nutrients.

10. Use vegetables in their raw form, like in salads and raithas, as then the vegetables will have their nutritional value in full. Also, use sprouts whenever possible, which again gives additonal nutrition.

Banana (Raw)

Grown in plenty all over India, specially in the southern states, banana is taken both as a vegetable as well as a fruit. Rich in carbohydrate and vitamins A and B. It also contains protein besides traces or iron and salt. Medicinal value is attributed to it as well. Taken as a fruit, it is good for prevention of constipation.

Banana (fruit) with milk, honey and dates every day is a good tonic, supplying energy and nourishment to the body. Both banana stem and flowers have very high medicinal properties and figure in home remedies.

A number of preparations are made using the raw banana, specially in the southern regions. The flower of the banana plant as well as its tender stem are also used in cooking.

Preparations

1. **Vazhai thandu Dry Curry/Thair Pachadi** (Tamil Nadu)
2. **Vazhaippu Paruppu Usli** (Tamil Nadu)
3. **Banana Flower Gravy** (Maharashtra)
4. **Vazhaikai Eriseri** (Kerala)
5. **Vazhaikai Kalan** (Kerala)
6. **Vazhaikai Podimas** (Tamil Nadu)
7. **Vazhaikai Roast** (Tamil Nadu)
8. **Vazhaikai Milaguttal** (Tamil Nadu-Kerala)
9. **Raw Banana Koftas in Gravy** (North India)
10. **Raw Banana Stuffed Parathas** (North India)

Vazhai thandu Dry Curry/Thair Pachadi

(Banana Stem Dry Curry and Raitha)

Ingredients

1 kg piece banana stem
2 green chillies, chopped
½ cup moong dal
½ tsp turmeric powder
A pinch of sugar
Juice of ½ lemon
1 tbsp coriander leaves

Seasoning

2 tbsp oil
½ tsp mustard seeds
1 tsp urad dal
1 red chilli, broken
A pinch of asafoetida
2 sprigs curry leaves
1 tbsp grated coconut

Method

1. Peel 2-3 layers of the stem, cut into thin circles. Remove as much of strands as possible and cut them into small pieces. Sprinkle lemon juice, leave aside. Boil dal with ¼ tsp turmeric powder and just enough water to make it soft, but not mushy.

2. Heat oil, add seasonings in the order given except coconut. When dal is golden brown, add chopped coriander leaves, curry leaves, stir fry. Add banana stem pieces, turmeric powder, fry for a min., add little water, salt. Cover and cook till tender. Do not add *too much* water.

3. When vegetable is done, add cooked moong dal, coconut gratings, chopped coriander leaves and sugar. Stir for 2-3 min., remove from fire.

Serve with rice and rasam.

Thair Pachadi (Raitha)

For this, omit dal, turmeric powder and lemon juice. Work **only step 2** and, when the banana stem is cooked, cool. Beat 1 cup curds, add to cooked stem, mix.

If the banana stem is very tender, it can be used raw – chop fine, add curds and seasonings.

Serve as an accompaniment.

Vazhaippu Paruppu Usli
(Banana Flower with Tuvar Dal)

Ingredients

1 medium banana flower
½ tsp turmeric powder
1 tbsp butter milk
A pinch of sugar

Seasoning

3-4 tbsp oil
½ tsp mustard seeds
1 tsp urad dal
1 red chilli, broken into two (optional)
2 sprigs curry leaves

Grind to a rough paste

1 cup tuvar dal
2 red chillies
2 green chillies
Small piece of asafoetida
Salt to taste

Method

1. Remove 2-3 layers of the banana flower, break the flowers from the stem, remove the hard pistil. Chop the flowers, sprinkle butter milk, set aside.

2. Add enough water, turmeric powder and salt; cook, sprinkling butter milk till flowers are tender.

3. Heat oil, add seasonings and when dal is golden brown, add curry leaves and the ground paste. Stir fry this for a while till dry.

4. Add cooked flowers, continue to fry till blended; remove from fire.

Serve with 'morkuzambu' (South Indian kadhi) or North Indian kadhi.

Banana Flower Gravy

Ingredients

1 banana flower
½ tsp turmeric powder
½-1 tsp chilli powder
¼ cup moong dal
2 tbsp oil
A large pinch of asafoetida
2 sprigs curry leaves
¼ cup curds

For Garnish

1 tbsp chopped coriander leaves
A pinch of garam masala

Grind to paste

2 medium onions
6 cloves garlic
1″ piece ginger
1 tsp poppy seeds
½ tsp cinnamon powder
1 tbsp chopped coriander leaves
1 tbsp chopped mint

Method

1. Prepare banana flowers as in previous recipe. Cook with ¼ tsp turmeric powder and just enough water.

2. Soak dal in a little water.

3. Heat oil, add asafoetida and curry leaves. Add ground paste, stir fry for 2-3 min., adding turmeric and chilli powders.

4. Strain water from dal, add to ground paste, stir for a while, cover and cook on low heat till done.

5. Add cooked banana flower; beat curds smooth, add to this. Mix thoroughly, cover and cook till well blended.

6. Garnish with the coriander leaves, sprinkle garam masala.

Serve hot with rotis.

Vazhaikai Eriseri
(Raw Banana Coconut Gravy)

Ingredients

2 raw bananas, medium
1½ tsp pepper, ground fine
8 tbsp grated coconut
1 tsp rice
¼ tsp turmeric powder
Salt to taste

Seasoning

2 tbsp coconut oil
1 tsp mustard seeds
2 sprigs curry leaves
2 tbsp coconut gratings

Method

1. Peel and cut raw bananas into 1″ by 1″ long pieces, add turmeric powder, pepper powder, 1 sprig curry leaf, salt and enough water; bring it to boil.

2. Grind coconut with rice to a fine paste. When bananas are sufficiently cooked add coconut paste, cook further for 2-3 min.

3. Heat oil, add mustard seeds and 1 sprig curry leaf and when done add coconut gratings and fry this on very low heat to a light brown colour.

4. Add this seasoning to cooked bananas, mix well, remove from fire. If gravy is too thick, add some water and mix.

Serve with rice.

Vazhaikai Kalan
(Raw Banana in Curds)

Ingredients

1 raw banana
1½ cups curds
3 green chillies
½ small coconut, grated (about cup)
¼ tsp turmeric powder
Salt to taste

Seasoning

2 tsp coconut oil
1 tsp mustard seeds
1 red chilli (broken into 2-3 pieces)
2 sprigs curry leaves

Method

1. Peel and cut bananas into finger length pieces. Add enough water, turmeric powder and salt, set to boil.
2. Grind coconut and chillies to paste. Churn curds, add coconut-chilli paste, mix thoroughly.
3. When bananas are cooked soft, add curds-coconut mixture, boil just once, remove from fire.
4. Season in oil the ingredients given, add to kalan.

Serve hot with rice and papadams.

Note

Both the above recipes can be prepared with yam (suran) also or a mixture of both the vegetables.

Vazhaikai Podimas
(Raw Banana Dry Curry)

Ingredients

2 raw bananas	**Seasoning**
4 green chillies	1½ tbsp oil
1 tbsp chopped coriander leaves	1 tsp mustard seeds
Juice of 1 lemon	1½ tsp urad dal
Salt to taste	1½ tsp chana dal
	2 sprigs curry leaves

Method

1. Boil bananas in their jackets, preferably in a pressure cooker. When cool, peel skin, grate the banana on a coarse grater. Cut chillies into 2-3 pieces each.
2. Heat oil add seasonings in the order given; when dals are golden brown add grated banana, green chillies, salt and coriander leaves. Fry 2 min., remove from fire. Sprinkle lemon juice, mix thoroughly.

Serve with rice and rasam.

Vazhaikai Roast

(Raw Banana Roast)

Ingredients

2 raw bananas
½ tsp turmeric powder
Salt to taste

Seasoning

3-4 tbsp oil
½ tsp mustard seeds
2 sprigs curry leaves

Fry in 2 tsp oil and powder roughly

1 tbsp urad dal
3 red chillies
A small piece of asafoetida

Method

1. Peel and cut bananas into thin rounds, cut these further into half, then again into half. You will get thin triangular slices. Keep these in water to which a pinch of turmeric powder has been added – this prevents discolouration.

2. Heat oil, season mustard and curry leaves, add banana slices (after pressing them between the palms of your hand to remove all water). Fry 2-3 min. adding turmeric powder, sprinkle some water. Cover and cook on low heat till done.

3. Remove cover, raise heat and fry slices crisp, adding some more oil if necessary. Add prepared powder, mix thoroughly, fry 1-2 min. more, remove from fire.

Serve with rice and sambar.

Vazaikai Milaguttal

(Raw Banana-Moong Dal Gravy with Pepper)

Ingredients

2 bananas
½ cup moong dal
½ tsp turmeric powder
2 sprigs curry leaves
Salt to taste

Grind to paste

4 tbsp coconut gratings
2 green chillies
1½ tsp cumin seeds
½-1 tsp pepper corns

13

Seasoning

   2 tsp til oil
   $\frac{1}{2}$ tsp mustard seeds
   1 tsp urad dal

Method

1. Peel and cut bananas into small cubes, add $\frac{1}{4}$ tsp turmeric powder, salt, curry leaves and enough water; cook, set aside.

2. Cook dal with $\frac{1}{4}$ tsp turmeric powder. When done add cooked banana, ground paste. Add some more water, if too thick. Simmer 2-3 min.

3. Season in oil the ingredients given, pour into kootu, mix well, remove from fire.

Serve hot with rice.

Raw Banana Koftas in Gravy

Ingredients

For Koftas

   2 raw bananas
   1 large potato
   1 onion, chopped
   2 tbsp chopped coriander leaves
   2 tbsp gram flour
   Salt to taste
   Oil for frying

Grind to paste

   1 medium onion
   1″ piece ginger
   3 green chillies

Powdered Masalas

   $\frac{1}{4}$ tsp turmeric powder
   $\frac{1}{2}$ tsp chilli powder
   $\frac{1}{2}$ tbsp coriander powder
   1 tsp cumin powder
   $\frac{1}{2}$ tsp garam masala

Method

1. Boil banana and potato in their jackets, peel and mash while still warm.

2. Heat 2 tbsp oil, add chopped onions, fry till browned. Add ground paste, continue to fry for some time, adding dry masalas.

3. Add mashed vegetables, salt and chopped coriander leaves. Mix thoroughly. Remove from fire, allow to cool.

4. Break·dough into lemon-sized balls, roll in gram flour, deep fry in hot oil, set aside.

14

Gravy for koftas

Ingredients

1 tbsp coriander powder
1 tsp cumin powder
$\frac{1}{2}$ tsp turmeric powder
$\frac{1}{2}$ tsp chilli powder
$\frac{1}{2}$-1 tbsp chopped coriander leaves
Salt to taste
1 tbsp garam masala

For garnish

$\frac{1}{2}$ cup cream (optional)
2 tbsp chopped coriander leaves

Grind to paste

1 medium onion
1″ piece ginger
5 cloves garlic

Seasoning

3 tbsp oil
3 green chillies, slit
1 onion, chopped

Method

1. After frying koftas, remove excess oil from the 'kadai', retaining about 3 tbsp. Heat this, add slit chillies and chopped onions, fry till onions are browned.

2. Add ground paste, fry; add powdered masalas, continue frying till oil surfaces.

3. Add 2-2$\frac{1}{2}$ cups water, salt and 1 tbsp chopped coriander leaves; allow the gravy to simmer on low heat. Cover and let it remain till serving time.

4. When about to serve, heat gravy, add koftas, simmer for 5 min. Pour gravy into a bowl.

5. Beat cream smooth, pour over gravy; sprinkle rest of the coriander leaves.

Serve with phulkas or parathas.

Raw Banana Stuffed Parathas

Ingredients

For Parathas

2 cups wheat flour
2 tsp oil to mix
Salt to taste

For Filling

Same as for koftas, omitting gram flour.

Method

1. Add oil and salt to flour; add enough water to make a fairly stiff dough. Keep covered for $\frac{1}{2}$-1 hr.

2. Prepare filling as for koftas up to step 3 only (omit gram flour).

3. Take a big lemon size dough and, using some oil, shape the dough into a cup. Keep filling in centre, close the cup. Roll out into a round very carefully, dusting with flour.

4. Heat tava, place the paratha on it and cook till done.

Serve hot with dal or raitha.

Note

Koftas thus prepared can be served as 'tikkis' with mint or coriander chutney.

Serve them very hot as bananas tend to get hard when cold.

Beans

There are innumerable varieties of beans all over the world. Many are grown in India, too. Beans, specially dried ones, are rich in proteins and minerals and, therefore, should form part of a vegetarian diet. Fresh green beans, fresh bean pods and dried beans yield themselves to simple and not so simple methods of cooking. Sometimes they can form a meal by themselves – like the bean pulav or as an accompaniment like a bean salad. Both fresh and dried beans are used in western cooking also, specially Mexican and Chinese.

Here, some very common beans have been selected at random. These have been listed alphabetically and their preparations given in detail. The vernacular names of the beans have also been given for easy reference to the dish.

Preparations

A. BROAD BEANS
1. **Avaraikai Paruppu Curry** (Tamil Nadu)
2. **Spicy Beans Gravy** (Maharashtra)

B. CLUSTER BEANS
3. **Kothavarangai Paruppu Usli** (Tamil Nadu)
4. **Kothavarangai Thoran** (Kerala)

C. DOUBLE BEANS
5. **Double Beans Layered Rice**
6. **Double Beans Masala Gravy**

D. FIELD BEANS
    7. **Mochakka Sundal** (Tamil Nadu)

    8. **Idhukubele Sar** (Karnataka)

E. FLAT BEANS
    9. **Sukha/Surthi Papdi** (Gujarat)

F. FRENCH BEANS
    10. **Beans Curry** (South India)

    11. **Beans-Potato Stew** (Karnataka & Kerala)

    12. **Beans Soup** (Western)

    13. **Beans Casserole** (Western)

    14. **Green Bean Salad**

G. LIMA BEANS
    15. **Lobia Gravy** (North India)

    16. **Beans Ambat** (Karnataka)

Avaraikai Paruppu Curry

(Broad Beans with Tuvar Dal)

Ingredients

½ kg avarakai
½ cup tuvar dal
½ tsp turmeric powder
2 tbsp coconut gratings
Salt to taste

Seasoning

1½ tbsp sesame seed oil
1 tsp mustard seeds
2 tsp urad dal
2 red chillies
2 sprigs curry leaves

Method

1. Boil dal with turmeric powder and just enough water, so that when done, the dal is cooked, but dry (and not soggy).

2. String and cut avarakai into small pieces; add salt and steam cook or cook sprinkling a little water, on low heat – *do not over-cook*.

3. Heat oil, add mustard and when done add dal and red chillies broken into 2-3 pieces each. When urad dal turns brown add curry leaves and cooked tuvar dal; stir fry 1-2 min.

4. Add beans and coconut, fry a while till water, if present, gets absorbed and the curry is absolutely dry.

Serve hot with rice and sambar.

Note

The above preparation can be made with any one of the beans listed. This is a simple way of preparing a dry vegetable and is common to all the southern states. Almost all kinds of vegetables, greens and some of the root vegetables can be made in the same way.

Spicy Beans Gravy

Ingredients

½ kg broad beans
1 medium onion, chopped
3 tbsp oil
½ tsp cumin seeds
½ tsp turmeric powder
1 tsp garam masala
2 tsp lemon juice (or) amchoor
A pinch of sugar
Salt to taste

Grind to paste

½" piece ginger
4 green chillies
3 cloves garlic (optional)
2 tbsp coriander leaves
2 tbsp fresh coconut gratings

Method

1. String and cut beans into large pieces.
2. Heat oil, season with cumin seeds, add onion along with turmeric powder and fry till browned.
3. Add ground paste, fry till oil surfaces; add beans, stir fry for a while.
4. Add salt, 1½ -2 cups water, cover and cook in low heat. When almost done, add amchoor, a pinch of sugar and garam masala, simmer 1-2 min. (If you are adding lemon juice, add later.)
5. Remove from fire, add lemon juice and sprinkle some coriander leaves.

Serve hot with chapathis.

Note

Cubed fried potatoes or boiled peas can be added to gravy in step 4.

Kothavarangai Paruppu Usli
(Cluster Beans with Tuvar Dal)

Ingredients

¼ kg kothavarangai
1 cup tuvar dal
3 green chillies
2 red chillies
2 sprigs curry leaves
Salt to taste

Seasoning

3 tbsp sesame seed oil
1 tsp mustard seeds
2 tsp urad dal
A pinch of asafoetida
2 sprigs curry leaves

Method

1. Soak dal 2-3 hrs. Strain all water, add ingredients (given on left hand side) except the beans. Grind to a rough paste adding very little water (if necessary).

2. String and cut beans into very fine pieces. Mix the ground paste with the beans, steam cook in a pressure cooker. Allow to cool.

3. Remove from cooker and loosen the mixture (as it would have caked by now) by breaking it into fine pieces with your hands. See that there are no lumps.

4. Heat oil, season ingredients in the order given, add cooked dal-bean mixture and on moderate fire, fry for a while turning now and then till the curry is dry. If necessary you can add some more oil (1-2 tbsp), fry till crisp.

Served with "morkuzhambu" (a South Indian kadhi), makes an excellent combination.

Note

This usli can be prepared with other types of beans – avarakai and French beans or fenugreek leaves, cabbage and capsicum (chopped fine).

Kothavarangai Thoran
(Cluster Beans with Coconut)

Ingredients

¼ kg kothavarangai
3 tbsp grated coconut
3 green chillies
1½ tsp cumin seeds
Salt to taste

Seasoning
1½ tbsp oil
½ tsp mustard seeds
1 tsp urad dal
2 sprigs curry leaves

Method

1. String and cut beans fine; add salt and enough water and cook. When done, there should be no traces of water. Set aside.

2. Grind to a rough paste the chillies, coconut and cumin seeds.

3. Heat oil, add seasonings and when dal turns brown add ground paste and stir for a while.

4. Add cooked beans, fry 1-2 min. more till the water, if any, is absorbed and the curry is dry.

Serve hot with rice and rasam.

Double Beans Layered Rice

Ingredients

3 cups basmathi rice
3 cups shelled beans
2 onions, chopped
4 tomatoes, pureed
4 green chillies, slit
3 tbsp chopped coriander leaves
$\frac{1}{2}$ tsp turmeric powder
1 tsp chilli powder (optional)
Salt to taste

Seasoning

3 tbsp ghee
1 tsp cumin seeds

Roast in 2 tsp ghee and grind to paste

1 tbsp coriander seeds
1 tsp cumin seeds
2 tsp poppy seeds
1 tsp aniseeds
2 red chillies
$\frac{1}{2}$ tsp pepper corns
2 stick cinnamon
2 cardamoms

Grind to paste separately

1″ piece ginger
6 cloves garlic

3 tbsp ghee (extra)
A large casserole dish

Method

1. Cook rice with some salt (preferably in a rice cooker) so that each grain is separate. Cool the rice sprinkling some ghee on it.

2. Cook beans with some salt and when done cool, peel the outer skin, set aside the beans.

3. Boil tomatoes till skin gets soft. Cool, discard water. Peel the skin, mash thoroughly, set aside puree.

4. Heat 3 tbsp ghee, add cumin seeds and, when done, the slit chilies. Add onions and fry till browned. Now add ginger-garlic paste. Fry for a while.

5. Add ground masala along with turmeric powder. Keep frying till oil surfaces. Add tomato puree, half of the chopped coriander leaves, the cooked beans. Mix thoroughly. Simmer 2-3 min., remove from fire.

6. Grease the casserole dish thoroughly with some ghee. Divide rice into two portions; spread one portion covering the entire bottom of the bowl. On this pour the bean curry, even out surface. Spread the second portion of rice on this, evenly.

7. Sprinkle all over the surface 2 tbsp of melted ghee and rest of the coriander leaves. Cover the bowl with a tight lid or foil and leave it in the hot oven for 20 min.-½ hr. till it gets steaming hot.

Serve with a vegetable salad and curds – makes a complete meal.

Double Beans Masala Gravy

Ingredients

2 cups shelled double beans	**Grind to paste**
1 large onion, chopped	1 small onion
2 medium tomatoes, chopped	1″ piece ginger
2 tbsp chopped coriander leaves	3 cloves garlic
4 tbsp oil or vanaspathi	4 tbsp grated coconut
1 tsp mustard	2 tsp poppy seeds
3 split green chillies	1 tsp chilli powder
2 sprigs curry leaves	1 tsp garam masala
Salt to taste	½ tsp turmeric powder

Method

1. Cook beans in a pressure cooker with salt, till soft.
2. Heat oil, add mustard and, when done, the green chillies, curry leaves and onions; fry till onions are browned. Add tomatoes, fry for some time.
3. Add ground masala, fry till oil surfaces.
4. Add cooked beans, half of the chopped coriander leaves; simmer till masalas are well blended.
5. Pour curry into a bowl, garnish with the rest of the chopped coriander leaves.

Serve with either rice or rotis.

Note

Any shelled beans – field beans, lima (chawlai or lobia) can be prepared this way.

Mochakka Sundal
(Field Beans Dry Curry)

Ingredients

2 cups shelled mochakka
$\frac{1}{2}''$ piece ginger
3 green chillies
2 tbsp grated coconut
1 tbsp chopped coriander leaves
Salt to taste

Seasoning

2 tbsp sesame seed oil
$\frac{1}{2}$ tsp mustard seeds
$1\frac{1}{2}$ tsp urad dal
A pinch of asafoetida
2 sprigs curry leaves

Method

1. Cook mochakka in a pressure cooker with salt.

2. Cut chillies into 2-3 pieces each, chop ginger fine.

3. Heat oil, add seasonings and, when dal turns brown add chillies and ginger, fry $\frac{1}{2}$ min., add cooked mochakka, grated coconut, chopped coriander leaves mix; stir 1-2 min. before removing from fire. A dash of lemon juice may be added if desired.

Serve with rice as an accompaniment or as a tea time snack.

Note

Sundal can be prepared with brown chana, Kabuli chana, chana dal, dried peas, whole moong or whole masoor. For this, soak them overnight before cooking the next day. Highly nutritious with proteins. A very common dish in Tamil Nadu, specially during Navarathri celebrations.

Idhukubele Sar
(Field Beans Gravy)

Ingredients

2 cups shelled avarekalu
2 tbsp groundnut (optional)
3 green chillies (slit)
1 medium onion, chopped
2 tbsp chopped coriander leaves
3 tbsp oil
½ tsp mustard seeds
2 sprigs curry leaves
¼ tsp turmeric powder
Salt to taste

Fry in 2 tsp ghee and grind to paste
4 tsp chana dal
2 tsp urad dal
1 tbsp coriander seeds
1 tsp poppy seeds
2 red chillies
1 tsp cumin seeds
¼ tsp pepper corns
A pinch of asafoetida
4 tbsp grated coconut

Method

1. Cook avarekalu in a pressure cooker till done. Cool, peel skin, set aside the 'kalu'.

2. Fry groundnuts in 2 tsp oil, set aside.

3. Heat rest of the oil, add mustard and, when done, the curry leaves, chillies and onions; fry onion till browned adding turmeric powder.

4. Add ground masala, stir 1-2 min., add cooked dal, 1- 1½ cups water, add salt. Allow to simmer on low heat till gravy is well blended adding groundnuts and chopped coriander leaves.

Served with ragi balls is a healthy, nutritious meal – both are the staple food of Karnataka.

Sukha/Surthi Papdi
(Flat Beans Dry Curry)

Ingredients

½ kg papdi
2 tbsp gram flour

Seasoning

3 tbsp oil
½ tsp mustard seeds
½ tsp cumin seeds
A pinch of asafoetida
2 sprigs curry leaves

2 tsp cumin powder
4 tsp coriander powder
1 tsp chilli powder
½ tsp turmeric powder
½ tsp garam masala
Salt to taste

Garnish

1 tbsp chopped coriander leaves
½ tbsp lemon juice

Method

1. String, wash and cut papdi lengthwise, then again into two making long, thin pieces of the vegetable.

2. Heat oil, season with ingredients given on the left hand side and, when done, add gram flour and fry to a golden brown.

3. Add papdi, stir fry 1-2 min. Now add all the powders in the order given; fry for some more time, sprinkling a little water. Add salt, cover and cook on low heat, turning vegetables now and then.

4. When done, remove, garnish with coriander leaves and lemon juice.

Serve hot – a good side dish for any meal.

Note

Cluster beans and French beans can also be prepared in the same way. Keep cluster beans whole, snipping off only the two ends.

Beans Curry

(French beans is generally referred to as beans, in South India)

Ingredients

½ kg beans
2 tbsp grated coconut
½ tbsp sesame seed oil
Salt to taste

Seasoning
½ tsp mustard seeds
1 tsp urad dal
2 red chillies, broken
2 sprigs curry leaves

Method

1. Wash, string and cut beans into small pieces.
2. Cook with salt and very little water – when cooked there should be no traces of water. Alternatively steam cook in a vegetable steamer.
3. Heat oil, season ingredients in the order given and when dal turns brown add cooked vegetable and coconut, stir 1-2 min.

Serve with rice and sambar or rasam.

Note

Most vegetables (e.g. cabbage, cauliflower, carrot, beet root, etc.) can be cooked this way and is a common preparation in South India.

Beans-Potato Stew

Ingredients

300 gm French beans
2 medium potatoes
1 medium onion, chopped
3-4 green chillies, slit
1 cup coconut, grated
2 tbsp chopped coriander leaves
Salt to taste

Grind to paste
1″ piece ginger
5 pods garlic

Seasoning
3 tbsp ghee or vanaspathi
2 bay leaves
2 large cardamoms
2½ pieces cinnamon
½ tsp pepper corns

Method

1. String and wash beans, cut slantwise into 2 inch long pieces. Peel and cut potatoes to $1\frac{1}{2}''$ length strips.

2. To grated coconut add $\frac{1}{2}$ cup boiling water, leave aside 10-15 min. When sufficiently cool, squeeze gratings to get the "thick milk"; strain, set aside. Now add $1\frac{1}{2}$ cups of boiling water; cool, run through a liquidiser, strain the resultant liquid – this is the "thin milk" (it can be extracted by squeezing also as before). Discard the used gratings, keep the "milk" aside.

3. Heat ghee, season in the order given and, when done, add green chillies and onions, fry to a light pink colour.

4. Add ginger-garlic paste, keep frying adding the vegetables; fry till they turn soft, keeping them covered, in between frying.

5. Add "thin" milk, salt, cover and cook on low heat till vegetables are done.

6. Before serving add thick milk, chopped coriander leaves simmer just **once**, remove from fire.

Serve hot with puris or pulav.

Note

The same can be prepared using chawlai (Karamani) which is commonly grown in Kerala.

Beans Soup

Ingredients

$\frac{1}{4}$ kg French beans	2 tbsp butter
1 small onion	2 tbsp corn flour
2 small carrots	1 tbsp thick cream or sour cream
A little fresh parsley or dill	2 cloves
Salt to taste	$\frac{1}{2}$ tsp pepper powder

Method

1. String beans, cut slantwise into small pieces. Cut carrots into thin rounds, chop onion and parsley.

2. Cook beans, carrots and parsley with some salt and enough water till vegetables are tender.

3. Melt butter, add cloves and onion, fry till onion turns light pink in colour.

4. Add cooked vegetables along with the water (if any) and stir for a while.

5. Mix corn flour with 1 cup water, add salt and pepper. Pour into the vegetables and simmer for sometime. If too thick, add some more water to get the required soup consistency.

6. Before serving, remove the cloves. Add cream or sour cream, serve immediately.

Note

If parsley is not available, use dill (*suva bhaji*) which is a common green.

Beans Casserole

Ingredients

½ kg very tender, fresh beans
1 small, minced onion
1 tsp finely minced parsley or dill
1½ cup milk or ½ cup sour cream
½-1 cup grated cheese

For White Sauce
2 tbsp butter
1½ tbsp flour
½ tsp pepper
Pinch of sugar
Salt to taste

Method

1. Wash, string and cut beans into very small pieces. Add salt and enough water to cook or steam cook sprinkling salt and water.

2. Melt butter in saucepan, add minced onion, fry on low heat till onion turns pink in colour. Add flour, keep frying till done (slightly fried but not browned).

3. Add cooked beans, pepper, some more salt if necessary and sugar; mix thoroughly.

4. If you are using milk, add at this stage and cook 1-2 min. till a thick consistency is obtained.

5. Add half the cheese and the herbs, mix well. Pour into a greased casserole dish. Sprinkle rest of the cheese, dot with some butter.

6. Bake at 400°F or 190°C for 20-25 min. or till top is browned.

Serve with toasted bread.

Note

If you are using sour cream, add in step 5.

Green Bean Salad

Ingredients

1 cup cut French beans
1 tbsp minced onion (optional)
1 tsp minced parsley or dill
2 tsp oil (refined oil or
   refined groundnut oil)
1 tbsp vinegar or fresh lemon juice

$\frac{1}{2}$ tsp fresh mustard (powdered fine)
$\frac{1}{2}$ tsp pepper
1 tsp sugar
Salt to taste

Method

1. Cook beans in a vegetable steamer with a little salt and a pinch of sugar, transfer to a salad bowl.
2. Mix all ingredients except onion, add half the herbs and shake thoroughly, pour over beans, mix; chill.
3. When about to serve, sprinkle minced onion and the rest of the herbs.

Serve chilled.

Lobia Gravy

(Cuba Beans or Chawlai or Lobia Gravy)

Ingredients

½ kg lobia
1 medium tomato, chopped
1 tbsp gram flour
2 medium onions, chopped
1 tbsp chopped coriander leaves
3 tbsp oil
Salt to taste

Grind to paste
1 onion
1″ piece ginger
5-6 pods garlic

Powdered Masala
2 tsp coriander powder
1 tsp cumin powder
1 tsp chilli powder
1 tsp garam masala
½ tsp turmeric powder

Method

1. String, wash and cut lobia into 2″ pieces.

2. Heat oil, fry chopped onions till browned, add ground paste, fry 1-2 min. more, add tomatoes. Keep frying.

3. Add powdered masalas, continue to fry till oil surfaces. Add lobia, fry on slow fire till they turn soft.

4. Add 1-1½ cups water mixed with gram flour, salt, a little bit of the chopped coriander leaves. Cover and cook on low heat till done.

5. Remove from fire, pour into a bowl, garnish with the rest of the coriander leaves.

Serve hot with phulkas.

Tips ....   **Ginger-Garlic Paste**

To save time, keep ginger-garlic paste refrigerated and use when necessary.

Beans Ambat

(Here, the tender seeds of beans are used – any beans where seeds have formed can be used.)

Ingredients

½ kg shelled beans
4 tbsp grated coconut
3 red chillies, fried
1 small piece of tamarind
Salt to taste

Seasoning

2 tbsp oil
1 tsp mustard seeds
1 sprig curry leaf
1 onion, chopped
2 tbsp chopped coriander leaves

Method

1. If beans are tough, soak overnight. Otherwise (pressure) cook with some salt till they turn soft.

2. Grind to paste coconut, red chillies and tamarind.

3. Heat oil, add seasonings and when done add chopped onion, fry till browned. Add ground masala, cooked beans, a little salt if necessary, and a little coriander leaves. Simmer till done. Garnish with rest of the coriander leaves.

Serve hot with rice or phulkas

Note

Dried peas can also be prepared in the same way.

Tips....   **Soups**

Always serve soups sizzling hot; cold soups should be served very chilled.

Left over vegetable peels can be used in soups.

Cut vegetables into large chunks for soups.

Vegetables sauted in butter add flavour to soups; also addition of herbs, particularly fresh ones.

Soups are served with a variety of *accessories*. They can be simple, toasted/buttered slices of bread or crisp, fried croutons. They can be bread sticks or fresh bread rolls.

You can serve cream, cheese or wafers or even potato chips. You can also serve macaroni shells or rings sprinkled over the soup.

For cream soups, add whipped cream and slivered almonds. Garnish soups according to the recipe. Garnsih can be fresh parsley, dill or any dried herb.

Dumplings can be added to soup while the soup is boiling.

Cheese can be sprinkled direct on soup or the soup can be served with cheese toast.

Beet root

Has a high nutrition value as well as medicinal properties. Rich in carbohydrate, protein and vitamins, beets are good for liver, spleen as well as kidney ailments. In ayurveda, these are used for arthritis. They have a laxative property and thus prevent constipation. Used plenty in salads – both in raw form as well as cooked.

Raw beet root with honey is a good source of vitamin C – helps in treating gastric ulcer. Mixed with lemon juice has high medicinal properties and used in the case of piles, nausea and jaundice. Beet is used for the preparation of sugar in western countries.

Preparations

1. **Beet root Coconut Dry Curry** (Tamil Nadu)
2. **Beet root Thair Pachadi** (Tamil Nadu)
3. **Beet root in Coconut Milk** (Karnataka)
4. **Beet root Salad (Boiled)**
5. **Beet root Salad (Raw)**
6. **Beet root Coconut Chutney** (Tamil Nadu)
7. **Beet root Cutlets** (North India)
8. **Beet root Parathas** (North India)
9. **Beet root Halwa**
10. **Beet root Aspic Salad** (Western)

Beet root Coconut Dry Curry

Ingredients

2 medium beet roots
2 tbsp grated coconut
A little chopped coriander leaves
Juice of ½ lemon
Salt to taste

Seasoning
2 tsp oil
½ tsp mustard seeds
1 tsp urad dal
1-2 red chillies
1 sprig curry leaf

Method

1. Boil, peel and cut beet into cubes.

2. Heat oil, add mustard and when done the dal and chillies (broken into 1-2 pieces each). When dal turns golden in colour add curry leaf, boiled beet, salt; stir fry 1-2 min.

3. Add chopped coriander leaves sand grated coconut, sprinkle lemon juice before serving.

Serve with rice as an accompaniment.

Beet root Thair Pachadi

(Beet root Raitha)

Ingredients

1 large beet root
1½ -2 cups curds
1 tbsp chopped coriander leaves

Seasoning
2 tsp oil
½ tsp mustard seeds
1 sprig curry leaf

Grind to paste
2 green chillies
½ tbsp chopped ginger
1½ tbsp coconut gratings
Salt to taste

Method

1. Cook the beet root, peel and grate.

2. Beat curds smooth, add ground paste, mix well.

3. Season in oil mustard seeds and curry leaf, pour into pachadi. Add chopped coriander leaves, mix thoroughly.

Serve chilled as an accompaniment to seasoned rice – lemon or coconut rice.

Beet root in Coconut Milk

Ingredients

1 large beet root	**Grind to paste**
1 carrot, medium	1 medium onion, minced
2 tbsp ghee	3 green chillies
1 cup grated coconut	½ ″ piece ginger
1 tsp pepper powder	A little coriander leaves, chopped
1 tsp chilli powder (optional)	Juice of ½ lemon
1 tsp mustard powder	
1 tbsp flour or rice flour	
½ -1 tsp sugar	
Salt to taste	

Method

1. Boil beet root and carrot, peel and cut into cubes.
2. Add ½ cup boiling water to coconut gratings; leave aside. When sufficiently cool, pass through a liquidiser – the coconut should be ground to a very fine paste. Squeeze gratings, take out 'milk'. Repeat process and take out milk a second time. Discard gratings, mix both the 'milks', add sugar, mustard and flour, mix thoroughly, set aside.
3. Heat ghee, add minced green chillies, onion and ginger; fry till onions are browned.
4. Add beet-carrot cubes, stir fry adding salt, pepper and chilli powders.
5. Add coconut milk, chopped coriander leaves and simmer on low heat for a min. or two.
6. Remove from fire, add lemon juice.

Serve immediately with pulav or puris.

Beet root Salad (Boiled)

Ingredients

1 beet root, boiled

1 carrot, boiled

1 large tomato

1 medium onion

Juice of 1 large lemon

$\frac{1}{2}$-1 tsp pepper

Salt to taste

Method

1. Peel and cut beet root and carrot into cubes.

2. Cut tomatoes into small pieces, chop onion.

3. Mix all the vegetables together adding salt, pepper and lemon juice. Transfer to a glass bowl.

Serve chilled.

Beet root Salad (Raw)

Ingredients

1 large beet root

1 large carrot

Juice of 1 large lemon

Salt to taste

Seasoning

$\frac{1}{2}$ tbsp oil

$\frac{1}{2}$ tsp mustard powder

A pinch of asafoetida

1 tsp chilli powder

$\frac{1}{2}$ tsp turmeric powder

Method

1. Wash, peel and cut beet root and carrot into very small pieces. Put them in a bowl. Make a well in the centre of the vegetables, put in chilli and turmeric powders.

2. Heat oil, add mustard and, when done, the asafoetida. Pour this hot oil onto the chilli and turmeric powders so that they get done.

3. Add salt, lemon juice and mix thoroughly.

Serve as a pickle with curd rice.

Note

Keeps 2-3 days in the refrigerator.

Beet root Coconut Chutney

Ingredients

1 large beet root
2 sprigs curry leaves
4 tbsp grated coconut
1 small ball of tamarind
1 small piece of jaggery (optional)
Salt to taste

2 tbsp oil
1 small piece of asafoetida
1 tsp urad dal
3-4 red chillies

Method

1. Peel and grate beet root.

2 Heat oil, fry asafoetida, dal and red chillies; when dal becomes golden brown, remove from kadai.

3. To the same oil, add curry leaves, grated coconut and beet root; stir fry for some time, remove from kadai.

4. Boil tamarind in a little water, take out thick pulp. Add this to the fried ingredients along with salt and jaggery (if you are using). Grind all together to a rough paste.

Serve with dosas or vadas.

Note

1 finely minced onion may be added (in step 3) while frying (if desired).

Beet root Cutlets

Ingredients

1 large beet root
1 medium onion
4-5 green chillies
1 tbsp chopped coriander leaves
1 tbsp chopped mint

1 tsp garam masala
4 slices bread
2-3 tbsp bread crumbs
Salt to taste
Oil for frying

Method

1. Cook and grate beet root; chop onion and chillies.

2. Heat 1½ tbsp oil, add chopped onion and chillies, fry till onion is browned lightly. Add grated beet root. Stir fry till dry; remove from fire.

3. Add chopped coriander leaves, mint, garam masala and salt. Mix thoroughly. Allow to cool.

4. Soak bread slices in water, squeeze dry, crumble. Add to beet root, mix thoroughly. Take lemon size balls of the beet root, flatten in the palm of your hand, roll in bread crumbs and shallow fry (preferably in a non-stick pan).

Serve hot with spinach soup.

Beet root Parathas

Ingredients

2 cups wheat flour
1 beet root, boiled and grated fine
1 tbsp chopped coriander leaves
1 tsp chilli powder
2 tsp oil for mixing
Salt to taste
Oil/ghee for frying

Method

1. Except for the oil (for frying) mix all the ingredients to a soft dough using very little water. Set aside 15-20 min.

2. Divide dough into 10 balls. Flatten each ball spread into a small circle on a rolling surface (either marble or wooden board), dusting your hands with some flour. Spread some oil/ghee on the surface, fold into a triangle, roll again using fat or flour while doing so. Transfer on to a 'tava', cook on low heat, turn, cook the other side also. When done, increase the heat, spread some ghee, cook on both sides.

Serve hot with dal or vegetable gravy.

Beet root Halwa

Ingredients

1 large beet root	$\frac{1}{2}$ tbsp raisins
2 cups milk	$\frac{1}{2}$ tbsp almonds or cashew nuts
2 tbsp khova	3 cardamoms (powder)
2 tbsp sugar (or to taste)	Few drops of rose essence
1-1$\frac{1}{2}$ tbsp ghee	

Method

1. Peel, grate and pressure cook beet root in very little water. Remove from cooker, keep aside.

2. Boil milk with sugar till quite thick, add beet root, cook further till almost dry.

3. Add khova and ghee, keep stirring till it starts to leave the sides of the vessel; remove from fire.

4. Fry in $\frac{1}{2}$ tbsp ghee the raisins and nuts, add to halwa along with cardamom powder and rose essence. Mix thoroughly.

Serve hot.

Beet root Aspic Salad

Ingredients

1 medium beet root	2 tbsp gelatine
2 tomatoes	2 tbsp lemon juice
1 small cucumber	$1\frac{1}{2}$ cups boiling water
2 carrots	$\frac{1}{2}$ tbsp sugar
A small piece of cabbage	$\frac{1}{2}$ tsp salt
$\frac{1}{2}$ tsp finely chopped mint	A fluted mould
A few lettuce leaves	A large salad plate

Method

1. Cook beet root, peel skin, grate, set aside. Wash all the vegetables. Keeping lettuce aside, slice tomatoes and cucumber into rounds. Shred cabbage, grate carrots. Keep each separate.

2. Soak gelatine in $\frac{1}{2}$ cup boiling water. When thoroughly soaked, add 1 cup more water. Add sugar, pepper and salt along with 1 tbsp lemon juice, mix thoroughly. Add grated beet root, chopped mint to the gelatine, mix; pour into a wet fluted mould, cover and set in the refrigerator till serving time.

3. On the salad plate arrange vegetables thus: Make a bed of lettuce. On this arrange tomato and cucumber slices alternately. Sprinkle grated carrots, shredded cabbage, keeping the centre of the plate free.

4. Before serving, loosen edges of the gelatine by holding the mould under a tap for a minute or so. Run a knife all around the mould. Carefully invert the mould in the centre and remove quickly leaving the jelly in the centre.

5. Mix together the remaining lemon juice, add salt, pepper and sugar to taste, shake well. Pour this over the vegetables (be careful not to pour over the jelly).

Serve immediately. Makes a lovely centre piece for the table!

Brinjal

(Also known as egg plant or Aubergine)

Brinjal comes in various shapes, sizes and colours – from very small finger-length green brinjals of the South to large, purple brinjals of the North. A versatile vegetable, it lends itself to any form of cooking including western preparations. It is grown in all parts of the country and almost throughout the year.

Has carbohydrate, protein and iron of equal content, as well as vitamins, specially vitamin B. Has a high content of calcium as well as potassium.

Being a popular vegetable, any number of dishes are prepared from brinjal. Here are given some regional preparations with its vernacular names.

Preparations

1. **Vangi Bath** (Karnataka)
2. **Badanekai Gojju** (Karnataka)
3. **Ennai Katharikai** (Tamil Nadu)
4. **Rasavanghi** (Tamil Nadu)
5. **Katharikai Thair Pachadi and Baigan Raitha**
   (Tamil Nadu & North India)
6. **Brinjal Moilee** (Kerala)
7. **Vankai Pachadi** (Andhra Pradesh)
8. **Bhagara Baigan** (Hyderabad)
9. **Baigan Burta** (North India)
10. **Paneer Stuffed Brinjal** (North India)

11. **Brinjal in Curds Gravy** (Maharashtra)
12. **Fried Brinjal Slices** (Gujarat)
13. **Baigan-Alu Charchari** West Bengal)
14. **Baigan Dali** (Orissa)
15. **Brinjals baked in Vegetable Sauce** (Western)
16. **Stuffed egg plant (Brinjals)** (Italian)
17. **Egg plant Parmesan** (Italian)

Vangi Bath

(Brinjal Masala Rice)

Ingredients

¼ kg long, green brinjals
2 cups rice
½ tsp turmeric powder
4 tsp sesame seed oil
1 small lemon-size ball of tamarind
4 tbsp grated copra
1 tbsp chopped coriander leaves
　(optional)
Salt to taste

Fry in 2 tsp oil and powder

2 tbsp coriander seeds
1 tbsp chana dal
1 tbsp urad dal
2-3 red chillies
2 cloves
1 small piece cinnamon
1 small piece asafoetida

Seasoning

4 tbsp oil
1 tsp mustard seeds
1½ tsp urad dal
2 tsp chana dal
3 sprigs curry leaves

Method

1. Cook rice so that each grain is separate (preferably in a rice cooker). Cool on a plate sprinkling 4 tsp oil, set aside.

2. Soak tamarind in boiling water, take out thick extract, set aside.

3. Cut brinjals by slitting through, then cutting each half into 3-4 pieces each about 1″ long.

4. Heat oil, add seasonings in the order given and when dals have turned golden brown, add brinjal, curry leaf and turmeric powder; stir fry for a while on low heat till brinjals have turned soft. Add salt, tamarind extract and allow to cook till almost dry. Add powdered masalas and stir on gentle heat, remove from fire.

5. Pour onto rice, mix lightly using tips of your fingers so that the rice and brinjals are mixed properly. Sprinkle copra, mix. Garnish with coriander leaves.

Note

If desired, 1 capsicum cut into small pieces may be added along with brinjal.

Serve with any pachadi and fried appalams (pappads).

Badanekai Gojju
(Brinjal in Tamarind Sauce)

Ingredients

¼ kg brinjals

2-3 green chillies, slit

2 sprigs curry leaves

1 tbsp chopped coriander leaves

¼ tsp turmeric powder

1 lemon-size ball of tamarind

A small piece of jaggery

Salt to taste

Grind to paste

2 tbsp grated coconut

2 red chillies

½ tsp mustard seeds

Broil and powder separately

1 tbsp sesame seeds

Seasoning

2 tbsp oil

½ tsp mustard seeds

Method

1. Wash and cut brinjals into cubes. Boil tamarind in water, take out extract, set aside.

2. Heat oil, add mustard seeds and, when done, the curry leaves, slit chillies and brinjals; fry on low heat till they turn soft adding turmeric powder.

3. Add salt, jaggery, tamarind extract and ground paste, chopped coriander leaves; simmer for a while.

4. Just before removing from fire, add sesame seed powder, mix.

Serve as an accompaniment with curd rice.

Ennai Katharikai
(Stuffed Brinjal in Oil)

Ingredients

½ kg round, purple brinjals
½ tsp turmeric powder
1 small ball of tamarind
Salt to taste

Seasoning

4-6 tbsp sesame seed oil
½ tsp mustard seeds
1 tsp urad dal
2 sprigs curry leaves

Fry in 2 tsp oil and powder

2 tbsp coriander seeds
1 tbsp chana dal
1 tbsp urad dal
3-4 dried red chillies
½ tsp fenugreek
1 small piece asafoetida
2 tbsp grated copra (optional)

Method

1. Wash and slit brinjals into fours up to the end of the stalk without breaking the stem.

2. Boil tamarind in water, take out extract, set aside.

3. Mix salt with the powdered masala and stuff brinjals carefully. If any masala is left over, keep aside.

4. Heat oil, add seasonings and, when done, add brinjals carefully. Lower heat and stir fry turning over every now and then; sprinkle left over powder as well. Cover and cook on low heat.

5. When brinjals have turned soft add tamarind extract, some more salt (if necessary) and stir. If necessary, add some more oil while frying.

Serve hot with rice and rasam.

Rasavanghi

(Brinjal Gravy with Dal and Masala)

Ingredients

¼ kg tender brinjals
2 green chillies, slit
2 sprigs curry leaves
¾ cup tuvar dal
½ tsp turmeric powder
1 lemon-size ball of tamarind
1½ tbsp oil
Salt to taste

Fry in 2 tsp oil and powder

1 tbsp coriander seeds
A large pinch of asafoetida
¾ tbsp chana dal
2-3 red chillies
4 tbsp grated coconut

Seasoning

2 tsp oil
½ tsp mustard seeds
1½ tsp urad dal
1 red chilli, broken into two

Method

1. Heat 2 tsp oil, add masalas one by one in the order given and when done, remove from kadai. Add coconut gratings and keep stirring on low heat till they get light brown in colour. Add to the rest of the fried masalas and powder, set aside.

2. Wash and cut brinjals into small pieces. Boil tamarind in water, take out extract, set aside.

3. Boil dal with ¼ tsp turmeric powder.

4. Heat oil, add green chillies, curry leaves and brinjal along with ¼ tsp turmeric powder; fry on low heat till they become soft. Cover vessel in-between frying – this cooks the vegetable faster.

5. Add tamarind extract and salt; boil 3-5 min. Now add cooked dal, prepared powder and some water. Simmer for a while, remove from fire.

6. Season ingredients in oil in the order given, pour into rasavanghi, mix well.

Serve hot with rice.

Katharikai Thair Pachadi and Baigan Raitha

(Brinjal in Seasoned Curd)

Ingredients

1 large brinjal
1½-2 cups curds
1 tbsp chopped coriander leaves
Salt to taste

Seasoning (for Pachadi)
  2 tsp oil
  ½ tsp mustard seeds
  2-3 green chillies, cut
  1 sprig curry leaf
For raitha
  1 green chilli, minced
  ½ tsp each chilli, coriander, cumin
    powders

Method

1. Smear oil all over brinjal, make slits. Cook on direct flame. Keep turning the brinjal every now and then till skin gets dark and wrinkled. When cooked, the skin will peel off easily. Cool, peel skin and mash thoroughly.

2. Beat curds smooth, add mashed brinjal, salt and chopped coriander leaves; mix.

3. a) **For Pachadi**: Season in oil the ingredients given, pour into curds mix.

   b) **For Raitha**: Mix into curds and brinjal mash the ingredients given.

Serve with seasoned rice or pulav.

Brinjal Moilee
(Brinjal in Coconut Milk)

Ingredients

½ kg medium purple brinjal
1 cup grated coconut
4 green chillies, slit
½ tsp turmeric powder
4 tbsp ghee or refined oil
Salt to taste

Seasoning

2 bay leaves
3 cloves
2 small piece cinnamon sticks
2 large cardamoms

Chop fine

2 medium onions
2 medium tomatoes
A handful of coriander leaves

Grind to paste

6-8 cloves garlic
1″ piece ginger

Garnish

2 tbsp chopped coriander leaves

Method

1. Add ½ cup boiling water to coconut gratings, set aside 15- 20 min. When cool, squeeze gratings. Extract thick milk, keep aside. Repeat process, adding 1½ cup boiling water, take out 'thin milk', keep separately.

2. Wash, cut brinjals into longish pieces, 6-8 per brinjal.

3. Heat oil, add seasonings and, when done, add chopped onions, fry till browned. add ginger-garlic paste, fry till oil surfaces.

4. Add tomatoes, continue frying on low heat 3-5 min. adding brinjal pieces and turmeric powder.

5. Add thin coconut milk, salt, some of the coriander leaves. Cover pan with a lid, allow to cook or 'sim'. When sufficiently cooked, add 'first' milk, boil once, remove from fire. Garnish with the rest of the coriander leaves.

Serve hot with pulav or puris.

Vankai Pachadi
(Spicy Roasted Brinjals)

Ingredients

1 large brinjal
1 tsp oil

Seasoning

1½ tsp oil
½ tsp mustard seeds
1 tsp urad dal

Grind to a fine paste

3 cloves garlic
2-3 green chillies
A little coriander leaves
Salt to taste

Method

1. Smear oil all over brinjal, make slits. Cook on direct flame turning the brinjal every now and then, till skin gets dark and wrinkled. When it has cooked, the skin will peel off easily. Cool, peel skin and mash.

2. Add ground paste, mix thoroughly.

3. Season in oil the ingredients given, add to pachadi.

Serve with curd rice as an accompaniment.

Note

Variations to the above recipe:

Prepare brinjal mash as in step 1.

a) Add ½ cup of thick tamarind extract and a little jaggery along with salt, mix thoroughly.

b) Add 1 cup curds (beaten smooth) along with one minced onion.

Bhagara Baigan
(Spicy Brinjal Curry)

Ingredients

½ kg tender, round brinjals
1 large onion, chopped
3 green chillies, slit
1 lemon-size ball of tamarind
1 tbsp powdered jaggery
2 sprigs curry leaves
1 tbsp chopped coriander leaves
½ tsp turmeric powder
6 tbsp oil
Salt to taste

Fry in 2 tsp oil and grind

1 tbsp coriander seeds
1 tsp cumin seeds
2-3 red chillies
1 tbsp sesame seeds
3 cloves
1″ stick cinnamon
3 tbsp coconut gratings
4 cloves garlic
1″ piece ginger
1 tbsp coriander leaves

Method

1. Wash, slit brinjals without breaking them, into 4 or 8 slits (according to size). Boil tamarind in water, take out extract, set aside.

2. Add salt to the ground masala, stuff brinjals carefully with this masala, keeping aside any left over masala paste.

3. Heat half the oil, add stuffed brinjals and carefully fry them on low heat, occasionally turning them over. When brinjals are done, remove them carefully from the kadai (while cooking brinjals, cover the pan).

4. Heat rest of the oil, add curry leaves, slit chillies and chopped onion; fry till onion is browned. Add the left over masala along with turmeric powder, fry till oil surfaces.

5. Add tamarind extract and jaggery (some salt if necessary) and cook on low heat for a few minutes. Add fried brinjal, simmer 2-3 min. (see that the brinjals do not break). Transfer onto a serving bowl, garnish with the chopped coriander leaves.

Serve hot with rice or chapathis.

Baigan Burta
(Brinjal Mash)

Ingredients

1 large brinjal
1 medium onion, chopped
2 cloves garlic, minced
2 medium tomatoes, chopped
3 green chillies, minced
1 tbsp chopped coriander leaves
1½ tbsp oil

2 tsp coriander powder
1 tsp cumin powder
½ tsp garam masala powder
½ tsp turmeric powder
Salt to taste
1 tbsp ghee

Method

1. Cook brinjal on direct flame as in previous recipe (**Vankai Pachadi**). Set aside the mash.

2. Heat oil, add green chillies, garlic and onion; fry till onion is browned.

3. Add tomatoes, stir fry till they turn soft.

4. Add all the ingredients on the right hand side (except ghee), fry till oil surfaces. If found dry, add some more oil (½ -1 tbsp), while frying.

5. Add mashed brinjal and chopped coriander leaves, mix thoroughly.

6. Just before serving, heat ghee, pour into burta, mix well.

Serve hot with phulkas.

Paneer Stuffed Brinjal

Ingredients

6-8 brinjals (large, round variety)
1 medium potato, boiled
1 large onion, finely chopped
3-4 green chillies, minced
1 tbsp minced coriander leaves
5-6 tbsp oil

$\frac{1}{2}$-1 cup paneer
1 tsp pepper
1 tsp garam masala
3-4 slices bread
Salt to taste

Method

1. Cut brinjals in halves, parboil in salted water – do not over cook. Remove cooked brinjal carefully from water, leave on a plate to cool. When cooled, scoop out pulp carefully, set aside both pulp and 'cases'. Mash the potato (boiled) and crumble the paneer. Keep everything separate.

2. Heat 2 tbsp oil, add minced chillies and onion, fry till onion turns pink. Add brinjal pulp, mashed potato, pepper, garam masala, salt, mix, stir 1-2 min.; lastly add paneer and coriander leaves. Mix everything thoroughly, remove from fire, allow to cool.

3. Stuff brinjal 'cases' with this filling, smooth out surfaces. Discard edges of bread slices, crumble fine. Take a little of the crumbs, press down on the stuffing. Sprinkle some water to moisten the crumbs so that they may hold. Fill all cases thus.

4. When ready to serve, fry brinjals in a shallow fry pan (preferably non-stick), stuffed side downwards. Pour oil all over with a teaspoon. When golden brown, carefully turn over for the other side to be done.

5. Transfer onto a serving plate and serve immediately.

Serve at a buffet dinner. If you want to serve this for a western menu, substitute cheese for paneer, parsley for coriander leaves, pepper and mustard powders for garam masala.

Brinjal in Curds Gravy

Ingredients

½ kg purple brinjals
1 cup curds
4 tbsp oil or ghee
1 tbsp gram flour
1 tsp sugar
½ tsp turmeric powder
4 tsp coriander-cumin powder
1 tsp chilli powder
½ tsp garam masala
Salt to taste

Grind to paste

4-5 green chillies
6 cloves garlic
1″ piece ginger
4 tbsp grated coconut
A little coriander leaves

Method

1. Wash, cut brinjals into fours or eights, according to size.

2. Heat half of the oil, fry brinjal slices, turning them over all the time, cover and cook on low heat.

3. When brinjals get tender, remove from kadai, set aside. Pour the rest of the oil, fry ground paste, adding dry masalas one at a time, continuing to fry all the time till masalas are done.

4. Put back brinjals, add about a cup of water, cover and cook for 2-3 min. till brinjals turn soft and masalas are blended.

5. Beat curds smooth with sugar, pour into brinjal gravy, simmer just once, remove. Garnish with chopped coriander leaves.

Serve hot with rice or rotis.

Fried Brinjal Slices

Ingredients

1 large brinjal
4 tbsp curds
2 tbsp minced coriander leaves
½ tsp each turmeric powder,
   chilli, pepper and garam masala
   powders

2 tsp coriander powder
1 tsp cumin powder
2 tbsp gram flour
Salt to taste
Oil for frying

Method

1. Wash and cut brinjals into fairly thick slices. Sprinkle some turmeric powder, salt, set aside.

2. Mix all ingredients (except oil) to form a thick paste.

3. When about to fry take brinjal slices between your palms, press gently to remove all water, leave on a cloth or paper towel.

4. Heat oil, coat slice with the paste and shallow fry (preferably in a non-stick pan) till crisp.

Serve hot with chapathis or rice.

Baigan-Alu Charchari
(Brinjal Potato Dry Curry)

Ingredients

¼ kg brinjals
2 medium potatoes
6 cloves garlic, minced
1″ piece ginger, minced
2 tbsp mustard oil

2 bay leaves
2 tsp panchforon
3 red chillies, broken
½ tsp turmeric powder
1 tsp chilli powder
½ tsp sugar
Salt to taste

Method

1. Cut brinjals into medium size pieces; peel potato and cut into cubes.

2. Heat oil to smoking point, cool a little, then add bay leaves, red chilli pieces and panchforon. When done, add minced ginger and garlic; fry till garlic is browned; add potatoes, stir fry.

3. When potatoes are slightly soft, add brinjals and turmeric powder; keep frying on low heat adding chilli powder after a while.

4. Add salt and sugar, sprinkle some water, cover and cook on low heat till vegetables are done. Remove lid, fry a little longer till dry.

Serve hot with rice and dal.

Note

Panchforon is a mixture of spices used for seasoning in Bengal, Orissa and some Bihar preparations.

Mix together 2 tsp each aniseeds, onion seeds (kala jeera), mustard seeds, cumin seeds and ½ tsp of fenugreek seeds. Store and use when required.

Baigan Dali
(Brinjal with Moong Dal)

Ingredients

¼ kg brinjals
½ cup moong dal
½ tsp turmeric powder
1 large onion
2 tbsp oil
2 bay leaves
. Salt to taste

Grind to fine paste

3 cloves
6-8 pepper corns
2 large cardamoms
1″ piece cinnamon
1 tsp cumin seeds
1-2 red chillies

Seasoning

1 tbsp ghee
1 red chilli, broken into 2-3 pieces
3 cloves garlic (optional)

Method

1. Boil dal with ¼ tsp turmeric powder, set aside.

2. Cut brinjals into 1″ long pieces, chop onion, slit garlic, keep each separate.

3. Heat oil, add bay leaves and onion, fry till browned; add brinjal pieces and ¼ tsp turmeric powder, fry on low heat. Cover and cook till brinjals turn soft.

4. Add ground paste, fry for a while till oil surfaces. Now add dal, salt, some water (about 1 cup); simmer for a while.

5. Season red chilli and garlic in ghee. When garlic is browned pour into dal, mix.

Serve with rice and ghee.

Brinjals baked in Vegetable Sauce

Ingredients

4-6 round brinjals	4 tbsp oil
2 medium onions	2 tbsp butter
1 large capsicum	2 tbsp flour
4 medium tomatoes	1 tsp sugar
5 cloves garlic	1 cup grated cheese
2 tsp mixed herbs	1½ -2 cups water
(fresh or dried)	2 tbsp bread crumbs
1 tsp chilli powder	**Optional**
1 tsp pepper powder	1 cup cooked pasta
Salt to taste	2 tbsp tomato sauce
A large casserole dish	

Method

1. Wash vegetables; cut brinjals into cubes, mince onions, crush garlic, chop capsicum and tomatoes; keep each separate. Thoroughly grease the casserole dish with some oil.

2. Pour some of the oil, fry brinjal cubes to a golden colour, remove from kadai, set aside.

3. Pour rest of the oil into kadai, add garlic and onions, fry till onions turn light pink in colour. Add capsicums, fry for a while, add tomatoes. Continue frying till oil surfaces.

4. Add seasonings, herbs and the flour, fry 1-2 min. longer, add little water, cover and cook on low flame till a thick sauce is obtained. Remove from fire.

5. Add ¾ of the cheese, brinjal cubes, mix well, pour into casserole dish. Even out surface by shaking gently. Sprinkle cheese and bread crumbs all over the vegetable layer, dot with butter.

6. Bake in a hot oven (190°C – 375°F) for 30-40 min. or till top is browned.

Serve hot with buns or toasted bread.

Note

If you are using pasta add to the cooked sauce in step 5 along with the tomato sauce.

Stuffed Egg plant (Brinjals)

Ingredients

2 large brinjals
1 medium onion, minced
1 medium tomato, minced
1 tsp chopped parsley
  or dried herbs

2 tbsp grated cheese
2 tbsp butter
1 tsp pepper powder
1/2 cup bread crumbs
Salt to taste

Method

1. Parboil brinjals with 1 tsp lemon juice. Remove from water and leave on a plate to cool.

2. Scoop out pulp carefully (so as not to break the cases). Mash thoroughly adding all ingredients except butter.

3. Fill cases with this, smoothen out surface. Melt butter, brush sides and top of brinjal cases with butter, place on a greased dish.

4. Bake at 190°C for 20-30 min. or till top is browned.

Egg plant Parmesan

Ingredients

4-5 medium brinjals
½ cup flour (maida)
Oil for frying
2 cups cheese
½-1 cup fine bread crumbs
3-4 tbsp butter
2 tsp of dried, mixed herbs
    (like oregano, basil, etc.)

A large grease-proof dish

For the sauce

½ kg tomatoes
1 2" piece celery stalk (optional)
3 cloves garlic
1 large carrot
1 large onion
1 tsp sugar
½ -1 tsp chilli powder
1 tbsp flour
2 tbsp olive oil
1 tsp pepper
Salt to taste

Method

1. Cut brinjals into fairly thick slices. Coat with flour and shallow fry in very hot oil till soft. Set aside the fried slices.

2. Chop onion, celery, garlic, tomatoes and carrots. Add enough water and pressure cook. When cool, puree the vegetables, strain, discard peel and seeds.

3. To strained puree add herbs, some water and simmer 3-5 min.; remove, cool, add half the cheese and mix.

4. Grease the casserole dish thoroughly. Pour some of the sauce covering the entire bottom of the dish. On this arrange fried brinjal slices. Sprinkle some of the cheese kept by, a little bit of butter. Pour a second layer of sauce, repeat process topping with cheese.

5. Sprinkle bread crumbs on cheese layer, dot with butter, bake at 190°C for ½ hr. or till browned.

Serve hot as a main dish for a buffet dinner with some salad.

Cabbage

Cabbage belongs to the same botanical family as cauliflower. Cultivated extensively all over the world, cabbage is very high in vitamin A and contains vitamin C, carbohydrate and proteins. They help fight haemorrhage. Latest studies reveal they also help to fight cancer and heart disease.

Fresh cabbage juice taken with honey every day is a cure for gastric problems, diabetes, bleeding gums and excessive acidity. With such nutritional value one or the other should be included in the daily diet.

Cabbage lends itself to various modes of preparation. Here are some of them.

Preparations

1. **Cabbage Sadam** (Tamil Nadu)
2. **Cabbage Thoran** (Kerala)
3. **Cabbage Stew** (Karnataka, Kerala)
4. **Cabbage Gashi** (Karnataka)
5. **Cabbage Banvade** (Maharashtra)
6. **Cabbage Muthia** (Gujarat)
7. **Cabbage Rasedar** (Pun jab)
8. **Cabbage Cutlet** (North India)
9. **Paneer Stuffed Cabbage Rolls** (North India)
10. **Cabbage Koftas in Peas Gravy** (West Bengal)
11. **Cabbage Soup** (Western)

12. **Cabbage Au-gratin** (Western)

13. **Cabbage Salad** (Western-Italian)

14. **Cabbage Pan Rolls** (Chinese)

Note

Two very common preparations in the South are 'Cabbage-Coconut Dry Curry' and 'Cabbage Kootu'. These have not been mentioned here separately because these have already been listed under 'French beans' and 'Amaranthus'. Cabbage can be substituted for beans in 'Beans Curry' and for amaranthus in 'Amaranthus Kootu'.

Cabbage Sadam
(Cabbage Masala Rice)

Ingredients

1 cup fine rice (cooked)
2 cups chopped cabbage
½ cup boiled peas (optional)
1 tbsp chopped coriander leaves
½ tsp turmeric powder
2 tbsp sambar powder
Juice of lemon
Salt to taste

Seasoning

3 tbsp sesame seed oil
6 cashew nuts
½ tsp mustard seeds
1 tsp urad dal
1 tsp chana dal
2 sprigs curry leaves
1-2 green chillies, slit

Method

1. Cook rice so that each grain is separate (a rice cooker is best for this). Transfer cooked rice onto a plate, sprinkle some oil, allow to cool.

2. Heat oil, fry cashew nuts (broken into 2-3 pieces each), remove from kadai, set aside. Now season rest of the ingredients and when dal turns golden brown add curry leaves and green chillies; fry.

3. Add cabbage, salt and turmeric powder, stir for 3-5 min. on 'sim'; keeping pan covered allow to cook (sprinkling some water, if necessary).

4. When cabbage has turned soft, add boiled peas, sambar powder and half of the coriander leaves; mix thoroughly, frying all the while till dry. Remove from fire. Cool.

5. Transfer the cabbage onto the rice, mix very lightly using only the tips of your fingers adding lemon juice. Transfer rice to a serving bowl, garnish with the cashew nuts and the rest of the coriander leaves.

Serve with any pachadi.

Note

Sambar powder (See 'Ennai Katharikai' under Brinjal – Page 47).

Cabbage Thoran
(Cabbage-Coconut Dry Curry)

Ingredients

2 cups chopped cabbage
1 small onion, minced
3 green chillies, minced
3 tbsp grated coconut
Salt to taste

Seasoning
1 tbsp oil
1 tsp mustard seeds
$1\frac{1}{2}$ tsp urad dal
2 sprigs curry leaves

Method

1. Boil or steam cook cabbage with salt. When done there should be no traces of water and cabbage should be crisp – *not over cooked.*

2. Heat oil, season in the order given and when dal is done add chillies and onion, fry till onion turns brown in colour. Add coconut, stir fry for a minute.

3. Add cooked cabbage, stir fry 1-2 min., remove from fire.

Serve hot with rice and rasam or sambar.

Cabbage Stew

Ingredients

2 cups chopped cabbage
1 onion, chopped
3 cloves garlic, minced
4 green chillies, slit
1 tbsp chopped coriander leaves

1 cup grated coconut
$\frac{1}{4}$ tsp turmeric powder
1 tbsp ghee
Salt to taste

Method

1. Add 1 cup boiling water to coconut gratings, leave aside to cool. Squeeze gratings to get 'thick milk'. Repeat process to get 'thin milk'. Keep both separate (gratings can be passed through a liquidiser to get maximum amount of coconut milk).

2. Cook cabbage with half of the onion, chillies, garlic and salt along with the 'thin milk' (second milk), till done.

3. Heat ghee, add the rest of the chillies, garlic, onion and turmeric powder. Fry till onion is browned.

4. Add cooked cabbage, half of the coriander leaves and the 'thick milk'. Simmer 1-2 min., remove from fire. Garnish with the rest of the coriander leaves.

Serve with pulav or puris.

Cabbage Gashi
(Cabbage-Tuvar Dal-Coconut Gravy)

Ingredients

2 cups chopped cabbage
½ cup shelled peas
½ cup tuvar dal
¼ tsp turmeric powder
1 tbsp tamarind extract

Seasoning

2 tbsp oil
½ tsp mustard seeds
1 onion, chopped
2 green chillies, slit
2 sprigs curry leaves

Fry in 2 tsp oil and grind

1 tbsp coriander seeds
½ tsp cumin seeds
1 tsp urad dal
¼ fenugreek seeds
2 red chillies

Adding

4 tbsp grated coconut

Method

1. Boil dal with turmeric powder. Boil cabbage and peas separately with salt, set aside.

2. Season in oil mustard seeds and when done add chilli, curry leaves and onion; fry till onion is browned.

3. Add cooked dal, vegetables, tamarind extract, ground masala and some water if too thick. Simmer 3-5 min., remove from fire.

Serve with rice or chapathis.

Cabbage Banvade

(Savoury Cabbage Steamed Rolls)

Ingredients

2 cups chopped cabbage
1 large onion, minced
3 green chillies, minced
1 tbsp chopped coriander leaves
2 tbsp grated coconut
½" piece ginger, minced
3 cloves garlic, minced (optional)
Little coconut and coriander leaves
    for garnish

½ tsp chilli powder
½ tsp turmeric powder
A large pinch asafoetida
½ tsp baking soda
1 cup gram flour
2 tbsp oil
Salt to taste

Method

1. Put all ingredients into a large bowl, except oil. Heat 1 tbsp oil, pour into bowl, mix with all the other ingredients. Add just enough water to hold.

2. Transfer the thick batter onto a greased container. Even out the surface. Pour 1 tbsp oil all over and bake ½ hour in moderate oven or steam cook till done.

3. Cut into pieces, keep on a plate, garnish with coconut and coriander leaves.

Serve as a tea time snack or as a side dish at dinner.

Cabbage Muthia
(Steamed Cabbage Rolls)

Ingredients

2 cups chopped cabbage
½ cup gram flour
½ cup flour
2 tsp sesame seeds
3 green chillies, minced
½" piece ginger, minced
1 tbsp chopped coriander leaves
4 tbsp curds
Salt to taste

¼ tsp turmeric powder
½ tsp chilli powder
A pinch of sugar
Seasoning
2 tbsp oil
A pinch of asafoetida
½ tsp mustard seeds
Garnish
1 tbsp grated coconut
1 tbsp chopped coriander leaves

Method

1. Dry roast sesame seeds, powder.
2. Mix all ingredients (except those of seasoning and garnish) in a large bowl to a smooth batter adding just enough water.
2. Form this into long rolls, steam cook for about ½ hr. or till firm. Cool and cut into pieces.
4. Heat oil, add seasonings and when done add muthia pieces and stir fry on low fire carefully till they turn a light brown colour.
5. Transfer muthias onto a plate, garnish with coconut and coriander leaves.

Serve as a snack or at lunch.

Cabbage Rasedar
(Cabbage Gravy with Cream)

Ingredients

1 small cabbage
1 cup shelled peas, boiled
2 medium tomatoes, chopped
3 green chillies, slit
2 tbsp chopped coriander leaves
3 tbsp cream
2 bay leaves
2 tbsp coriander-cumin powder
1 tsp garam masala powder
1 tsp chilli powder
1 tsp turmeric powder
Salt to taste

Grind to paste
1 large onion
6 clover garlic
1″ piece ginger

For pakodas
4 tbsp gram flour
1 tsp chilli powder
½ tsp turmeric powder
Salt to taste
Water to mix
Oil for frying

Method

1. Wash and cut cabbage into strips, pat on a dry cloth so as to remove all water.

2. Mix together all ingredients for pakodas (except oil). The batter should be of a thin consistency.

3. Heat oil, take a handful of cabbage, shake well so as to remove any water left, dip in batter; deep fry to a golden brown colour. Leave on paper towels for oil to drain.

4. When cabbage has been fried, remove the excess oil, leaving about 2 tbsp in the kadai. Heat this, add bay leaves, slit chillies and ground paste; fry till masala is browned.

5. Add tomatoes and the powdered masalas, continue to fry till oil surfaces.

6. Add 1-1½ cups water and salt. Cover and cook on low heat till a gravy is formed.

7. Add fried cabbage, cooked peas, 1 tbsp coriander leaves, simmer 1-2 min.; remove from fire, pour into a serving bowl.

8. Beat cream smooth, pour over curry, sprinkle rest of the coriander leaves.

Serve hot with puris or parathas.

Cabbage Cutlet

Ingredients

2 cups chopped cabbage
2 medium carrots
2 medium potatoes
2 tbsp flour
2 slices bread, crumbled
½ cup bread crumbs
Salt to taste
Oil for frying

Mince very fine
1 medium onion
3 green chillies
½" piece ginger
Few mint leaves
A little coriander leaves

Method

1. Boil, peel and mash potatoes and carrots; crumble bread slices, set aside both.
2. Heat oil (2 tbsp), add minced onion, ginger and green chillies, fry to a light brown.
3. Add chopped cabbage, fry for a while; add salt, cover and cook on low heat till cabbage is done.
4. Add 1 tbsp flour, fry 1-2 min. longer, remove from fire. Add mashed potatoes, carrots, chopped mint and coriander leaves. Mix thoroughly.
5. Remove from fire, add crumbled bread and make into a soft dough; divide dough into 8-10 balls, flatten each ball on the palm of your hand, shape into a cutlet.
6. Mix 1 tbsp flour with ½ cup water into a thin paste. Dip cutlet in this, roll in bread crumbs and shallow fry on a non-stick fry pan or deep fry in a kadai.

Serve hot with tomato ketchup.

Paneer Stuffed Cabbage Rolls

Ingredients

12 large cabbage leaves
$\frac{1}{2}$ cup boiled, mashed potatoes
$\frac{1}{2}$ cup boiled peas
1-1$\frac{1}{2}$ cups crumbled paneer
$\frac{1}{2}$ tsp chilli or pepper powder
1 tbsp lemon juice
1 cup bread crumbs
Salt to taste
Oil for frying

For batter
4 tbsp flour
$\frac{1}{4}$ tsp salt
1 cup water

Chop very fine
1 large onion
3 green chillies
A few mint leaves
A handful of coriander leaves

Broil and powder
1 tsp cumin seeds
3 cloves
$\frac{1}{2}$" piece cinnamon
3 small cardamom

Method

1. Boil water with some salt. Immerse cabbage leaves, 2 at a time, cover and cook 3-5 min. Drain, remove and set aside. Blanch all leaves thus.

2. Heat 2 tbsp oil, add chopped onion and chillies, fry till onion turns light brown. Add mashed potatoes and peas; fry 1-2 min.

3. Add freshly powdered garam masala, salt, chilli powder and paneer. Continue frying 2-3 min. more; remove from fire.

4. Add chopped herbs, lemon juice; mix thoroughly, cool. Divide filling into 12 portions.

5. Keep the blanched cabbage leaf on a plank and carefully remove core of the leaf very thinly by slicing. Put one portion of the stuffing on one edge and roll carefully turning in the edges gently.

6. Prepare batter by mixing all the ingredients, beat to a smooth paste. Dip each roll in this, roll in bread crumbs and shallow fry, carefully turning it over when one side is done.

7. Arrange rolls on a plate, garnish with mint.

Serve hot with ketchup, for a buffet dinner.

Note

If you want to serve these for a western menu, substitute cheese for paneer, parsley for coriander leaves and pepper and mustard powder for garam masala. **Serve** as an accompaniment with baked pasta.

Cabbage Koftas in Peas Gravy

Ingredients

For Koftas

2 cups chopped cabbage
1 medium onion, minced
1" piece ginger, minced
2 green chillies, minced
1 tbsp minced coriander leaves
4 tbsp flour
Salt to taste
Oil for frying
1 tbsp ghee

For gravy

2 cups boiled peas
2 medium tomatoes, chopped
1 tsp cumin seeds
2 bay leaves
1 tsp chilli powder
½ tsp turmeric powder
½ tsp garam masala
1-1½ cup curds
½ tsp sugar
Salt to taste

Method

1. Mix all ingredients for koftas except oil and ghee to a soft dough, sprinkling a little water. Make koftas, deep fry, set aside.

2. After frying koftas, remove excess oil, leaving about 2 tbsp in the kadai; add bay leaves and cumin seeds. When done, add tomatoes and fry on low heat adding all the powdered masalas in the order given along with sugar and salt.

3. Continue to fry till tomatoes are cooked. Add boiled peas, simmer for a while.

4. **Beat** curds smooth, add to gravy along with peas, simmer 3-5 min. Add koftas, pour into bowl.

5. Just before serving, heat ghee, pour over gravy, sprinkle some pepper powder if desired.

Serve hot with rice.

Note

You could substitute boiled, cubed potatoes instead of peas for the gravy.

Cabbage Soup

Ingredients

3 cups chopped cabbage
2 cups water
1 small onion, minced
2 tbsp butter
1 tbsp flour
2 cups milk

Seasoning
1 tsp. minced dill or parsley
1 tsp pepper powder
½ tsp chilli powder (optional)
Salt to taste

Method

1. Cook cabbage in water till soft, cool, puree, set aside.

2. Melt butter, add onion, fry to a light pink colour. Add flour, frying all the while (on low heat) so no lumps are formed.

3. Remove from fire, add milk gradually stirring all the while. Put back on fire, add cabbage puree, seasonings and simmer 2-3 min. or till soup is thick and well blended.

Serve very hot with cheese toast.

Cabbage Au-gratin

Ingredients

1 small cabbage
1 medium potato, boiled
$\frac{1}{2}$ cup boiled peas
4 tbsp grated cheese
A generous pinch of herbs
Butter (about 2 tbsp)
Bread crumbs (about 2 tbsp)

For White Sauce

2 tbsp butter
1 tbsp flour
2 cups milk
1 tsp pepper powder
Salt to taste
A pinch of sugar (optional)

Method

1. Remove leaves of cabbage, cut away thick ribs (if any) and blanch leaves in boiling water to which some salt has been added. When leaves have turned soft, drain out all water, shake the leaves to remove any traces of water. Chop leaves into chunks, keep aside.

2. Cut potatoes into cubes, fry in some butter, sprinkle a little salt and pepper powder while frying. Remove when brown, set aside.

3. *To prepare white sauce:* Melt butter on low heat, add flour, fry to a light pink, remove from fire. Add milk gradually, mixing all the while, so that there are no lumps. Put sauce on fire and cook to custard constancy, adding cabbage, salt, pepper powder and herbs. Simmer 1-2 min.

4. Add potato cubes, peas and half of the cheese; mix thoroughly, remove from fire.

5. Pour into a greased casserole dish, even out surface. Add rest of the cheese, dot with some butter, sprinkle bread crumbs and bake in a hot oven for 20-30 min. or till lightly browned.

Serve with soup and toast.

Cabbage Salad

Ingredients

½ small cabbage
1 medium capsicum
1 small onion

Seasoning

¼ tsp pepper
½ tsp dry mustard powder
A pinch of sugar
Salt to taste

Dressing

3 tbsp white vinegar
1½ tsp sugar
2 tbsp olive oil or refined oil

Method

1. Wash vegetables; shred cabbage fine into thin strips. Cut capsicum also into fine strips, mince onion, mix all together in a bowl, cover and chill.

2. Boil the ingredients for dressing along with seasonings for 3-5 min. Cool, refrigerate.

3. When about to serve, pour dressing over vegetables, mix thoroughly; remove at once.

Serve as an accompaniment for a western meal.

Cabbage Pan Rolls
(Chinese Style)

Ingredients

For Filling
    1 cup chopped cabbage
    ½ cup boiled, mashed potatoes
    1 large onion, minced

Seasoning
    1 tsp soy sauce
    1 tsp chilli sauce
    A pinch of sugar
    Salt to taste

For sealing Rolls (mix together)
    2 tbsp flour
    A pinch of salt
    1 tbsp water

    Oil for frying rolls

For Rolls (without eggs)
    1 cup flour
    ½ tsp baking powder
    4 tbsp sour curds
    Salt to taste
    2 cups water to mix

For Rolls (with eggs)
    1 cup flour
    1 egg
    A pinch of salt
    A pinch of baking powder
    Milk to mix

Method

For Filling

1. Heat 2 tbsp oil in a kadai, fry minced onions to light pink. Add cabbage, stir fry, sprinkle some water, cover and cook till tender.

2. Add mashed potatoes and seasonings, mix thoroughly, remove from fire, set aside to cool.

3. **For rolls (Without eggs)**
   Sieve flour, salt and baking powder, add curds, beat batter smooth; add enough water to form a smooth batter of dropping consistency. Keep aside ½ hour.
   For rolls (With eggs)
   Mix batter as before, substituting egg for sour curds and milk for water.

4. Heat oil in a non-stick pan, pour a ladleful of batter (if thick, add some water), turn pan around quickly so that batter spreads. Cover and cook on one side, flip over, cook the other side too.

5. Transfer roll onto a board (wooden), put some filling in the center; fold ⅓ roll over filling, then the other ⅓ over first. Seal edge with flour paste. Make all pan rolls thus.

6. When about to serve, shallow fry rolls, putting in the sealed edge on the pan, pour some oil, fry 1-2 min. gently turn rolls over, fry the other side. Cut each roll into 2-3 pieces.

Serve hot with chilli or tomato sauce for a Chinese menu.

Capsicum

Capsicums come in different colours – green, red, yellow and even a light purple. In the West, they are known as green or red peppers. They are rich in carbohydrate, protein, vitamins A and C. They lend themselves to various kinds of preparations (like the brinjals) and are used both in Indian and Western cooking, specially Mexican. As far as possible, they should be eaten raw to retain their nutritive value. They are steamed, sauted or baked – exotic preparations of capsicum are the stuffed capsicums with various fillings.

Preparations

1. **Capsicum Shahi Pulav** (North India)
2. **Capsicum Salad/Raitha** (North India)
3. **Capsicum in Coconut Milk** (Karnataka)
4. **Capsicum Gojju** (Tamil Nadu)
5. **Capsicum Besan – Dry or Gravy Curry** (Gujarat)
6. **Stuffed Capsicum**

    a) **Chana Dal**

    b) **Peas-Paneer**

    c) **Eggs-Cheese**

    d) **Rice-Peas (*Chinese style*)**
7. **Shells baked in Capsicum Sauce** (Western)
8. **Mexican Rice**

Capsicum Shahi Pulav

Ingredients

2 cups fine rice
4 large capsicums
2 large onions
6 tbsp ghee
6-8 cashew nuts
A few raisins
A large pinch of saffron
1 tbsp hot milk
2 cups fresh curds (not sour)
2 tbsp chopped coriander leaves
Salt to taste

Seasoning
2 bay leaves
4 cloves
2 1″ piece cinnamon
4 small cardamoms
$\frac{1}{4}$ pepper corns

Powdered Masalas
$\frac{1}{2}$ tsp turmeric powder
4 tsp coriander powder
1 tsp cumin powder
1 tsp chilli powder

Method

1. Wash rice, allow to dry on a muslin cloth.

2. Chop one onion, slice the other. Cut capsicums into small pieces, keep each separate. Soak saffron in hot milk.

3. Heat 2 tbsp ghee in a pressure cooker; fry cashew nuts (broken into 2-3 pieces each) and raisins; remove; set aside.

4. Fry sliced onion in the same ghee to a dark brown colour, remove, set aside.

5. Add 1 more tbsp ghee to the cooker, add bay leaves and spices; fry till done. Add rice, stir fry 1-2 min. Add saffron, 4 cups hot water and salt. Cook without weight on low heat (or you could use a rice cooker which is better). When done, each grain of rice should be separate.

6. Heat rest of the ghee in a kadai, add chopped onion, fry till browned; add capsicum and turmeric powder, stir fry till capsicums turn soft. Now add all the dry masala powders along with some salt; fry 2-3 min. more. Add 1½ cup curds with half of the chopped coriander leaves; stir 1-2 min., remove from kadai; set aside.

7. Grease a large oven proof dish, transfer half of the rice into it, sprinkling some of the nuts and raisins, even out surface. Pour capsicum curry, spread evenly. On this transfer the second portion of the rice, even out surface. Beat ½ cup curds, sprinkle on the rice layer along with fried onion, nuts and coriander leaves and a little ghee.

8. Cover dish tightly with an aluminium foil. Keep in a moderate oven till serving time.

Serve with any raitha.

Capsicum Salad/Raitha

Ingredients

For Salad
2 capsicums, chopped
Juice of 1 lemon
2 tsp oil
$\frac{1}{2}$ tsp pepper powder
$\frac{1}{2}$ tsp sugar
Salt to taste

For Raitha
Ingredients same as
for Salad – in addition
1 cup curds
2 tsp chopped coriander leaves
A pinch of cumin powder
(Omit lemon juice)

Method

For Salad

1. Heat oil, fry capsicum on low heat for 1-2 min. or till capsicums start getting soft. Add salt, pepper powder, stir; remove from fire. Cool.
2. Add lemon juice, sugar, chopped coriander leaves, mix, chill.

Serve chilled as an accompaniment.

For Raitha

Method

1. Preparation same as above up to step 1.
2. Beat curds, add cooked and cooled capsicums along with coriander leaves and cumin powder, chill.

Serve as an accompaniment to any pulav.

Note

If desired, the salad can be prepared without cooking. Do not fry capsicum – mix all ingredients, serve chilled.

Capsicum in Coconut Milk

Ingredients

4-5 medium capsicums

4 tbsp grated coconut

1 large onion, chopped

½ tsp garlic paste

A handful of coriander leaves

1 tsp sugar

Salt to taste

2 tbsp refined oil

2 bay leaves

1 tsp chilli powder

½ tsp turmeric powder

1 tbsp rice flour

1 tbsp tamarind extract

Method

1. Wash and cut capsicum into fairly large size pieces, chop coriander leaves.
2. Add 1 cup boiling water to coconut gratings, keep aside for 15-20 min. When cool, squeeze gratings to extract 'thick' milk. Repeat process by adding 1½ cups boiling water to coconut, take out 'thin' milk. Keep both separate.
3. Heat oil, add bay leaves and onion. Fry till onion turns light brown in colour.
4. Add garlic paste along with turmeric and chilli powders, fry till oil surfaces.
5. Now add capsicum pieces and continue frying on low heat till they turn soft.
6. Add 'thin' (second) coconut milk with half the coriander leaves, salt, sugar and tamarind extract. Simmer for a while.
7. Mix rice flour with a little water, add to capsicums and allow to cook till gravy is thick and well blended.
8. Now add 'thick' milk, rest of the coriander leaves, simmer just once, remove from fire.

Serve hot with puris.

Capsicum Gojju
(Capsicum in Tamarind Sauce)

Ingredients

¼ kg capsicums
6-8 green chillies
2 sprigs curry leaves
½ tsp turmeric powder
1 small ball of tamarind
A small piece of jaggery
Salt to taste

Seasoning

4 tbsp sesame seed oil
1 tsp mustard seeds
½ tsp fenugreek seeds
¼ tsp asafoetida
2 sprigs curry leaves

Method

1. Cut each chilli into 2-3 pieces each. Cut capsicums to medium size pieces. Boil tamarind in water, squeeze to extract pulp. Set aside each of these.

2. Heat oil, add seasonings and, when done, add curry leaves and green chillies, fry 1 min.

3. Add capsicums and turmeric powder, continue to fry till they get soft. Add tamarind pulp, salt, jaggery and 1-1½ cups water. Cook on low heat till a thick consistency is formed.

Serve with curd rice or dosas.

Capsicum Besan – Dry or Gravy Curry

Ingredients

4 capsicums, chopped
1 tbsp chopped coriander leaves
½ tsp turmeric powder
1 tsp chilli powder
2 tbsp gram flour
1 cup curds (optional)
1 tsp sugar
Salt to taste

Seasoning

2 tbsp oil
½ tsp fenugreek seeds
¼ tsp sesame seeds
A large pinch of asafoetida
2 sprigs curry leaves

Method

1. Heat oil, add ingredients in the order given, one at a time as each gets done.
2. Add capsicums and fry adding turmeric and chilli powder as also sugar and salt.
3. Sprinkle gram flour, stir fry 2-3 min., cover and cook on low heat till capsicums are tender. Add chopped coriander leaves, mix, remove from fire. This is the dry curry.
4. If you require a gravy, beat curds, add to capsicums after they are done. Simmer once and remove.

Serve either with rice or chapathis.

Stuffed Capsicum

Prepare capsicum for stuffing, thus:

Cut the tops of capsicums and carefully remove seeds. Smear the insides with salt and leave them upside down for sometime. Boil some water, immerse capsicums in this for about 5- 8 min. or till they turn little soft. Remove capsicums from water, shake off all excess water. Set aside.

Alternatively, place capsicums on a trivet with the cut side down in a pressure cooker. Allow to cook about 5 min. (without weight). When cool, remove lid, lift out capsicums, leave on a plate. Follow any one of these two methods for the stuffed capsicum recipe.

Note

After stuffing, capsicums can be shallow fried or baked as desired.

A Wide Variety of Vegetables to Choose from

Stuffed Capsicum and Tomatoes

Spices and Vegetables

a) Chana Dal

Ingredients

4-6 medium capsicums
1 cup chana dal
1 large onion, minced
1 tbsp chopped coriander leaves
1 tsp garam masala powder
½ tsp turmeric powder
3 slices of bread crumbled
Oil for frying
Salt to taste

Grind to paste
4 green chillies
1″ piece ginger
6 cloves garlic

Method

1. Cook dal with turmeric powder and salt. While still warm, mash roughly, set aside.

2. Heat 2 tbsp oil, add onion, fry till browned; add ground paste, fry till oil surfaces.

3. Add cooked dal, garam masala powder and chopped coriander leaves. Stir fry 1 min., remove from fire.

4. Stuff capsicums with this mixture. Take a small portion of bread crumbs, place this on top of filling and press down with wet fingers so that the crumbs are moist and they hold. Stuff all capsicums thus, set aside till required.

5. Pour a little oil in a fry pan (preferably a non-stick one). Place capsicums upside down (the filling side should be at the bottom), reduce heat, cover pan with a tight-fitting lid and allow to cook 2-5 min. Remove cover and fry by basting some oil on top of the capsicums. Carefully turn and fry the other side as well.

   Alternatively, grease thoroughly a baking tray, smear capsicums with some oil and place them on the tray with the filling side at the bottom. Bake in a moderate oven for 10-20 min. Remove tray, invert the capsicums and leave them in the oven for another 10 min., drizzling some more oil if necessary.

Note

You may substitute 1½ cups boiled, mashed potato for chana dal.

b) Peas-Paneer

Ingredients

6-8 capsicums
1 cup paneer, crumbled
1 cup boiled peas
1 large onion, chopped
2 green chillies, minced
1 tbsp chopped coriander leaves
Salt to taste

$\frac{1}{4}$ tsp turmeric powder
$\frac{1}{2}$ tsp garam masala
Oil for frying
Bread crumbs

Method

1. Prepare capsicum for stuffing, as in previous recipe.
2. Heat 2 tbsp oil, fry green chillies and onion till onion is browned, adding turmeric powder.
3. Add paneer, peas, chilli, garam masala and salt. Stir fry 1-2 min. adding coriander leaves. Mix, remove from fire, cool.

Follow steps 4 and 5 of the previous recipe for the rest of the recipe.

c) Eggs-Cheese

Ingredients

8 capsicums
4 eggs
$\frac{1}{2}$ cup boiled peas (optional)
$\frac{1}{2}$ cup grated cheese
1 large onion, chopped
3 green chillies, minced

$\frac{1}{2}$ tsp pepper powder
$\frac{1}{2}$ tsp turmeric powder
$\frac{1}{2}$ tsp chilli powder
Oil for frying
Bread crumbs
Salt to taste

Method

1. Heat $1\frac{1}{2}$-tbsp oil, add chillies and onion, fry till onion is browned.
2. Beat eggs with turmeric powder, add salt, pour into onion, fry till eggs are cooked adding chilli and pepper powders.
3. Add peas and cook till mixture is quite dry. Add grated cheese, mix, remove from fire, cool.

Follow steps 4 and 5 given in (a) for the rest of the recipe.

d) Rice-Peas (*Chinese Style*)

Ingredients

8 capsicums
1-1½ cups cooked rice
1 cup cooked peas
1 medium onion
4 cloves garlic, minced
1 tbsp minced onion leaves

Seasoning

¼ tsp pepper
2 tsp soy sauce
1 tsp chilli sauce
A pinch of ajinomoto (optional)
Salt to taste
Oil for frying
Bread crumbs

Method

1. Sprinkle some oil on the cooked rice. Each grain should be separate.
2. Heat 2 tbsp oil, add garlic and onion, fry till onion is brown.
3. Add all the seasonings along with the minced onion leaves, stir fry for 2 min. Add rice and peas, mix thoroughly, remove, cool.

    Follow steps 4 and 5 as in (a) for the rest.

Shells baked in Capsicum Sauce

Ingredients

2 cups cooked macaroni shells
4 capsicum, minced fine
6 tomatoes
1 large onion, minced
3 cloves garlic, minced
4 tbsp butter
1½ tbsp flour
1 cup grated cheese

1 tsp chilli powder
1 tsp sugar
2 tsp minced dry herbs
A pinch of nutmeg
Salt to taste
A greased casserole dish

Method

1. Boil tomatoes, cool, pass through a liquidiser, strain, set aside resultant puree.
2. Melt 3 tbsp butter, add minced onion and garlic, fry to a light pink colour. Add flour, stir constantly so that no lumps are formed.

3. Add capsicums along with seasonings including sugar and salt; continue to fry till capsicums turn soft.

4. Add tomato puree, boil briskly for 2-3 min. or till sauce is quite thick, remove from fire.

5. Add cooked shells, ¾ of the cheese, mix thoroughly, pour into the casserole dish.

6. Bake at 190°C (375°F) for ½ hour or till top is browned.

Serve as a main dish for a western meal along with soup and toasted bread.

Mexican Rice

Ingredients

1 cup fine rice
3-4 medium capsicums
6-8 cloves, garlic
1 cup shelled peas
2 tbsp casera sauce
2 cups water
4 tbsp oil
Salt to taste

Casera Sauce
4 cloves garlic, crushed
1 small onion, minced
1 medium tomato, chopped
6 green chillies, minced
1 tbsp chopped coriander leaves
2 tsp lemon juice
1 tsp refined oil or olive oil
½ tsp pepper
A pinch of dried oregano
Salt to taste

Method

1. Mix together all the ingredients for the casera sauce, refrigerate at least 3-5 days before preparing the rice.

2. Wash rice, leave on a clean muslin cloth to dry.

3. Cut capsicums into thin 1½″ long strips, crush garlic.

4. Heat half of the oil in a cooker, add capsicum, some salt, stir fry till they turn soft. Remove from cooker, set aside.

5. Heat rest of the oil in the cooker, add garlic, fry till browned; add rice, stir fry for 1-2 min.

6. Add casera sauce, 2 cups water and some salt; cook till rice is done (for good results use a rice cooker).

7. While rice is still in the cooker, add cooked capsicum and mix in lightly using a fork. Cover cooker and leave it for a while.

Serve hot with a salad.

Note

Casera sauce can be used as a dip for finger chips, onion fry, etc.

Tips ....   **Salad Dressings**

Dressings for salads should always be prepared in advance as ageing improves flavour.

Keep dressings refrigerated in a bottle or jar; shake them once a while. Just before use, shake thoroughly and then pour over salad.

        Salads

No meal is complete without a **salad** – a simple one of sliced onions and tomatoes or a complicated 'aspic' salad served decoratively.

Salads can be served either as an accompaniment or even as a main dish with bread.

For weight-watchers, salads with curds (yoghurt) form a nutritious afternoon snack.

Always use fresh and crisp vegetables. Wash them thoroughly in running water a couple of times, leave in a colander to drain, then dab them with a paper or cloth towel to remove excess water. Then use them as directed in the recipe.

If you are using lettuce for salads *do not* chop or cut but tear the leaves to desired size.

If you are not going to use the vegetables immediately, wipe them with a fresh kitchen cloth or paper napkin. Then put them in different packets (plastic) and refrigerate.

All containers for salad should be chilled before assembling the salad.

Do not leave cut vegetables in water for too long as this will drain away the nutrients.

Salad should always be prepared last – just before serving time. Since the 'dressing ingredients' tend to make the vegetables limp, it is advisable to keep the vegetables and dressing separate in the refrigerator and mix them only just before serving.

For cold salads, the basic 'dressing' is the same. Oil, vinegar or lemon juice, salt, pepper and mustard. Onion, garlic, herbs, nuts, sprouts, honey and fruit juices (orange or pineapple) add extra flavour and nutrition.

Carrot

Like cabbage and cauliflower, a common vegetable with a very high content of vitamins A and B. Also has protein and carbohydrate. Contains beta carotene which prevents night blindness.

Chewing carrots after food prevents bleeding of gums and tooth decay. Cures constipation and other digestive problems. Prevents stone formation in kidneys. A glass of carrot juice mixed with honey taken every morning is a cure for gastritis, acidity and helps as a general tonic for the body.

Best taken raw in the form of salads or mildly cooked as in soups. Used extensively in both Indian and Western cooking. Since it has a sweetish taste, it is used in plenty in the preparation of sweets. Here are many ways to cook carrots.

Preparations

1. **Gajar-Badam Halwa** (North India)
2. **Carrot-Cashew Payasam** (South India)
3. **Carrot Poli** (South India)
4. **Carrot Raisin Loaf** (Western)
5. **Carrot Soup** (Western)
6. **Carrot Salad** (Western)
7. **Carrot Cutlets** (North India)
8. **Carrot Puris** (North India)
9. **Gajar Masala** (North India)

10. **Carrot Dhokla** (Gujarat)
11. **Carrot Rice** (South India)
12. **Carrot Rasam** (Tamil Nadu)
13. **Carrot Sundal** (Tamil Nadu)
14. **Carrot Kosamalli** (Tamil Nadu)

Gajar-Badam Halwa

Ingredients

½ kg carrots (finely grated)
½ cup almonds (about 100 gms)
1½-2 cups sugar (to taste)
6 cups milk (1 litre)

5-6 cardamoms, powdered
A large pinch of saffron
Few drops of almond essence
½ cup ghee
½ cup khova (optional)

Method

1. Blanch and skin almonds; keeping aside a few, grind the rest to a fine paste using some milk. Soak saffron in 1 tbsp hot milk.

2. Boil rest of the milk, add carrots, and cook till they turn soft.

3. Add almond paste, khova, saffron and sugar and continue to cook stirring all the while till the mixture starts to get thick.

4. Add ghee gradually and continue to cook on 'sim' till the mixture starts to leave sides of the vessel. Remove vessel from fire.

5. Add cardamom powder, essence, mix thoroughly. Chop almonds set aside, mix in half of it.

6. Grease a serving bowl with 1 tsp ghee, transfer halwa into it, smoothen out surface. Garnish with the rest of the nuts.

Serve very hot as a dessert or at tea-time.

Note

If desired, the cooked carrots can also be ground with the almonds.

Carrot-Cashew Payasam
(Carrot-Cashew Kheer)

Ingredients

¼ kg carrots, grated fine
2 litres milk
1-1½ cups sugar (to taste)

½ cup cashew nuts (100 gms)
A large pinch of saffron
6 cardamoms

Method

1. Keeping aside a few nuts for garnish, grind the rest to a fine paste with some milk.

2. Boil the rest of the milk along with carrots, saffron and 2 of the cardamoms till they turn soft, stirring all the while so that no cream is formed on top.

3. Add sugar, ground paste and simmer on low heat till quite thick and creamy. Remove from fire.

4. Powder 4 of the cardamoms and chop the cashew nuts set aside. Add both these to payasam and mix.

Serve hot or chilled.

Carrot Poli
(Carrot filled, Sweet Parathas)

Ingredients

For the outer covering
1 cup flour
¼ tsp salt
¼ tsp turmeric powder
2-2½ tbsp oil for mixing
Ghee for frying

For Filling
1½ cups grated carrots
½ cup grated coconut
1-1½ cups jaggery
2 tbsp ghee
3-4 cashew nuts, powdered
A few almonds or cashew nuts

Method

1. Knead all the ingredients for the covering (except the ghee), adding 1-1½ tbsp of water to a smooth dough. Cover and set aside.

2. Boil carrots with just enough water, remove from fire cool.

3. Grind cooked carrots, coconut, jaggery, nuts and cardamom to a fine paste with little water, if necessary.

4. Heat ghee, add ground mixture, fry on low heat till quite dry, stirring all the while. Cool, make lemon-size balls, set aside.

5. Make equal number of balls of the dough and with a little oil sprinkled on your hand, shape into a cup. Put 1 carrot ball into the cup, bring edges together and seal at the top. Pat the cup flat, set aside. Use up all the dough and filling.

6. Using a little flour or oil, roll out the flattened dough into thin rounds (polis).

7. Heat a tava, cook polis on both sides turning over carefully when one side is done. Add some ghee and fry both sides till light brown in colour.

Serve very hot with ghee or milk.

Carrot Raisin Loaf

Ingredients

1 cup finely grated carrots	**Sift together**
1 cup butter	2 cups flour
1 cup sugar	1 tsp baking powder
1 cup raisins	1 tsp baking soda
2 eggs	1 tsp cinnamon powder
	A pinch of salt

Method

1. Cream butter and sugar until light and creamy. Add eggs and carrot, continue beating till well blended.

2. Add sifted flour to the creamed butter-carrot mixture along with raisins; blend thoroughly to form batter of dropping consistency.

3. Grease a loaf tin, pour batter into it, even out surface.

4. Bake at 190°C (375°F) for 45 min.-1 hour.

Serve with hot coffee.

Carrot Soup

Ingredients

3 medium carrots, chopped
1 large onion, minced
½ tbsp chopped celery
   (or) a pinch of celery seeds
½ cup cream

2 tbsp butter
1 tbsp flour
2 cups milk
1 tsp pepper powder
Salt to taste

Method

1. Cook carrots and celery with 2-2½ cups water till tender. Pass through a liquidiser, set aside puree.
2. Melt butter, fry onion to a light brown colour.
3. Add flour, stir fry, seeing no lumps are formed. Remove from fire, add milk gradually, stirring all the while till well blended.
4. Put back on fire, add carrot puree, seasonings and cook 2-3 min. more.

To serve: Beat cream lightly, pour soup into cups, add a big dollop of cream to each cup and **serve** with garlic toast.

Carrot Salad

(Italian Style)

Ingredients

4 carrots, cubed
1 small onion, minced
1 clove garlic, crushed
A few lettuce leaves (optional)
1 tbsp raisins for garnish
   (optional)

For dressing
2 tbsp olive oil
1 tbsp white vinegar
1 tbsp lemon juice
1 tsp pepper powder
1 tsp fresh or dried basil or oregano
Salt to taste

Method

1. Parboil carrots with a pinch of salt, 3-5 min., drain, cool, cover and refrigerate.
2. Mix together ingredients for dressing, refrigerate.

3. When about to serve, transfer carrot into a salad bowl, mix in minced onion, crushed garlic; shake and pour dressing over. Mix once again. If desired, the carrots can be served on a bed of lettuce garnished with raisins.

Carrot Cutlets

Ingredients

¼ kg carrots
1 large potato
1 medium onion, minced
2 tbsp chopped mint
1 tsp chilli powder
½ tsp pepper powder

1½ tbsp flour
2 slices bread, crumbled
Salt to taste
Oil for frying
Bread crumbs

Method

1. Boil carrots and potato, cool and mash.
2. Heat 2 tbsp oil, fry onion to brown, add mashed vegetables along with chopped mint, chilli, pepper and salt. Add crumbled bread and mix into a dough.
3. Make lemon-size balls of dough, pat into a round, set aside.
4. Mix flour with some water. Dip cutlets in this, roll in bread crumbs and shallow fry, preferably in a non-stick pan.

Serve sizzling hot with tomato ketchup.

Carrot Puris

Ingredients

For outer cover
- 2 cups flour
- 2 tbsp vanaspathi/oil
- ½ tsp salt
- Water to mix
- Oil or vanaspathi for frying

For Filling
- 2 cups grated carrots
- 4 green chillies, minced
- ½" piece ginger, minced
- 2 tbsp coriander leaves
- ½ tsp pepper
- 1 tsp cinnamon powder
- Salt to taste

Method

1. Sift flour with salt, add vanaspathi and mix lightly until flour is crumbly. Add some water to make a very stiff dough. Cover, set aside.

2. Heat 2 tbsp oil, add filling ingredients one by one stirring all the while. Sprinkle some water, cover and leave on 'sim' till carrots are done and you get a soft mixture. Remove from fire, cool.

3. Take a lemon-sized ball of dough, work it into a cup, keep 2-3 tsp of filling, close 'cup'. Dust 'cup' with flour, roll into a fairly thick puri.

4. Deep fry puris to golden brown, drain on absorbent paper.

Serve piping hot with mint chutney.

Tips ....   **Stuffed Parathas/Puris**

While making stuffed parathas/puris, when you are rolling and you see the filling spilling out, dust that portion generously with flour and seal; then roll as before. This applies to puris also.

Gajar Masala

Ingredients

¼ kg carrots, cubed
1 large tomato, chopped
1 tbsp chopped coriander leaves
1 tsp chopped mint
2 tbsp oil or ghee
1 tsp cumin seeds
½-1 tsp chilli powder
1 tsp cinnamon powder
1 tbsp flour
Salt to taste

Grind to paste

3 green chillies
¼" piece ginger
1 tbsp coriander leaves
1 small onion
A few pepper corns
  (or ½ tsp pepper powder)

Method

1. Cook carrots with some salt and enough water or alternatively steam cook in a vegetable steamer.

2. Heat oil/ghee, add cumin seeds and, when done, the ground paste; fry till oil surfaces.

3. Add chopped tomatoes, chilli powder, half the coriander leaves and mint; stir fry for sometime.

4. Add flour, continue to fry 1-2 min. more. Now add 1- 1½ cups water, some more salt (if necessary). Simmer till gravy is well blended. Just before removing add cinnamon powder mix.

5. Pour into a serving bowl, garnish with the rest of the coriander leaves. If desired, some cream can be whipped and poured over curry.

Serve with hot puris or parathas.

Carrot Dhokla

Ingredients

2 cups grated carrots
½ cup chana dal
2 tsp grated coconut
2 tbsp chopped coriander leaves
3 green chillies, minced
½" piece ginger, minced

¼ tsp baking soda
2 tbsp sour curd
¼ tsp turmeric powder
A pinch of sugar
Salt to taste
2 tbsp oil
1 tsp mustard seeds

Method

1. Soak dal ½ hr., grind to a rough paste.

2. Beat curds, add baking soda, mix into dal, leave aside for about 2 hours.

3. To ground dal add carrots, half of the coconut and coriander leaves, chillies, ginger, turmeric powder, sugar and salt. Mix thoroughly.

4. Pour mixture in a well greased plate or flat vessel. Even out surface, sprinkle some oil on top, steam cook.

5. When cool, remove from cooker, cut into small squares, transfer onto a plate.

6. Heat oil, season with mustard seeds, pour onto dhokla. Garnish with the rest of the coriander leaves and coconut.

Serve as a tea-time snack.

Tips ....   **Stuffed Parathas**

While cooking the parathas, first cook on low flame on both sides, when brown spots appear and it looks like done; then raise heat, pour oil/ghee all around and fry crisp.

Carrot Rice

Ingredients

1 cup rice
2 cups grated carrots
2 green chillies, slit
2 sprigs curry leaves
2 tbsp chopped coriander leaves
¼ tsp turmeric powder
2 tbsp roasted, powdered peanuts
Juice of 1 lemon

Seasoning

4 tbsp oil (sesame seed oil preferably)
1 tsp mustard seeds
1 tsp chana dal
1 tsp urad dal

Fry in tsp oil and Powder roughly

1 tbsp sesame seeds
2 tbsp coriander seeds
2 tsp chana dal
1 tsp urad dal
A pinch of fenugreek seeds
1-2 red chillies

Method

1. Cook rice, preferably in a rice cooker, so that each grain is separate. Transfer rice onto a plate. Sprinkle some oil. Keep aside.

2. Heat oil, add seasonings, when done, add chillies, curry leaves and carrot; fry on low heat 2-3 min., sprinkle some water, add salt, cover and cook till carrots are tender.

3. Add powdered masala, half of chopped coriander leaves, stir fry for a minute or so. Pour this onto the rice, add peanut powder and lemon juice and mix delicately with the tips of your fingers.

4. Transfer rice onto a rice plate, garnish with rest of the chopped coriander leaves.

Serve with any pachadi (raitha).

Carrot Rasam

Ingredients

½ cup cooked tuvar dal
½ tsp turmeric powder
1 medium carrot, chopped
1 medium tomato, chopped
1 tbsp chopped coriander leaves
1 tbsp tamarind pulp
    or juice of ½ lemon
Salt to taste

Powder roughly

1 tsp cumin seeds
½ tsp pepper powder

Seasoning

2 tsp ghee
½ tsp mustard
1-2 green chillies, slit
2 sprigs curry leaves
3 cloves garlic (optional)

Method

1. Mash cooked dal thoroughly, add enough water to make 2 cups, churn, set aside.
2. Pressure cook carrots and tomatoes, cool, pass through a liquidiser, set aside puree.
3. Heat ghee, add mustard seeds, cumin and pepper powder and, when done, add green chillies, curry leaves and garlic. Stir fry till garlic is browned.
5. Add carrot-tomato puree, dal water, tamarind pulp and salt with ½ tbsp coriander leaves; simmer 3-5 min. or till rasam starts to foam. Remove from fire, garnish with the rest of the coriander leaves (if you are using lemon juice, use now).

Serve very hot as an appetiser or with rice.

Note

If you are serving rasam as an appetiser, add extra water (about 1-1½ cups) with required seasonings (in step 5).

Carrot Sundal

Ingredients

2 cups moong dal
$\frac{1}{4}$ tsp turmeric powder
2 cups grated carrots
2 tbsp grated coconut
1 tbsp chopped coriander leaves
Juice of 1 lemon
Salt to taste

Seasoning

1 tbsp sesame seed oil
$\frac{1}{2}$ tsp mustard seeds
1 tsp urad dal
A pinch of asafoetida
2 green chillies, cut
2 sprigs curry leaves

Method

1. Boil dal with turmeric powder and just enough water. When done, dal should be cooked not mushy.
2. Heat oil, add seasonings, then add carrots, salt; stir fry 1-2 min., sprinkle some water. Cover and cook on low heat for 2-3 min. (till carrots get tender).
3. Add dal, coconut, half the coriander leaves, mix, stir fry for a minute. Be careful not to fry too much – otherwise dal will get mushy.
4. Remove from fire, add lemon juice and garnish with rest of the coriander leaves.

Serve as an accompaniment to a South India meal.

Note

Even though this by itself is a nutritious preparation, you could make it even more nutritious by using sprouted moong dal instead of the plain one. The method is the same but cook just right so that the sprouts are tender and crisp.

Carrot Kosamalli

(Carrot Salad/Pickle)

Ingredients

3 carrots, minced
1 tsp chilli powder
½ tsp turmeric powder
Juice of 1 lemon
Salt to taste

Seasoning

2 tsp til oil
½ tsp mustard seeds
½ tsp fenugreek seeds
A large pinch of asafoetida

Method

1. Place carrot pieces in a bowl. Put turmeric and chilli powder in the centre of the carrot pieces.
2. Heat oil, fry fenugreek seeds and ascafoetida, remove and powder.
3. In the same oil, fry mustard seeds. Pour this along with the oil onto the chilli-turmeric powder. Add salt, lemon juice and the prepared powder, mix well.

Serve after 2-3 hours, with curd rice.

Note

Can be stored in the refrigerator for at least a week.

Tips ....   **Rasam**

If you are serving rasam with rice, it should be of a thicker consistency.
Serve with hot rice and a dash of pure ghee.

Cauliflower

Belongs to the same botanical family as the cabbage. Hence the nutritional value of both are about the same. Also, recipes of both can be interchanged but there are some recipes which go well with cauliflower only. There are many ways to cook this vegetable. It is used extensively in Western cooking as well.

Preparations

1. **Cauliflower Rice** (South India)
2. **Cauliflower Dry Curry** (Tamil Nadu)
3. **Cauliflower Stew** (Mangalore- Kerala)
4. **Cauliflower Garam Masala Kootu** (Karnataka)
5. **Cauliflower- Potato with Greens**
6. **Phool Gobi-Alu Charchari** (West Bengal)
7. **Phool Gobi-Alu Rasedar** (Punjab)
8. **Cauliflower Puris** (North India)
9. **Cauliflower Pakodas in Gravy**
10. **Cauliflower Kheer** (North India)
11. **Cauliflower Soup** (Western)
12. **Cauliflower Au-gratin** (*Indian Style*)
13. **Cauliflower baked in Cheese Sauce** (Western)
14. **Cauliflower Sour Cream Salad** (Western)
15. **Cauliflower & Noodles baked in Tomato Sauce** (Western)

Cauliflower Rice

Ingredients

1 cup fine rice
1 cup shelled peas
1 medium cauliflower
2 green chillies, slit
1 cup coconut gratings
$\frac{1}{2}$" piece ginger, chopped
2 tsp roasted poppy seeds
2-3 tbsp chopped coriander leaves
Salt to taste

Seasoning

2 tbsp ghee
A few raisins
A few almonds
2 bay leaves
3 cloves
1" piece cinnamon
3-4 cardamoms
$\frac{1}{2}$ tsp pepper corns

Method

1. Wash rice, leave on a cloth to dry. Wash and break cauliflowers into medium-size florets, set aside.

2. Soak coconut gratings, ginger and poppy seeds in 1 cup boiling water, leave aside for a while. Cool, grind to a puree in a liquidiser. Squeeze the gratings, strain through a sieve and keep the resultant liquid aside. Repeat process to get $2\frac{1}{2}$ cups.

3. Heat ghee, fry the raisins and almonds (slivered) remove. Keep aside. To the same ghee, add bay leaf and spices, fry adding slit chillies, cauliflower and rice. Stir fry for some more time (2-3 min.).

4. Add coconut milk, peas, half of the chopped coriander leaves and salt. Cook in a pressure cooker (without the weight) or preferably in a rice cooker.

Garnish with raisin, almonds and rest of the coriander leaves.

Serve with any raitha or plain curds.

Cauliflower Dry Curry

Ingredients

1 small cauliflower
$\frac{1}{2}$ cup shelled peas
2 tbsp chopped coriander leaves
2 tbsp grated coconut
$\frac{1}{4}$ tsp turmeric powder (optional)
$\frac{1}{2}$ tsp chilli powder (optional)

Seasoning

2 tbsp oil
$\frac{1}{2}$ tsp mustard seeds
$\frac{1}{2}$ tsp cumin seeds (optional)
$\frac{1}{4}$ tsp asafoetida
2 minced green chillies
2 sprigs curry leaves
Salt to taste

Method

1. Wash and break cauliflower into very small sprigs.

2. Heat oil, add mustard seeds, cumin seeds and asafoetida and, when done, the green chillies and curry leaves. Stir fry, add cauliflower along with turmeric and chilli powder. Fry 1-2 min. longer.

3. Add peas, salt, sprinkle some water, half of coriander leaves and cook on low heat till done. Add grated coconut, the rest of the coriander leaves, mix remove from fire.

Serve hot with rice and rasam.

Cauliflower Stew

Ingredients

1 large cauliflower
1 cup grated coconut
2 tbsp chopped coriander leaves
1 tbsp tamarind water
   (or juice of 1 lemon)
1 tbsp gram flour
Salt to taste

2 tsp coriander seeds
2 tsp chilli powder
$\frac{1}{2}$ tsp turmeric powder
A pinch of pepper powder

Seasoning

2 tsp ghee
$\frac{1}{2}$ tsp mustard seeds
1 sprig curry leaf

Method

1. Add ½ cup boiling water to coconut gratings. Keep aside for a while. Squeeze gratings to get 'thick' coconut milk. Repeat process with 2 cups more boiling water to get thinner milk. Set aside this too. Discard the gratings.
2. Wash and chop cauliflower into small pieces.
3. Dry roast coriander seeds, powder; set aside.
4. Mix gram flour with 'second' milk, turmeric powder and chilli powder, add cauliflower. Cook on 'sim' till the cauliflower is partly done, adding some water if necessary.
5. Add coriander powder, tamarind water (if you are using), salt, half of the chopped coriander leaves and cook till cauliflower is tender.
6. Season in ghee the mustard seeds and curry leaves, add to cauliflower gravy along with 'first' milk, mix simmer once. Remove from fire. Garnish with the rest of the coriander leaves, add lemon juice (if necessary) at this stage.

Serve hot with rice or rotis.

Cauliflower Garam Masala Kootu

Ingredients

1 medium cauliflower	**Fry in 2 tsp oil and powder**
1 medium onion, minced	2 red chillies
3 green chillies, slit	¼ tsp pepper
½ cup tuvar dal	¼ cumin seeds
¼ tsp turmeric powder	½" piece cinnamon
3 tbsp grated coconut	2-3 cloves
1 tbsp chopped coriander leaves	**Seasoning**
1 tbsp oil	1 tsp mustard seeds
Salt to taste	2 sprigs curry leaves

Method

1. Boil dal so that it is cooked but not mushy; each dal should be separate.
2. Boil cauliflower separate with salt and just enough water, so that it is cooked, but not overdone.

3. Heat oil, season with mustard seeds and curry leaves, add onion; fry to a light brown colour.

4. Add cooked dal and cauliflower, stir fry for a while. Add prepared powder, chopped coriander leaves, stir to mix thoroughly, adding some water if necessary. Simmer 1-2 min.

Serve hot with rice or chapathis.

Note

If desired, ½ cup shelled peas may be added in step 2.

Cauliflower-Potato with Greens

Ingredients

1 large cauliflower	**Seasoning**
2 medium potatoes	3 tbsp oil
1 large onion, chopped	1 tsp cumin seeds
3 green chillies, minced	½ tsp turmeric powder
1″ piece ginger, minced	½-1 tsp chilli powder
1 cup chopped fenugreek leaves	2 tsp coriander powder
½ cup chopped coriander leaves	Salt to taste
½ cup chopped mint	

Method

1. Wash and cut cauliflower into small pieces (medium). Cut potato into cubes.

2. Heat oil, add cumin seeds and when done add onion and fry till browned adding turmeric powder.

3. Add potatoes, fry for a while, add cauliflower. Continue frying for some time. Add chilli and coriander powders, stir fry.

4. Now add all the greens, fry for some time more. Sprinkle ½ cup or so of water, cover and cook on 'sim' till done.

Serve hot with phulkas.

Note

You can substitute (1 cup) peas for potatoes.

Phool Gobi-Alu Charchari

Ingredients

1 medium cauliflower
2 medium potatoes
1 tbsp chopped coriander leaves
1 tsp mustard seeds
1 medium onion
2 green chillies
½ tsp turmeric powder
½-1 tsp chilli powder
Salt to taste

Grind to a paste
1 onion
2 green chillies
½" piece ginger
½ tsp poppy seeds (broiled)
Seasoning
4 tbsp oil (mustard)
2 bay leaves

Method

1. Break cauliflower into small sprigs, cut potatoes into cubes, slit 2 green chillies.
2. Soak mustard in some water; grind to a fine paste with 1 onion.
3. Heat oil, add bay leaves, green chillies and ground paste along with turmeric and chilli powders, fry till oil surfaces.
4. Add cauliflower and potatoes, continue to fry till they turn soft; add some water, salt, cover and cook on 'sim' till nearly done.
5. Mix the mustard paste with some water, add to vegetables; cook for another 2-3 min. more. Add chopped coriander leaves and mix. Remove from fire.

Serve hot with rice.

Tips ....   **Dry Curry**

When you are making roasted vegetables (plantain, yam, etc.), first cook vegetables on low heat; if necessary, sprinkle some water and cover the pan. When the vegetable is cooked, remove cover, raise the heat, add some more oil and fry crisp.

Phool Gobi-Alu Rasedar

Ingredients

1 large cauliflower
4 medium potatoes
1 large onion, chopped
2 medium tomatoes, chopped
2 tbsp coriander powder
$\frac{1}{2}$ tbsp cumin powder
$\frac{1}{2}$ tsp turmeric powder
1 tsp chilli powder
1 tsp garam masala
Salt to taste

Grind to a fine paste
1 onion
1 tomato
1" piece ginger
6 cloves garlic
4 green chillies

Seasoning
8 tbsp oil
2 bay leaves
2 tbsp chopped coriander leaves

Method

1. Wash and break cauliflower into fairly large pieces. Peel and cut potatoes into big pieces.
2. Heat half the oil, add vegetables, fry for a while on low heat keeping vessel covered in-between frying till vegetables are a little soft. Remove from kadai, keep aside.
3. Heat rest of the oil, add bay leaves and chopped onion, fry till browned; add tomatoes and fry till they turn soft.
4. Add ground masala, continue to fry till oil surfaces. Add dry masala powders one by one, continuing to fry all the while.
5. Add vegetables, half the coriander leaves, stir fry for 3-5 min. Now add water, salt, cover and cook on low heat till a gravy is formed. Add the rest of the coriander leaves, mix thoroughly.

Serve hot with phulkas.

Cauliflower Puris

Ingredients

For puris
- 2 cups wheat flour
- $\frac{1}{2}$ cup maida
- 2 tsp oil to mix
- Salt to taste
- Oil for frying

For filling: Mix together
- $1\frac{1}{2}$-2 cup grated cauliflower
- 2 minced green chillies
- 1 tbsp minced coriander leaves
- $\frac{1}{2}$ tsp cumin powder
- $\frac{1}{2}$ tsp garam masala powder
- Little salt

Method

1. Mix together ingredients for puri, with very little water, to a stiff dough.
2. Break dough into small pieces, two at a time, roll them into 2 puris. Put 1-2 tsp of filling on the puris, spread evenly, cover with the second puri. With wet fingers, seal the two puris.
3. Fry in hot oil till browned on one side, carefully turning over so second side is also done.

Serve very hot with mint chutney (refer to mint).

Tips ....　　　　　　　**Curries**

Always prepare fresh masala as far as possible.

While frying vegetables (on low heat) for curries, keep pan covered in-between frying – this cooks the vegetable with less oil.

Cauliflower Pakodas in Gravy

Ingredients

1 large cauliflower
2 tbsp chopped coriander leaves
1 tsp chilli powder
½ tsp turmeric powder
Oil for frying pakodas
Salt to taste
½-1 cup thick cream

Seasoning

2 bay leaves
3-4 cloves
1" piece cinnamon

Grind to paste

2 medium onions
2 medium tomatoes
3 green chillies
1" piece ginger
4 cloves garlic
2 tsp poppy seeds (slightly roasted)

For pakodas

6 tbsp gram flour
3 tbsp rice flour
4 minced chillies
1 tbsp minced coriander leaves
Salt to taste

Method

1. Wash and break cauliflower into medium-size florets. Leave in boiling water to which some salt has been added. After about 10 min., drain out all water, shake the florets and leave on a cloth to dry.

2. Mix all the ingredients for pakodas with 2 tsp hot oil and some water to a thick batter.

3. Heat oil, dip florets in batter, deep fry to golden brown, set aside.

4. After frying pakodas, remove excess oil from kadai leaving about 3-4 tbsp. Heat this oil, add bay leaves and spices. when done add ground paste along with turmeric and chilli powders. Fry till oil surfaces.

5. Add 2 cups water, half of the coriander leaves and salt, simmer 5-7 min. till a thick gravy is formed.

6. Pour gravy into a bowl, add pakodas. Beat cream smooth, pour over pakodas, sprinkle rest of the coriander leaves.

Serve hot with phulkas.

Note

Pakodas can be served separate as a tea time snack.

Cauliflower Kheer

Ingredients

1 large cauliflower
2 litre milk
1-1½ cup sugar (to taste)
½ cup cream (optional)

15 almonds
15 cashew nuts
3 cardamoms (powdered)
½ tsp almond essence

Method

1. Soak 12 each of the nuts, grind to a paste with ½-1 cup milk. Chop the rest of the nuts for garnish.
2. Wash cauliflower thoroughly in hot water, grate on a thick grater to get about 2 cups of gratings. Wash gratings once again in hot water, leave in a container to drain.
3. Boil milk, add gratings continue to cook till they turn soft. Stir constantly so that no cream is formed on top.
4. Add sugar, ground nuts and simmer on low heat till thick and creamy. Remove from fire, cool.
5. Beat cream, add to kheer along with cardamom powder and essence; mix thoroughly.
6. Pour into a serving bowl, garnish with chopped nuts.

Serve chilled.

Cauliflower Soup

Ingredients

1 large cauliflower
1 small lemon
½ cup boiled peas
2 tbsp grated cheese
½ cup fresh cream

For white sauce
2 tbsp butter
2 tbsp flour
2 cups milk
1 tsp pepper
A large pinch of nutmeg
Salt to taste

Method

1. Wash, cut cauliflower into florets; cut lemon into half, add enough water to cover florets. Cook till florets are tender.

2. Discard lemon pieces, remove a few florets, keep aside for garnish. Put the rest through a liquidiser and set aside cauliflower puree.

3 *Make White Sauce:* Melt butter on low heat, fry flour to a light pink colour stirring all the while. Remove from fire, add milk gradually, mix thoroughly so there are no lumps. Put back on fire and cook to custard consistency.

4. Add cauliflower puree along with salt, pepper and nutmeg. Cook 1-2 min. more; remove from fire, add cheese.

To Serve: Pour soup into bowls, add a few florets and some peas. Beat cream smooth, add a dollop to each bowl. Serve sizzling hot with toasted bread.

Cauliflower Au-gratin (*Indian Style*)

Ingredients

1 large cauliflower
1 cup shelled peas
1 medium onion, minced
2 green chillies, minced
1 tbsp minced coriander leaves
$1\frac{1}{2}$ cups grated cheese
$1\frac{1}{2}$-2 tbsp bread crumbs
$\frac{1}{2}$ tbsp butter
Salt to taste

For White Sauce
3 tbsp butter
3 tbsp flour
3 cups milk
$1\frac{1}{2}$ tsp pepper
1 tsp mustard powder
A large, greased casserole dish

Method

1. Wash and break cauliflower into small florets. Chop stem into small pieces. Add enough water and salt, cook just right – the florets should be cooked but not overdone.Cook peas separate.

2. *Prepare white sauce:* Melt butter, add minced green chillies and onion, fry till onion turns a light pink colour. Add flour, stir fry till light brown in colour. Remove from fire, add milk gradually, stirring all the while so that no lumps are formed. Put back on fire and cook to custard consistency.

3. To white sauce, add seasonings, cauliflower, peas, 1 cup cheese and minced coriander leaves. Mix thoroughly.

4. Pour mixture into the casserole dish, sprinkle rest of the cheest and bread crumbs, dot with butter. Keep for a few minutes on a grill till top is lightly browned (you may this serve without grilling; also, omit butter and bread crumbs).

Serve as a main dish with soup and bread.

Cauliflower baked in Cheese Sauce

Ingredients

1 large cauliflower	**For white sauce**
Juice of 1 lemon	3 tbsp butter
1 cup cheese	3 tbsp flour
½ cup cream (optional)	2½ cups milk
1 tbsp chopped almonds	1 small onion, minced
Salt to taste	1 green chilli, minced (optional)
A little butter	1 tbsp minced parsley or dill
1 tbsp bread crumbs	1 tsp pepper

Method

1. Wash cauliflower thoroughly, place on a trivet and pressure cook without weight for 5 min. or till it has turned tender but crunchy.

2. Make white sauce as in previous recipe (step 2). Add salt, pepper, herbs, 1 cup cheese, slightly beaten cream; mix everything thoroughly.

3. Place the cooked (steamed) cauliflower in the centre of a well greased dish. Take a little of the white sauce in a teaspoon and place it in-between the florets. Pour the rest of the sauce covering the cauliflower completely.

4. Sprinkle rest of the cheese, chopped almonds, dot with some butter and bread crumbs, put the dish under a grill for cheese to melt and the top to brown.

Serve as a main dish in a western menu.

Note

If you are not using cream add extra ½ cup of milk to sauce.

Cauliflower Sour Cream Salad

Ingredients

1 medium cauliflower
1 minced onion (optional)
1 tsp minced parsley or dill
1 cup sour cream (chilled)
Salt to taste

For dressing

1 tbsp white vinegar
½ tsp lemon juice
2 tbsp olive or refined oil
1 tsp pepper
1 tsp mustard seeds
Salt to taste
A pinch of sugar

Method

1. Wash and cut cauliflower into medium sized florets, sprinkle salt and steam cook till done – florets should be tender but crisp. Transfer to a salad bowl, allow to cool.

2. Shake thoroughly the ingredients for dressing, pour over florets and allow to marinate for 30-40 min. Keep chilled, covering bowl.

3. When about to serve, beat sour cream, add minced onion and herbs; pour over florets.

Serve as an accompaniment to a western meal.

Cauliflower and Noodles baked in Tomato Sauce

Ingredients

1 large cauliflower
50 gm noodles
1 cup cheese
½ cup bread crumbs
2 tbsp butter
1 tbsp flour
A little extra butter
A greased casserole dish

For the sauce
½ kg tomatoes
1 medium onion, minced
4 cloves garlic, minced
1 tsp minced fresh herbs
A pich of dried oregano
½-1 tsp chilli powder
½ tsp pepper powder
1 tsp sugar
Salt to taste

Method

1. Cut cauliflower into florets, discard the hard stem. Steam cook florets, sprinkling some salt. When done, they should be tender but crisp.
2. Cook noodles according to instructions on packet, set aside.
3. *Make tomato sauce:* Boil tomatoes with enough water, cool, pass through a liquidiser, strain and take out thick tomato juice.
4. Melt butter, add minced onion and garlic, fry to a light brown, add flour, stir fry till lightly browned.
5. Add tomato puree, all the seasonings (from herbs downwards), cook till thick – sauce consistency.
6. Remove from fire, add cauliflower, noodles and ¾ of the cheese, mix thoroughly; pour into a greased casserole, even out surface.
7. Sprinkle rest of the cheese, the bread crumbs and dot the surface with butter. Bake in a moderate oven till cheese melts and the top is browned.

Serve hot as a main dish in a western menu.

Note

Instead of noodles, you could use any pasta – macaroni, shells or sphaghetti.

Colocasia

(Tubers and Leaves)

A common tuber, whose leaves are also used in cooking. Has a high content of carbohydrates and vitamin C as well as protein. The large green leaves of this plant make excellent stuffed rolls, a common dish in Maharashtra. The root (tuber), known as *Arvi*, is extensively used in North Indian cooking, and is quite popular in the South also.

Preparations

1. **Patrel** (Maharashtra)
2. **Sembu Elai Usli** Tamil Nadu)
3. **Arvi Cutlet/Roast** (Punjab)
4. **Masala Arvi – Dry or Gravy** (Uttar Pradesh)
5. **Dum Arvi** (Madhya Pradesh)

Patrel
(Colocasia Leaf Rolls)

Ingredients

6 arvi leaves
1 cup gram flour
1 small onion, minced
2 tbsp thick tamarind juice
1 small piece jaggery
1 tsp coriander powder
½ tsp cumin powder
½-1 tsp chilli powder
½ tsp turmeric powder
A pinch of salt
Salt to taste

Grind to paste
3 green chillies
1″ piece ginger
3 cloves garlic (optional)
1 tbsp chopped coriander leaves
1 tbsp grated coconut

For frying vadis
About 1 cup oil
A pinch of amchoor
A pinch of sugar

Method

1. Wash each leaf thoroughly, spread on a cloth to dry; keep aside.
2. Mix together in a bowl the ground paste with all the ingredients (on the left side) except the leaves, to form a thick batter. Heat a little oil (2 tsp), pour over batter; mix.
3. Spread a leaf on a plank, upside down. Apply batter all over the surface ½″ away from the edge. Carefully roll the leaf tightly pulling in the sides. Prepare all leaves thus.
4. Placing them side by side, steam the rolls in a pressure cooker, without putting on the weight, about 5-7 min. or till they turn soft.
5. Remove, cool, cut into 1″ thick slices – 'vadis'.
6. Heat little oil, preferably in a non-stick pan, fry 4-5 vadis at a time till they turn golden brown and crisp. Sprinkle amchoor and sugar on vadis.

Serve as a tea time snack or as an accompaniment to a meal.

Sembu Elai Usli
(Colocasia Leaf Usli)

Ingredients

1 cup tuvar dal

3 red chillies

3 green chillies

1 small piece asafoetida

Salt to taste

1 cup chopped colocasia leaves

3 tbsp oil

½ tsp mustard seeds

1 tsp urad dal

1 sprig curry leaves

Method

1. Soak dal for about an hour. Drain water, grind to a rough paste with all the ingredients given on the left hand column.

2. To ground batter mix the chopped colocasia leaves, place the mixture in a cooker and steam cook for 10-12 min. (till dal is cooked).

3. Heat oil, add mustard and, when done, add dal. When dal turns brown, add curry leaf and the cooked dal-leaf mixture. Stir fry till usli is dry and crisp. You may add some more oil if necessary.

Serve with rice and 'morkuzambu'.

Note

Instead of chopping the leaves, they can also be made into rolls. For this follow the first recipe (Patrel) from step 3 onwards. Season as for 'usli'.

Tips .... **Ginger-Garlic Paste**

Grind to a fine paste one whole garlic (pod) and a large piece of ginger (3-6″ piece). Keep this in an air-tight bottle and use when necessary.

Arvi Cutlet/Roast

Ingredients

6 pieces arvi, thick, long variety
2 tbsp curds
2 tbsp gram flour
1 tbsp chopped coriander leaves

4 tbsp oil
2 tbsp chilli powder
1 tbsp turmeric powder
1 tbsp powdered ajwain
Salt to taste

Method

1. Parboil arvi (boil till it is just soft – do not allow to get mushy). While still warm, peel, cut into two halves lengthwise, press between your palms to flatten, set aside.

2. Mix together all the ingredients except oil, to a thick batter.

3. Heat oil, preferably in a non-stick pan; coat arvi slices in batter, fry till crisp and brown, turning over when one side is done.

Serve garnished with some chopped coriander leaves.

Note

You could make this into a roasted curry:

1. For this, omit gram flour and curds.
2. Heat oil, add arvi (cut into slices), along with all the dry masalas; stir fry till browned.

Masala Arvi – Dry or Gravy

Ingredients

½ kg arvi
½ tsp turmeric powder
1 tsp chilli powder
2 tsp coriander powder
1 tsp amchoor
½ tsp garam masala
Salt to taste

For gravy
4½ cups curds (omit amchoor)

Grind to paste
2 green chillies
1″ piece ginger
4 cloves garlic
1 tbsp chopped coriander leaves

Seasoning
3-4 tbsp oil
2 tsp sesame seeds
A large pinch of asafoetida

Method

1. Boil arvi, cool and cut into round pieces.

2. To ground masala add all ingredients except seasoning ones. Coat arvi pieces with the masala. See that they don't get mushy.

3. Heat oil, add seasonings and, when done, add arvi, stir fry turning over and over carefully. If you like it very crisp and roasted, add 1-2 tbsp more of oil while frying.

    For gravy curry: Beat curds smooth and when arvi is sufficiently fried (do not add extra oil), pour curds into the kadai, simmer gently on low heat till gravy is well blended.

Serve curries with chapathis.

Dum Arvi

Ingredients

½ kg arvi
1 large onion, chopped
6 cloves garlic
1″ piece ginger
1 tbsp chopped coriander leaves
1½-2 cups curds
½-1 tsp sugar
6-8 tbsp oil
2 bay leaves
Salt to taste

Dry roast and powder
3 tsp coriander seeds
1 tsp cumin seeds
1″ piece cinnamon
2 large cardamoms
3 cloves
6 pepper corns
2-3 red chillies (additional)
½ tsp turmeric powder
A pinch of nutmeg

Method

1. Boil arvi, cool, peel skin and cut into thick slices, if large; otherwise, keep them whole. Prick pieces with a fork, set aside.

2. Heat 1 tbsp oil in a kadai, fry chopped onion to a dark brown colour, remove from kadai, cool and grind to a paste with ginger and garlic.

3. Add 3 more tbsp oil to kadai, fry arvi pieces till crisp and brown. Set aside.

4. Pour rest of the oil into kadai, add bay leaves and ground onion paste, stir fry 1-2 min.

5. Now add the powdered dry masalas along with turmeric powder, stirring till oil surfaces.

6. Beat curds smooth, adding sugar, some water if too thick; add to masalas along with salt and fried arvi.

7. Reduce heat and cook gravy on low heat till well blended. Sprinkle nutmeg and chopped coriander leaves, remove from fire.

Serve with phulkas.

Cucumber

This vegetable is mainly used in salads, either separately or in combination with other vegetables. Rarely is this vegetable cooked but here are a few recipes that call for cooking.

A glass of cucumber juice mixed with honey with a dash of lemon juice is very effective for reducing blood pressure. Cucumber juice with mint is an antidote for biliousness and indigestion. Mixed with buttermilk and salt, cucumber juice is a good summer drink.

These are used in plenty in cosmetics as face packs.

Preparations

1. **Cucumber Cold Soup** (Western)
2. **Cucumber Aspic Salad** (Western)
3. **Cucumber Salad** (Italian)
4. **Pickled Cucumber** (Chinese)
5. **Cucumber Cups – with Curds-Cheese Filling** (North India)
6. **Kakadi Raitha** (North India)
7. **Cucumber Kosamalli** (South India)
8. **Southekai Mosuru Gojju** (Karnataka)
9. **Southekai Ambat** (Karnataka)
10. **Vellarikai Puli Kuzhambu** (Tamil Nadu)
11. **Pickled Cucumber** (Chinese)

Cucumber Cold Soup

(A delicious Cold Soup)

Ingredients

2 medium cucumbers
1 stalk celery (or)
   A small bunch of dill
1 medium onion
½ a small capsicum
A little cream to serve (optional)

3 tbsp butter
2 tbsp flour
2 cups milk
1 tsp pepper
Salt to taste

Method

1. Pare cucumber, discard centre if too seedy, chop. Mince onion, capsicum, celery or dill.

2. Put all vegetables together in a large saucepan, add enough water to cover, cook till they turn soft. Pass through a liquidiser, set aside puree.

3. Melt butter, add flour, fry till light pink in colour, remove from fire. Add milk gradually so no lumps are formed. Put back on fire and cook on slow flame.

4. Gradually add cucumber puree to white sauce, stirring all the while till soup is quite thick. Add salt, pepper to taste. Remove from fire, cool.

To Serve: Beat cream, pour soup into bowls, add a dollop of cream to each bowl, garnish with a pinch of dill, serve cold with hot garlic toast.

Cucumber Aspic Salad

(Cucumber in Jelly Mould)

Ingredients

1 large cucumber
2 tomatoes, sliced
1 small carrot, grated fine
A piece of cabbage, shredded
½ tsp chopped mint (or) parsley
2 tbsp lemon juice
1½ cups boiling water

2 tbsp powdered gelatine
2 tsp sugar
½ tsp salt
½ tsp pepper powder
½ tsp mustard seeds
A pinch of green colour
A fluted mould

Method

1. Wash and prepare vegetables as specified. Peel and grate half the cucumber, slice the other half. Refrigerate vegetables until required.

2. Mix the gelatine, $1\frac{1}{2}$ tsp sugar, $\frac{1}{4}$ tsp salt and boiling water. Stir till dissolved, cool. Add 1 tbsp lemon juice, mint or parsley, grated cucumber. Mix thoroughly, pour into the mould (which has been rinsed in cold water). Set in a refrigerator.

To Serve: Unmould jelly onto a fairly big salad plate. Surround sides with cucumber and tomato slices. Sprinkle cabbage and carrot gratings. Mix together salt, pepper, mustard, pinch of sugar with the remaining lemon juice, pour over vegetables; serve.

Cucumber Salad
(Italian Style)

Ingredients

1 large cucumber	**For dressing**
2 tomatoes sliced (or)	1 tbsp white vinegar
A few lettuce leaves	2 tbsp olive oil
1-1$\frac{1}{2}$ tbsp grated Parmesan cheese	A dash of honey
	1 clove garlic, crushed (optional)
	Salt, pepper and mustard powders
	– to taste
	A large pinch of dried oregano
	or basil

Method

1. Mix the 'dressing' ingredients in a jar, shake well and leave in refrigerator till use.

2. Peel, de-seed and cut cucumber into small cubes. Cover and refrigerate vegetables in separate bowls.

To Serve: Arrange on a salad plate a bed of lettuce or tomato slices. Transfer cucumber pieces onto the middle of the plate. Shake dressing thoroughly. Pour over vegetables, sprinkle Parmesan cheese just before serving.

Cucumber Cups – with Curds-Cheese Filling

Ingredients

1 large cucumber
½ small, finely grated carrot
1 small onion, minced (optional)
1 cup thick curds (not sour)
2 tbsp grated cheese
1 tbsp chopped walnuts

1 tbsp minced dill
  or coriander leaves
1 green chilli, minced
  or chilli powder
1 tsp pepper
½ tsp mustard powder (optional)
Salt to taste

Method

1. Peel cucumber, cut into as many two inch pieces as desired. Scoop out the inside, leaving a little at the bottom to form the base, so that the 'cups' stand firm; immerse in cold water. When required drain out all water and shake well before use.

2. Hang curds in a muslin cloth for all water to drain. Keep aside.

3. Mix together in a large bowl all the ingredients along with curds (except walnuts); beat to a smooth consistency.

4. Fill cups with this curd mixture, garnish with chopped walnuts, serve chilled.

Note

The above mixture makes an excellent sandwich spread. Grate a 2″ piece of cucumber, add to mixture before spreading on slices.

Kakadi Raitha

Ingredients

1 medium cucumber
1-2 small green chillies
1 small onion
1 tbsp chopped coriander leaves

1½-2 cups curds
1 tsp cumin seeds
½ tsp chilli powder
Salt to taste

Method

1. Peel cucumber, discard centre seed portion, chop the rest. Mince green chillies and onion, add to cucumber along with coriander leaves.
2. Beat curds smooth, add salt and chilli powder, pour into cucumber.
3. Broil cumin seeds, powder, add to mixture, mixing everything thoroughly; pour into bowl. Garnish with some coriander leaves

Serve chilled with pulav.

Cucumber Kosamalli
(Seasoned Cucumber-Moong Dal Salad)

Ingredients

1 large cucumber	**Seasoning**
½ cup moong dal	2 tsp oil
2 tbsp grated coconut	½ tsp mustard seeds
Juice of 1 lemon	2 green chillies
1 tbsp chopped coriander leaves	2 sprigs curry leaves
Salt to taste	A pinch of asafoetida

Method

1. Wash and soak dal for half-an-hour. Strain and set aside.
2. Peel and chop cucumber, cut chilli into 2-3 pieces each.
3. Mix soaked dal, cucumber, coriander leaves, coconut and salt. Add lemon juice.
4. Season mustard seeds in oil and when done add asafoetida, green chillies and curry leaves. Add to cucumber, mix thoroughly, chill and serve.

Southekai Mosuru Gojju
(Cucumber-Butter Milk Chutney)

Ingredients

1 small cucumber
$1\frac{1}{2}$ cups curds
A small piece of jaggery (optional)
Salt to taste

Seasoning

2 tsp oil
$\frac{1}{2}$ tsp mustard seeds
2 sprigs curry leaves

Grind to fine paste

3 tbsp grated coconut
1 tbsp roasted gram
2 red chillies
1 tsp mustard seeds
$\frac{1}{4}$ tsp turmeric powder

Method

1. Wash, peel and chop cucumber.
2. Beat curds to smoothness, add salt, jaggery and the ground masala paste. Mix thoroughly adding cucumber.
3. Season mustard and curry leaves in oil, add to curds, mix. If desired add 1 tsp chopped coriander leaves and mix.

Serve with coconut or lemon rice.

Southekai Ambat

Ingredients

1 medium cucumber (preferably
   the Mangalore variety)
$\frac{1}{2}$ cup cooked masur dal
   (or moong dal)
$\frac{1}{2}$ tsp turmeric powder
4 tbsp grated coconut
3 red chillies
1 small piece tamarind

Seasoning

1 tbsp oil
1 tsp mustard seeds
2 sprigs curry leaves
A pinch of asafoetida
   (or 3 crushed garlic cloves)

Method

1. Peel, cut cucumber into small pieces, add enough water, turmeric powder, salt and cook till soft.

2. Fry in 1 tsp oil the red chillies, grind to paste with coconut and tamarind.

3. Add ground paste to cooked cucumber along with dal, simmer 2-3 min.

4. Season in oil the mustard seeds and curry leaves. Add either asafoetida or browned garlic, add to cucumber, mix, remove from fire.

Serve hot with rice.

Vellarikai Puli Kuzhambu
(Cucumber in Tamarind Sauce)

Ingredients

1 large cucumber
3-4 green chillies, slit
2 sprigs curry leaves
1 large lemon-sized ball, tamarind
A small lump of jaggery
1 tbsp sesame seeds
1 tsp turmeric powder
1 tbsp rice flour
Salt to taste

Seasoning
3 tbsp sesame seed oil
1 tsp mustard seeds
$1\frac{1}{2}$ tsp urad dal
$1\frac{1}{2}$ tsp chana dal
$\frac{1}{2}$ tsp fenugreek seeds
A large pinch of asafoetida

Method

1. Extract tamarind pulp by 'boiling' tamarind in hot water, set aside. Broil (dry roast) sesame seeds, powder, set aside.

2. Peel cucumber, discard centre seed portion, cut the rest into fairly large pieces.

3. Season in oil ingredients given, in the same order. When dals have turned golden brown, add curry leaves, green chillies and cucumber pieces along with turmeric powder. Fry on low heat till cucumber gets soft.

4. Add tamarind pulp, jaggery, salt and 2 cups water; cook for a while.

5. Mix rice flour with a little water, add to cucumber, boil 3-5 min. or till gravy is quite thick. Add sesame seed powder, mix, remove from fire.

Serve hot with rice.

Note

The same can be prepared with pumpkin or broad beans ($\frac{1}{4}$ kg of the vegetable).

Pickled Cucumber
(Chinese Style Pickle/Salad)

Ingredients

4 small cucumbers
3 green chillies, mined
3 cloves garlic, crushed
$\frac{1}{2}''$ piece ginger, minced

$1\frac{1}{2}$ tsp sugar
1 tsp pepper
2 tsp vinegar
Salt to taste

Method

1. Peel and cut cucumbers into cubes, add minced chillies, put them into a glass bowl.

2. Pour $1\frac{1}{2}$ cups water into a saucepan, add all seasonings, boil 3 min., cool.

3. Add the seasoned mixture to cucumber, mix, leave aside 2-3 hours before using.

Serve with Chinese or Mexican food.

Drumstick

A popular vegetable, especially in the South, where it is used extensively throughout the season when it is found in plenty. Not only the vegetable, but also the leaves and flowers are used in cooking. The leaves have a high content of vitamins A, B and C along with proteins, iron, calcium, phosphorous and carbohydrates. Medicinally also they have a high value, acting as a tonic as well as a cure in certain ailments.

A glass of fresh drumstick leaf juice mixed with 1 tbsp honey taken at bed time cures vertigo, piles and indigestion. Fresh juice of flowers with 1 tbsp butter milk is a cure for asthma and stones in the bladder. Drumsticks are a cure for rheumatism, colitis and act as a medicine for weak nerves. In summer, it cools the body. A quote from the book *Medicinal Secrets of your Food* by Dr. Aman – "Almighty God has treasured enormous nutritive health in these cheap and discarded leaves".

Preparations

1. **Drumstick Leaves with Sprouted Moong** (Maharashtra)
2. **Drumstick Flower Dry Curry** (Maharashtra)
3. **Drumstick Sambar** (South India)
4. **Drumstick in Coconut Cream**
5. **Drumstick Fry**
6. **Drumstick Leaf Adai** (Tamil Nadu)

Drumstick Leaves with Sprouted Moong

Ingredients

2 cups cleaned, picked
   and washed drumstick leaves
2 tbsp green moong dal
1 onion, chopped (optional)
Juice of 1 lemon
Salt to taste

Seasoning
3 tsp oil
1 tsp cumin seeds
A pinch of asafoetida
2 minced green chillies
$\frac{1}{2}$" piece ginger, minced

Method

1. Soak dal overnight; next day, tie loosely in a muslin cloth and hang it for a whole day. On the third day, you will see that the dal has sprouted. Remove the dal carefully from the cloth, transfer onto a vessel and steam cook for 5-7 min.

2. Heat oil, add seasonings; when cumin seeds are done, add chillies, ginger and onion; fry till browned.

3. Add drumstick leaves, saute for another 3 min.; allow to cook till tender, adding water only if necessary.

4. Add sprouted moong, salt and cook further 2-3 min. Remove, sprinkle lemon juice.

Serve as an accompaniment with rice or chapathis.

Drumstick Flower Dry Curry

Ingredients

2 cups freshly picked
   drumstick flowers
1 medium onion, chopped
$\frac{1}{2}$ tsp turmeric powder
1 tsp tamarind pulp
2 tsp powdered jaggery
Salt to taste

Grind to paste
2 tbsp coconut gratings
3 red chillies
2 tsp coriander seeds
$\frac{1}{2}$ tsp cumin seeds

Seasoning
2 tbsp oil
1 tsp mustard seeds
2 sprigs curry leaves

Method

1. Wash flowers, add water and salt, cook till soft, set aside.

2. Season mustard seeds and curry leaves in oil, add onion along with turmeric powder, fry till onion is browned.

3. Add ground paste, stir fry 1-2 min. Add tamarind pulp, jaggery and cooked flowers. Simmer on low heat 3-5 min., till quite dry.

Serve with rice and dal.

Drumstick Sambar

Ingredients

1 cup tuvar dal
1 tsp turmeric powder
4-5 drumsticks
1 lemon size ball tamarind
1½ tsp oil (sesame seed oil)
Salt to taste

For the masala
¼ tsp asafoetida
¼ tsp fenugreek seeds
1 tbsp gram dal
3-4 dried red chillies
2 tbsp coriander seeds
4 tbsp grated coconut

Seasoning
1 tsp mustard seeds
2 sprigs curry leaves

Method

1. Heat 1 tbsp oil in a kadai, fry asafoetida and fenugreek seeds till they turn brown; remove from kadai. Add gram dal and red chillies, fry till dal turns golden brown. Remove. Add coriander seeds, fry 1-2 min., add coconut and fry till coconut turns golden brown; remove. Grind all these together to a fine paste, set aside.

2. Boil tuvar dal with ½ tsp turmeric powder in a pressure cooker. Mash, set aside.

3. Boil tamarind with sufficient water. Cool. Extract thick pulp.

4. Boil drumsticks with salt, ½ tsp turmeric powder. Cook till soft.

5. To cooked drumsticks add tamarind extract, simmer 1-2 min.; add mashed, dal, ground paste, some water and allow the mixture to simmer 3-5 min.

6. Season mustard seeds in oil, add curry leaves, add to sambar, mix, remove from fire.

Serve hot with rice or iddlis.

Note

Sambar can be prepared with a variety of vegetables, the most popular being drumstick and small onions sambar.

For this, peel onion, fry in $1\frac{1}{2}$ tbsp oil before adding turmeric powder, salt and tamarind extract. Rest of the method is the same.

Drumstick in Coconut Cream

Ingredients

4 drumsticks	2 tsp coriander powder
1 medium onion, chopped	1 tsp cumin powder
2 tomatoes, chopped	1 tsp chilli powder
2 sprigs curry leaves	$\frac{1}{2}$ tsp turmeric powder
$\frac{1}{2}$ cup grated coconut	1 tsp ginger-garlic paste
3 tbsp oil	Salt to taste
	2 tbsp chopped coriander leaves

Method

1. Add 1 cup boiling water to coconut; when cool, pass through a liquidiser till you get a very soft puree – this is the coconut cream, set aside.

2. Wash, cut drumsticks to 3″ pieces; set aside.

3. Heat oil, add curry leaves, onion, fry till browned. Add ginger-garlic paste, continue frying till oil surfaces.

4. Add tomatoes, continue to fry on medium heat, closing pan with a cover every now and then. This way, tomatoes get cooked faster without much oil.

5. Add all the powdered masalas (except salt), fry on low heat; add drumstick pieces and continue frying till they turn slightly soft.

6. Add 1-1½ cups water, salt, cover vessel and allow to cook on low heat till a thick gravy is formed.

7. Add half the coriander leaves, coconut cream, mix and turn off fire after just a minute or so.

Serve garnished with the rest of the coriander leaves. A very tasty dish; can be served with both rice and rotis.

Drumstick Fry

Ingredients

4 drumsticks, cut into 3" pieces
2 tbsp minced coriander leaves
2 tbsp gram flour
4 tsp curds
Little salt
Oil for frying

Mix together

2 tsp coriander powder
1 tsp cumin powder
1 tsp chilli powder
½ tsp turmeric powder
½ tsp garam masala powder
½ tsp pepper powder
A little salt

Method

1. Boil drumsticks with salt and enough water so that when cooked, the vegetable is soft and dry (there should be no water left in the pan).

2. To the dry powders, add gram flour and salt; mix. Beat curd smooth, add to dry masala to form a thick paste.

3. Coat drumstick pieces with the paste.

4. Heat a little oil, preferably in a non-stick pan. Add a few of the batter-coated drumstick pieces at a time and fry till they turn brown and crisp.

Serve hot as an accompaniment for a rice meal.

Drumstick Leaf Adai
(Drumstick Leaves in Dal Dosas)

Ingredients

1½ cups parboiled rice
⅓ cup each tuvar dal,
   chana dal and urad dal
3 sprigs curry leaves
3 cups chopped drumstick leaves

4 red chillies
4 green chillies
1 small piece of asafoetida
Salt to taste
Oil for frying

Method

1. Soak rice and dals separately for a few hours, overnight if possible. Grind rice for a while, add dals, the rest of the ingredients (on the right hand side, except oil), grind to a rough batter (like rava). Add enough water to make a pouring consistency.

2. Wash drumstick leaves, discard all stems, chop fine, set aside.

3. Heat a tawa, grease with some oil, pour a large ladleful of batter onto tawa, quickly spread it into a circle. Pour oil all around and in the centre.

4. Sprinkle 2-3 tbsp of drumstick leaves all over adai, cover and cook over medium heat till done. If you desire adai very crisp, carefully turn over and cook the other side also, pouring 1-2 tsp more oil and cooking on high flame. (If desired, mix the leaves with the batter for making adais – this will make it easier to fry.)

Serve hot with coconut chutney – makes a nutritious breakfast dish.

Note

You could substitute fenugreek leaves for drumstick leaves.

Fenugreek Leaves
(Methi Sag)

A familiar variety of greens, it is grown extensively all over India. Both the leaves and the seeds of the plant are used in cooking. Fenugreek seeds, specially, form part of the Indian spices and are used in various masalas in all types of Indian cooking. Very high in vitamin A. Also has carbohydrate, proteins, calcium and traces of iron. Both the leaves and the seeds have high medicinal value.

Both cooked and fresh juice of leaves are a medicine for liver and lungs and also a cure in the early stage of diabetes. Paste of leaves applied over the scalp, preserves natural colour and texture of hair and are a cure for dandruff. Seeds ground and mixed in curds is an antidote for diarrhoea and stomach ailments.

Leaves are very palatable and can be prepared in various forms of curries – dry and gravy; the seeds when fried have an aroma. Here are a few ways to prepare fenugreek leaves (*methi sag*).

Preparations

1. **Vendhia Keerai Sadam** (Tamil Nadu)
2. **Vendhia Keerai Paruppu** (Tamil Nadu)
3. **Methi-Moong Dal** (Maharashtra)
4. **Methi-Besan Dry Curry** (Maharashtra)
5. **Methi-Alu** (North India)
6. **Methi-Gajar** (North India)
7. **Methi-Muthias** (Gujarat)
8. **Vendhia Keerai Masala Morkuzhambu** (Tamil Nadu)

Vendhia Keerai Sadam
(Methi leaf Masala Rice)

Ingredients

1½ cups fine rice

3 cups chopped fenugreek leaves

1 small ball of tamarind

½ tsp turmeric powder

3-4 tbsp oil

Salt to taste

Seasoning

2 cloves (optional)

½ tsp mustard seeds

1 tbsp urad dal

1 tbsp chana dal

1 red chilli (broken into 2-3 pieces)

2 sprigs curry leaves

Fry in 2 tsp oil and powder

½ tsp fenugreek seeds

1 small piece asafoetida

1½ tbsp coriander seeds

1 tbsp chana dal

3-4 red chillies

1″ piece cinnamon

Method

1. Fry masala ingredients one at a time, removing each item after it is over; mix all together, powder; set aside.

2. Cook rice, preferably in a rice cooker so that each grain is separate. Transfer onto a plate, sprinkle about 2 tsp oil; set aside.

3. Extract thick pulp of tamarind by boiling in water and squeezing dry.

4. Heat oil, add seasonings one at a time and, when done, add curry leaves along with chopped fenugreek and turmeric powder. Fry for 1-2 min. till leaves become soft.

5. Add tamarind extract and salt, cover and allow to cook till dry.

6. Add powdered masala, stir 1-2 min., remove from fire; cool.

7. Pour this chutney onto the rice and with the tips of your fingers mix very lightly. Add some more oil if necessary.

Serve with 'Thair Pachadi' (raitha) and fried appalams (papads).

Vendhia Keerai Paruppu
(Methi-Tuvar Dal in Tamarind Sauce)

Ingredients

2 cups chopped fenugreek leaves
½ cup tuvar dal
½ tsp turmeric powder
1 small ball of tamarind
1 tsp chilli powder
Salt to taste

Seasoning
½ tbsp oil
½ tsp mustard seeds
¼ tsp asafoetida
1 tsp urad dal
1 tsp chana dal
1 sprig curry leaf

Method

1. Boil dal with ¼ tsp turmeric powder, cool, mash, set aside.

2. Take out tamarind extract, add 2 cups water. To this add all ingredients on the left hand side (except dal) and boil all together till it is reduced to less than half the quantity and the leaves are cooked.

3. Add mashed dal, mix, simmer 1-2 min.; remove.

4. Heat oil, add seasonings in the order given; when done, pour into dal; mix.

Serve hot with rice.

Methi-Moong Dal
(Fenugreek Leaves in Moong Dal)

Ingredients

2 cups chopped fenugreek leaves
$\frac{1}{2}$ cup moong dal
$\frac{1}{4}$ tsp turmeric powder
1 onion, chopped
1 tbsp chopped coriander leaves
1 tbsp oil
Juice of $\frac{1}{2}$ lemon
$\frac{1}{4}$ tsp sugar
Salt to taste

Dry roast

2 tsp coriander seeds
1 tsp cumin seeds
1 tbsp sesame seeds
2 tbsp grated coconut

Add the following and grind to paste

2 green chillies
3 cloves garlic
$\frac{1}{2}''$ piece ginger

Seasoning

$\frac{1}{2}$ tsp mustard seeds
1 red chilli, broken into pieces

Method

1. Cook dal with $\frac{1}{4}$ tsp turmeric powder; set aside.

2. Heat oil, add seasonings, stir fry; Add onions and $\frac{1}{4}$ tsp turmeric powder; fry till onion is browned.

3. Add ground paste, stir fry till oil surfaces. Add leaves and continue frying. Add salt, cover and cook till leaves are done.

4. Add dal and sugar, cook 1-2 min. more. Add lemon juice, mix and remove.

Serve with roti or rice.

Methi-Besan Dry Curry
(Fenugreek Leaves with Gram Flour)

Ingredients

2 cups chopped fenugreek leaves
8 tbsp gram flour
2 minced green chillies
4 tbsp curds
Salt to taste

½-1 tsp chilli powder
½ tsp turmeric powder
A large pinch of asafoetida
1 tsp coriander powder
1 tsp cumin powder

Seasoning

2 tbsp oil
½ tsp mustard seeds
1 red chilli, broken into 2 pieces
1 sprig curry leaf

Method

1. Mix all ingredients, except those of seasoning, into a thick batter, adding water if necessary. Pour batter into a cooker vessel and steam cook (without the weight) till done.

2. Remove cooked batter, cool and break this into crumbs.

3. Season mustard and curry leaves in oil, add fenugreek-gram flour mixture and stir fry on low heat till dry and crumbly (if necessary, add some more oil while frying).

Serve as a snack or as a side dish with rice and 'kadhi'.

Methi-Alu
(Fenugreek Leaves with Potatoes)

Ingredients

3 cups chopped fenugreek leaves

2 large potatoes

2-3 tbsp oil

1 tsp cumin seeds

2 red chillies

½ tsp turmeric powder

Salt to taste

Method

1. Wash and cut potatoes (without peeling) into cubes.

2. Heat oil, add cumin seeds; when done, add chilli (broken into 2-3 pieces each), fry till browned, add potato cubes and turmeric powder and fry on low heat for 2-3 min., cover and allow to cook.

3. When potatoes have turned slightly soft add chopped fenugreek, stir fry for another 2-3 min. more till well mixed.

4. Add salt, cover and cook on low heat till potatoes and fenugreek leaves are done and curry is dry (if necessary, sprinkle some water).

Serve hot with phulkas.

Methi-Gajar
(Fenugreek Leaves with Carrots)

Ingredients

2 cups chopped fenugreek leaves

3 medium carrots, cut into cubes

½ cup shelled peas

2 green chillies, minced

½″ piece ginger, minced

½ tsp chilli powder

¼ tsp turmeric powder

Juice of ½ lemon

½ tsp sugar

Salt to taste

Seasoning

1 tbsp oil

1 tsp cumin seeds

1 red chilli, broken into two pieces

Method

1. Heat oil, add cumin seeds and red chilli, and after browned, add minced chillies and ginger, fry 1 min., add carrots, continue to fry adding turmeric and chilli powders. When carrots have turned slightly soft, add chopped fenugreek leaves, fry mixing thoroughly. Add peas, salt and sugar and cook on low heat till carrots and chopped fenugreek leaves are done.

2. Remove from fire, add lemon juice and mix.

Serve with rotis.

Methi-Muthias

(Fenugreek Leaves steamed Savoury)

Ingredients

2 cups chopped fenugreek leaves
1 tsp cumin powder
$\frac{1}{2}$ tsp turmeric powder
$\frac{1}{2}$-1 tsp chilli powder
$\frac{1}{2}$-1 tsp sugar
$\frac{1}{2}$-1$\frac{1}{2}$ tbsp sour curds
1 cup gram flour
1 tbsp wheat flour

Garnish

1 tbsp grated coconut
1 tbsp chopped coriander leaves

Mince fine or grind

3-4 green chillies
3-4 cloves garlic
$\frac{1}{4}''$ piece ginger

Seasoning

1 tbsp oil
1 tsp mustard seeds
A big pinch of asafoetida
1 sprig chopped curry leaf

Method

1. Mix all ingredients together (except those of seasoning and garnish) to form a smooth dough. Divide dough into 4; make rolls from each portion.

2. Steam cook these rolls in a pressure cooker without the weight. Cool, cut into $\frac{1}{2}''$ circles, arrange these on a serving plate.

3. Heat oil, add seasonings and, when done, pour over 'muthias'; garnish with coconut and coriander leaves.

Serve as a tea time snack or at lunch.

Vendhia Keerai Masala Morkuzhambu

(Fenugreek Leaves in seasoned Butter Milk)

Ingredients

2 cups chopped fenugreek leaves
2 large potatoes
2-4 small brinjals
3-4 green chillies, slit
1 large onion, sliced
3-4 cloves garlic, minced
2 cups butter milk
½-1 tsp chilli powder
½ tsp turmeric powder
Salt to taste

Grind to paste
6 tbsp grated coconut
2 tsp poppy seeds

Seasoning
3 tbsp oil or ghee
2 cloves
2 cardamom
½″ piece cinnamon
1 bay leaf

Method

1. Peel and cut potatoes into cubes, slit brinjals into fours.

2. Heat oil/ghee, add seasonings and, when done, add the chillies, onion and garlic. Fry till onion turns brown, adding turmeric powder. Add potatoes, fry 1-2 min., add brinjals and, lastly, add fenugreek leaves, frying all for a while. Sprinkle some water, add salt, cover and cook on low heat till vegetables are nearly done.

3. To ground paste, add butter milk, chilli powder, mix thoroughly and pour onto vegetables. Allow to cook till gravy is well blended.

Serve hot with pulav or puris.

Note

If gravy is not thick enough, you could mix 1-2 tsp rice flour with butter milk. Thickening gravy with rice flour applies to all South Indian gravy preparations.

Tips ....   **Cooking Vegetables**

"In order to retain both colour and vitamin content in vegetables, it is important to cook them with care. Unless stated to the contrary, vegetables should go into a small quantity of boiling, salted water and, in the case of a large amount of vegetables like cabbage, should be added steadily rather than all at once. By putting into the water in this way, the liquid keeps boiling."

Serving Vegetables

"Serve the vegetables immediately they are cooked, for keeping hot, even for a short time, causes a loss of vitamins. When cooking root vegetables, particularly potatoes, steady cooking, rather than too rapid, is considered advisable."

– Marguerite Patten
(From the book *Fruit and Vegetable Cookery*)

Garlic, Ginger & Green Chillies

All these three are used as spices in Indian cooking – no preparation is complete without the addition of one, two or all three of them. Combined with onion, they form the most important ingredient in our cuisine both in everyday cooking as well as making chutneys, sauces and pickles for preserving.

Garlic has a high content of carbohydrate. It also contains protein, calcium and vitamin C. Garlic is used extensively for its medicinal properties, specially in ayurveda and home remedies. It is considered a blood purifier, has very good carminative properties and is a nerve tonic as well. Boiled with milk and taken at bed time, it is an effective cure for asthma. It is a boon to patients with heart ailments, rheumatism and sciatica. Taken everyday, it increases longevity. Besides specific ailments, garlic is used for general body care.

Ginger is cultivated all over India for its aromatic root – it has been known from Vedic times for its extensive medicinal properties. Has a high content of vitamin A, carbohydrate, protein and traces of calcium and phosphorous. Ginger juice combined with mint and lemon juice is a cure for bronchitis, indigestion, piles, jaundice and even urtecaria (allergy).

Green and Red Chillies are used extensively in our culinary preparations. Green chillies have a high content of carbohydrate and protein besides vitamins A and C as well as calcium and phosphorus. Chillies are rich in Rutin, an enzyme of high pharmaceutical value.

Preparations

GARLIC

1. **Garlic Rice** (North India)
2. **Poondu Rasam** (Tamil Nadu)
3. **Garlic Chutney** (Andhra Pradesh)
4. **Garlic Toast/Croutons** (Western)

GINGER

5. **Ginger Lemon** (North India)
6. **Inji Pachadi** (Kerala)
7. **Inji Rasam** (Tamil Nadu)
8. **Puli Inji** (Tamil Nadu)

GREEN CHILLIES

9. **Green Chillies Gojju (Chutney)**
10. **Mirch-ke-salan** (Parsi)

Garlic Rice

Ingredients

1 cup cooked rice
½ tsp garlic paste
A few spring onions, chopped
  (about 1 cup)
2 green chillies, minced (Optional)
½ cup boiled peas
1 egg (optional)
2 tbsp oil

Seasoning

¼ turmeric powder
½ tsp chilli powder
1 tsp vinegar
1 tbsp chopped parsley or
  coriander leaves
Salt to taste

Method

1. Cook rice with a little salt, so that each grain is separate, preferably in a rice cooker.

2. Heat oil, brown garlic paste, add spring onions and chillies, stir fry -2 min. or till slightly done. Add peas, stir a min. more.

3. Beat egg, add turmeric and chilli powders, some salt; pour into masala, stir fry further till all water has evaporated; remove from fire.

4. Add rice and vinegar, mix lightly and thoroughly, adding parsley or chopped coriander leaves.

Serve hot with dal. Goes well with a Chinese meal also.

Note

If you wish to omit egg, delete step 3. Add turmeric powder, chilli powder in step 2.

Poondu Rasam

(Garlic Rasam)

Ingredients

½ cup tuvar dal
½ tsp turmeric powder
6-8 cloves garlic
1 small ball of tamarind
Salt to taste

Grind to paste

1 tsp pepper corns
1 tsp cumin seeds

Seasoning

2 tsp ghee
1 tsp mustard seeds
1 red chilli, broken into two
1 sprig curry leaf

Method

1. Boil dal with turmeric powder; while still hot, mash, add 2 cups water, set aside.

2. Take out extract of tamarind, add 1½ cups water, salt, curry leaves, ground paste and crushed garlic; boil till reduced to less than half the original quantity.

3. Add dal water, cook further 2-3 min., remove from fire.

4. Season ingredients in ghee, add to rasam.

Serve as an appetizer or with rice.

Note

Helps in digestion.

Garlic Chutney

Ingredients

12 cloves garlic
1 medium onion
3-4 red chillies
1 small ball of tamarind
Salt to taste

Seasoning

3 tbsp oil
½ tsp mustard seeds
A pinch of asafoetida
1 sprig curry leaf

Method

1. Grind to paste all ingredients on the right hand side.
2. Heat oil, add seasonings and, when done, add ground chutney and keep stirring till oil surfaces.

Serve with dosais or vadas – will keep for a long time.

Garlic Toast/Croutons

Ingredients

8 slices of bread	8-10 cloves garlic
2 tbsp soft butter	1 tsp pepper powder
2 tbsp grated cheese	$\frac{1}{2}$ tsp chilli powder
Salt (if necessary)	1 tsp mixed fresh or dried herbs
	(parsley, dill and basil)

Method

1. Crush or grate garlic, squeeze to extract juice.
2. Mix together all ingredients (except bread) with garlic juice. Beat mixture to smoothness.
3. Spread bread slices with a generous helping of garlic-butter-cheese mixture on one side only.
4. Grill in an oven toaster for 5 min. or till browned and crisp.

Serve hot with soup.

Garlic Croutons

Ingredients as above. Cut bread into cubes (after removing the edges). Mix all other ingredients with one tbsp butter. Heat a non-stick pan, melt one tbsp butter, put mixture into it and, on very low heat, add bread cubes and keep frying, turning over cubes all the while. When crisp and browned, remove. Add a little more butter if necessary to get it crisp.

Ginger Lemon

Ingredients

½ cup ginger juice (2 tbsp chopped ginger)

1 cup lemon juice (4-6 lemons)

2 cups sugar

Method

1. To chopped ginger add one cup water, grind to a smooth paste. Leave this in a cup for a while for juice to settle down. Take out the top portion and discard sediment.

2. Add sugar to ginger juice and some more water, if necessary. Boil to one-thread consistency, remove from fire, cool.

3. Add lemon juice and a few drops (2-3) of yellow food colour (optional), mix and bottle.

A very refreshing drink on a hot day!

Inji Pachadi
(Ginger Raitha)

Ingredients

2″ piece ginger
1-2 green chillies
3 tbsp grated coconut
Salt to taste
1 cup curds

Seasoning
1 tbsp oil
1 tsp mustard seeds
2 sprigs curry leaves
1 medium onion, chopped
2 clover garlic, minced (optional)

Method

1. Wash, scrape, chop ginger. Grind to a paste with all the ingredients given on the left side (except curds).

2. Beat curds smooth, add ground paste, mix.

3. Season in oil ingredients given. When onion turns brown (as well as garlic), pour seasonings into curds; mix thoroughly.

Serve with pulav or lemon rice.

Note

A piece of chopped cucumber or tomato may be added to pachadi, if desired.

Inji Rasam

Ingredients

½ cup cooked tuvar dal	**Seasoning**
1″ piece ginger, minced	2 tbsp ghee
2-3 green chillies, cut	1 tsp mustard seeds
1 tbsp chopped coriander leaves	A pinch of asafoetida
Juice of 1 lemon	2 sprigs curry leaves
1 tomato, chopped	
Salt to taste	

Method

1. Add 2 cups boiling water to dal, churn, set aside.

2. Heat ghee, add seasonings in the order given; when done, add chillies, ginger and tomato; fry for a while till tomatoes and ginger get soft.

3. Add dal water, salt, half of the coriander leaves, boil for a while; remove from fire.

4. Add lemon juice, rest of the coriander leaves, mix.

Serve very hot as an appetizer. Very welcome on a rainy day!

Puli Inji
(Ginger in Tamarind Sauce)

Ingredients

1 large piece ginger
5-6 green chillies
½ tsp turmeric powder
1 large ball of tamarind
1 small ball of jaggery
Salt to taste

Seasoning

3 tbsp sesame seed oil
½ tsp mustard seeds
A large pinch of asafoetida
2 sprigs curry leaves

Method

1. Scrape, wash and chop ginger to very small pieces. Cut chillies into 2-3 pieces each. Boil tamarind water, take out pulp. Set aside each separately.

2. Heat oil, add seasonings and, when done, add chillies, ginger and turmeric powder; fry 5-8 min. on low heat till ginger pieces turn soft.

3. Add tamarind pulp, jaggery and salt.and simmer on low heat till oil surfaces and a chutney consistency is obtained. Remove from fire, cool and bottle.

Serve with curd rice or dosas. Will keep for over a month.

Green Chillies Gojju (Chutney)

Ingredients

50 gm. green chillies
1 lemon size ball tamarind
1 large piece of jaggery
3 tbsp oil
½ tsp turmeric powder
Salt to taste

Seasoning

1 tsp mustard seeds
½ tsp fenugreek seeds
¼ tsp asafoetida
2 sprigs curry leaves

Method

1. Wash, cut chillies into 3-4 pieces each. boil tamarind in water, take out pulp, set aside.

2. Heat oil, add seasonings, in the order given. When done, add curry leaves and green chillies; fry 2-3 min. adding turmeric powder.

3. When chillies have become soft, add tamarind pulp, jaggery, salt, a little water ($\frac{1}{2}$-$\frac{3}{4}$ cup); cook on low heat till chutney consitency.

Serve with curd rice.

Note

Refrigerated, will keep for a month. If desired, you can add 1-2 capsicums; reduce chillies.

Mirch-ke-salan

Ingredients

125 gm green chillies
2 large onions
$\frac{1}{2}$ tsp turmeric powder
1 large lemon-size ball of tamarind
A small piece of jaggery
2 tbsp chopped coriander leaves
2 sprig curry leaves
6-8 tbsp oil
Salt to taste

Dry roast and grind
$1\frac{1}{2}$ tbsp coriander seeds
$\frac{1}{2}$ tbsp cumin seeds
1 tbsp sesame seeds
1 tbsp ground nut
2 tbsp grated copra
Grind to paste, separately
2″ piece ginger
12 cloves garlic

Method

1. Wash, dry and slit chillies right through, without breaking the stalk. If too long, cut into two, then slit each separate, keeping the ends intact.

2. Heat 3 tbsp oil, fry chillies 2-3 min., remove (when slightly soft), set aside.

3. Pour rest of the oil into kadai, season with curry leaves, add chopped onions, fry to a dark brown colour, add ginger-garlic paste along with turmeric powder, fry 2-3 min. more.

4. Add ground masala,, continue frying till oil surfaces.

5. Now, add chillies, stir fry; add tamarind extract, jaggery and salt; cook on low heat stirring once or twice till gravy is formed, adding coriander leaves. Simmer min. more, remove, cool and bottle.

Serve with chapathis or bread.

Note

1. For this recipe, use the long, light green chillies, generally used in making pickles.

2. You can substitute capsicum for green chillies.

Tips ....   **Rice Cooking**

When cooking rice for seasoned rice, layered pulav, etc., use a rice cooker. If you do not have one, cook rice in a pressure cooker without putting on the weight.

When rice is ready, cool by spreading it on a plate, sprinkling ghee/oil.

Gourds

Gourds come in all shapes and sizes and they all belong to the same botanical family. They are found in plenty all over India, especially during the monsoon. They are grown in abundance in the western countries too. Referred to as squash or marrow, gourds in this chapter include ash gourd, bitter gourd, bottle gourd, ridge gourd, snake gourd, pumpkin and vegetable marrow.

Gourds have a high content of nutritional, medicinal and therapeutic properties. They have been known since ancient times in folk medicines, ayurveda, unani and home remedies. They have a high content of vitamins, salts and minerals, and they provide the necessary roughage to the system. They also provide bulk food to the body with a low calorific content and are therefore recommended for diabetes, especially ash gourd and bottle gourd. Ash gourd has a blood clotting property and is used for specific medicinal purposes like bleeding nose and piles. Also, juice of ash gourd is used for treatment of arthritis in ayurveda. Bottle gourd is highly recommended for people suffering from diabetes, gastric ulcer, piles and high blood pressure. Bottle gourd juice is very valuable in dehydration and acts as a laxative in constipation.

Among the gourds, bitter gourd has the most nutritive as well as medicinal properties and therefore should be *part of your daily diet*. Since it has all the essential vitamins and minerals, regular intake of bitter gourd acts as a buffer in prevention of many ailments by increasing body resistance against infection. Bitter gourd juice is highly recommended for diabetes. Also, bitter gourd juice mixed with honey is a cure for asthma, gastric ulcer and other liver ailments.

Vegetable marrow (chow-chow), like the rest of the gourds, supplies bulk with low-calorie content. It is an ideal vegetable for invalids and children for its easily digestible property. Both ridge gourd and snake gourd, like other gourds, have similar properties in that both have low calorific content and are good for diabetics. Gourds with their high water content have a cooling effect on the system and therefore should be consumed daily during the hot summer days.

Gourds lend themselves for easy mode of cooking and are therefore a cook's delight. Preparations of different gourds are mentioned here. Except those of the bitter gourd, most of the recipes of gourd are interchangeable, specially those of bottle gourd and vegetable marrow. There are many, many ways of preparing gourds.

Preparations

ASH GOURD

1. **Pushanikai Morkuzhambu** (Tamil Nadu)
2. **Boodhkumblekai Kootu** (Karnataka)
3. **Kashi Halwa**

BITTER GOURD

4. **Pagakkai Pitlai** (Tamil Nadu)
5. **Hagalkai Gojju** (Karnataka)
6. **Pavakkai Moilee** (Kerala)
7. **Stuffed Karela** (Punjab)
8. **Fried Karela** (Punjab)
9. **Karela Nawabi**

BOTTLE GOURD

10. **Sorakkai Kootu** (Tamil Nadu)
11. **Bottle Gourd Stew in Milk**
12. **Lauki-Chana Dal in Coconut Milk**
13. **Doodhi Muthias** (Gujarat)
14. **Lauki Koftas in Tomato Gravy** (Punjab)
15. **Lauki Raitha** (Uttar Pradesh)
16. **Lauki Kheer** (North India)
17. **Lauki Parathas** (Gujarat)

PUMPKIN

18. **Parangikai Palkootu** (Tamil Nadu)
19. **Seekumblekai Gojju** (Karnataka)
20. **Mathan Puli Pachadi** (Kerala)
21. **Mathan Eriseri** (Kerala)
22. **Pumpkin – Sweet and Sour** (North India)
23. **Pumpkin Khorma** (North India)
24. **Pumpkin Halwa** (North India)
25. **Pumpkin-Nut Pie** (Western)

RIDGE GOURD

26. **Peerkangkai Chutney** (Tamil Nadu)
27. **Peerkangkai Paruppu** (Tamil Nadu)
28. **Turai Tomato** (Parsi)
29. **Jhinga-Posto Charchari** (West Bengal)

SNAKE GOURD

30. **Pudalangai Thair Pachadi** (Tamil Nadu)
31. **Padavalkai Kootu** (Karnataka)
32. **Stuffed Padaval** (Karnataka)

VEGETABLE MARROW

33. **Vegetable Marrow Soup** (Western)
34. **Vegetable Marrow – Sweet and Sour**
35. **Vegetable Marrow Puri**

Pushanikai Morkuzhambu

(Ash Gourd-Coconut Kadhi)

Ingredients

½ kg ash gourd
1½-2 cups curds
½ tsp turmeric powder
Salt to taste

Seasoning

2 tsp oil
1 tsp mustard seeds
A pinch of fenugreek seeds
2 sprigs curry leaves

Grind to fine paste

1½ tbsp coriander seeds
1 tsp cumin seeds
1 tbsp chana dal
4-5 green chillies
4 tbsp grated coconut

Method

1. Peel and cut ash gourd into medium size pieces; add water, turmeric powder, salt, 1 sprig curry leaf and boil.

2. Churn curds, add ground paste, mix thoroughly, add to boiled gourd with some water, if too thick. Simmer 1-2 min., remove from fire.

3. Season mustard, fenugreek and curry leaves in oil, add to kuzhambu.

Serve with rice and 'paruppu usli' (see under **Beans** – 'Kothavarangai Paruppu Usli', Page 21).

Note

The same preparations can be made using bottle gourd, vegetable marrow and snake gourd.

Boodhkumblekai Kootu

(Ash Gourd-Chana Dal Gravy)

Ingredients

½ kg ash gourd
½ cup chana dal
½ tsp turmeric powder
2 sprigs curry leaves
1 tsp tamarind pulp
Salt to taste
½ tsp rice flour

Fry in 1 tsp oil and grind to paste
2 tsp coriander seeds
½ tsp cumin seeds
¼ fenugreek seeds
½ tsp pepper corns
2 tsp chana dal
A pinch of asafoetida
4 tbsp coconut gratings
2-3 red chillies

Seasoning

2 tsp oil
1 tsp mustard seeds
1 sprig curry leaf

Method

1. Pare and cut ash gourd into small cubes, add ¼ tsp turmeric powder, salt and enough water to cook. Cook separately the chana dal with ¼ tsp turmeric powder. When cooked mix with the gourd.

2. Add ground paste, tamarind pulp, curry leaves; simmer 2-3 min. Mix rice flour with some water to smooth paste and cook a while longer till gravy is blended.

3. Season ingredients in oil, add to kootu, mix.

Serve hot with rice.

Note

This recipe can be prepared with bottle gourd and snake gourd also.

Kashi Halwa
(Ash Gourd Halwa)

Ingredients

2 cups grated ash gourd
1 cup milk
1 cup khova
2-2½ cups sugar
1 tsp powdered cardamom

2 tbsp ghee
1 tbsp cashew nuts
   (broken into small pieces)
1 tbsp raisins
A large pinch of cooking camphor

Method

1. Squeeze water from gratings; add boiled milk and cook till soft, remove from fire.

2. To sugar, add 1 cup water, boil till thick; remove any scum forming on top.

3. When syrup is one-thread consistency, add boiled gourd, crumbled khova and stir on low heat till mixture gets quite thick.

4. Add ghee gradually till well blended. Add cooking camphor, mix. When halwa starts to leave sides of vessel, remove from fire.

5. Fry nuts and raisins in 1 tbsp ghee, add to halwa, mix.

Serve hot as dessert.

Note

The same preparation can be made with bottle gourd or vegetable marrow.

Pagakkai Pitlai
(Bitter Gourd Sambar)

Ingredients

¼ kg bitter gourd
½ cup tuvar dal
1 tsp turmeric powder
1 lemon size ball of tamarind
A pinch of jaggery (optional)
Salt to taste

Fry in 1 tsp oil and powder

1 tbsp coriander seeds
¾ tbsp chana dal
½ tsp urad dal
1 small piece asafoetida
4 red chillies
3 tbsp grated coconut

Seasoning

1 tbsp oil
½ tsp mustard seeds
1 red chilli, broken
2 sprigs curry leaves

Method

1. Cook dal with ½ tsp turmeric powder, set aside. Wash, cut bitter gourd into 1″ pieces, set aside.

2. Fry masala ingredients in oil, in the order given, removing each after frying. Fry coconut last till brownish in colour. Powder all together slightly rough, set aside.

3. Heat oil, add seasonings and when done add bitter gourd pieces along with turmeric powder and fry till soft, stirring all the while.

4. Extract juice of tamarind, add to gourd along with salt; allow to simmer for a while; add jaggery.

5. When gourd is sufficiently cooked, add dal, simmer 1-2 min. Lastly add powdered masala with some water if necessary; cook 1-2 min. more.

Serve hot with rice and papads.

Hagalkai Gojju

(Sweet-Sour Bitter Gourd Chutney)

Ingredients

¼ kg bitter gourd
½ tsp turmeric powder
1 lemon-size ball tamarind
1 small lemon-size ball of jaggery
2 sprigs curry leaves
3 tbsp oil
Salt to taste

Fry in 1 tsp oil and powder
1½ tbsp urad dal
4-5 red chillies
2-3 tbsp grated copra

Method

1. Wash and cut bitter gourd into small pieces.
2. Heat oil, fry gourd pieces adding ½ tsp turmeric powder till pieces are crisp and dark brown in colour.
3. Boil tamarind in water, take out extract. Boil this along with turmeric powder, salt, jaggery and curry leaves. When sufficiently boiled, it will have reduced to half the quantity. Add bitter gourd pieces, prepared powder, simmer 2-3 min. till thick chutney consistency.

Note

Refrigerated, it will keep for a week.

Pavakkai Moilee

(Bitter Gourd with Coconut Milk)

Ingredients

¼ kg bitter gourd
1 small onion, minced
1 tsp chilli powder
½ tsp turmeric powder

2 sprigs curry leaves
½ cup thick coconut milk
2 tbsp oil
Juice of ½ lemon
Salt to taste

Method

1. Wash, cut bitter gourd into very small pieces.

2. Heat oil, fry gourd pieces along with salt, curry leaves, turmeric and chilli powder till crisp and brown. Remove and cool.

3. To gourd pieces add minced onion, lemon juice and coconut milk; mix.

Serve as an accompaniment like a salad.

Note

If you do not desire the bitterness of the gourd, follow this method: after cutting, sprinkle salt and turmeric powder, leave for some time. Squeeze pieces, discard water and then fry. But it may be mentioned here that you will be discarding the nutrients. This method (of removing bitterness) applies to all bitter gourd preparations.

Stuffed Karela
(Stuffed Bitter Gourd)

Ingredients

6 medium karela
1 small onion, minced
1 potato or carrot
   (boiled and mashed)
1 tbsp tamarind pulp
1 tomato chopped
4 tbsp oil
½ tsp turmeric powder
Juice of ½ lemon
Salt to taste

Grind to paste
   3-4 green chillies
   ½" piece ginger
   1 tbsp chopped coriander leaves
Powdered masala
   2 tsp coriander powder
   1 tsp cumin powder
   1 tsp chilli powder
   ½ tsp turmeric powder
   ½ tsp garam masala

Method

1. Scrape, wash and slit karela lengthwise; sprinkle salt and turmeric powder all over surface as well as inside; leave aside for an hour or so. Squeeze out as much juice as possible, wash karela 2-3 times in water. Now boil enough water, immerse karelas, add some salt, tamarind pulp and cook till they turn slightly soft – do not let them cook *fully*. Remove from water, carefully scoop out pulp and seeds, set aside.

2. Heat oil (half the quantity), add chopped onions, fry till browned. Add tomatoes, fry till soft.

3. Add ground paste, continue frying adding the dry masala one by one. Stir fry till oil surfaces.

4. Add mashed potato or carrot, mix well adding lemon juice and salt. Remove from fire, cool, divide into 6 portions.

5. Carefully stuff potato mixture into each of the karelas, secure the two pieces with a thread or stick with a thick coat of flour paste.

6. Heat some of the oil in a non-stick pan, carefully slide the karelas one by one, pour some oil over the karelas, fry 3-5 min. Cover and cook in 'sim' till done.

Fried Karela – Plain or Spicy
(Fried Bitter Gourd)

Ingredients

For Plain Karela
- ¼ kg karela
- ½ tsp turmeric powder
- ½ tsp chilli powder
- Salt to taste
- 2 tbsp oil

For Spicy Karela
- 3 red chillies
- 2 green chillies, chopped
- ¼ tsp asafoetida
- 1 tsp coriander-cumin seeds
- 2 tbsp coconut gratings
- 1 small piece tamarind

Method

Plain Karela

1. Wash and cut karela into thin rounds or into very small pieces. Add turmeric powder and some salt, leave aside for a while. If you do not like the bitter taste, squeeze dry the karela pieces, leave on a paper towel for 1-2 min. for water, if any, to be absorbed.

2. Heat oil, fry gourd pieces, stirring all the while. Add chilli powder and some more salt if necessary, fry till dark brown in colour.

Spicy Karela

1. Heat 1 tsp oil, fry red chilli, coriander-cumin seeds and asafoetida, remove from kadai. Add chopped chillies and coconut. Fry till coconut becomes light brown in colour. Remove from kadai. Add tamarind, salt (if required) and powder the whole lot of spices roughly, set aside.

2. Prepare karela as in previous recipe. Before removing the fried gourd from kadai add the prepared powder, mix thoroughly.

Note

For this recipe, do not use chilli powder while frying karela.

Karela Nawabi
(Bitter Gourd in Masala)

Ingredients

¼ kg karela	2 tsp coriander powder
2 tbsp chana dal	½ tsp cumin powder
1 onion, minced	1 tsp chilli powder
4-5 cloves garlic	½ tsp turmeric powder
½ cup curds	1 tsp amchoor
A piece of jaggery	1 tsp aniseeds
2 tbsp oil	**Seasoning**
Salt to taste	1 tbsp oil
	¼ tsp fenugreek seeds

Method

1. Remove bitterness of karela thus: wash, cut karela, remove the inner pulp and seeds; now cut karela into small pieces, sprinkle salt, ½ tsp turmeric powder, ½ tsp amchoor and leave aside for 3-4 hours. Now squeeze the pieces, discard the karela juice. Wash pieces in water 2 or 3 times; once again squeeze out all water, drain pieces on paper towel.
2. In a pressure pan put all ingredients except those of seasoning and pressure cook till done.
3. Heat oil, add fenugreek seeds, fry till dark brown. Add cooked karela and stir fry on low heat till oil surfaces .

Serve with puris.

Note: Refrigerated, it will keep for a week or more.

If you wish to retain the bitterness as well as the nutrients, omit step 1. Instead, add chopped karela with the rest of the ingredients in the pressure pan and cook.

168

Sorakkai Kootu

(Bottle Gourd and Moong Dal Gravy)

Ingredients

½ kg sorakkai
½ cup moong dal
½ tsp turmeric powder
Salt to taste
2 sprigs curry leaves

Grind to paste

3 tbsp grated coconut
3-4 green chillies
1 tsp cumin seeds

Seasoning

2 tsp oil
½ tsp mustard seeds
1 tsp urad dal

Method

1. Peel and cut sorakkai into small cubes, add ¼ tsp turmeric powder, some salt, curry leaves and cook. Cook dal with ¼ tsp turmeric powder.

2. Mix together the cooked dal, vegetables and ground paste, adding some water if too thick. Simmer 2-3 min. till well blended.

3. Season mustard and dal in oil, add to kootu.

Serve hot with rice or chapathis.

Note

'Kootu' can be prepared with any of the gourds except bitter gourd.

Bottle Gourd Stew in Milk

Ingredients

½ kg bottle gourd
1 onion, chopped
1 cup milk
1 tbsp flour
2 tbsp ghee
1 tbsp chopped coriander leaves
Salt to taste

Seasoing

2 cloves
2 small cardamom
½" piece cinnamon
½ tsp pepper corns
1-2 slit green chillies (optional)
¼" piece ginger, minced

Method

1. Peel and cut bottle gourd into medium size cubes.
2. Heat ghee, add spices and, when done, the chillies and ginger along with chopped onions. Fry till onion turns pink in colour – *do not let onion get brown.*
3. Now add gourd cubes, stir fry 1-2 min., add salt, sprinkle some water, cover and cook on low heat till done.
4. Blend flour with milk, add chopped coriander leaves and pour this into the cooked gourd, simmer for 1-2 min. or till well blended.

Serve hot with puris.

A mildly spiced gravy which is very nutritious and, therefore, best suited for children.

Lauki-Chana Dal in Coconut Milk

(Bottle Gourd and Chana Dal in Coconut Milk)

Ingredients

½ kg lauki
½ cup chana dal
½ cup coconut gratings
1 tsp rice
½ tsp chilli powder (optional)
¼ tsp turmeric powder
1 onion, chopped
2-3 tbsp oil
2 tbsp chopped coriander leaves
Salt to taste

Grind to paste
   1-2 green chillies
   ½" piece ginger
   3 cloves garlic

Seasoning
   ½ tsp cumin seeds
   A pinch of asafoetida
   2 cloves
   ¼ tsp pepper corns
   ½" piece cinnamon

Method

1. Boil chana dal with ¼ tsp turmeric powder, set aside.
2. Peel and cut lauki into cubes. Grind coconut with rice to a very fine paste. Add 1-1½ cups hot water, mix, set aside.
3. Heat oil, add seasonings and, when done, add onion, fry to brown. Add ground paste and fry till oil surfaces. Then add chill and turmeric powder, continuing to fry all the time.

4. Add lauki, stir fry 1-2 min., add salt, sprinkle some water, cover and cook on low heat till the vegetable gets soft.

5. Add coconut milk, chopped coriander leaves and cook till well blended.

Serve hot with puris or parathas.

Doodhi Muthias

(Bottle Gourd steamed Savoury)

Ingredients

1 cup grated doodhi
1 cup gram flour
1 tbsp flour
2 tsp coriander-cumin powder
$\frac{1}{2}$ tsp chilli powder
A pinch of sugar
A pinch of turmeric powder
Salt to taste
1 tbsp curds

Mince fine
2-3 green chillies
$\frac{1}{2}$" piece ginger
A handful of coriander leaves

Seasoning
1 tbsp oil
$\frac{1}{2}$ tsp mustard seeds
A pinch of asafoetida

Garnish
1 tbsp grated coconut
1 tsp chopped coriander leaves

Method

1. Mix all the ingredients together, except those of seasoning and garnish, to form a smooth dough. Divide the dough into 4 portions, make rolls from each portion.

2. Steam cook these rolls in a pressure cooker, without putting on the weight. Cool and cut into $\frac{1}{2}$" circles. Keep them on a plate.

3. Heat oil, add seasonings, pour over muthias. Garnish with coconut and coriander leaves

Serve as a tea time snack or as an extra item for your lunch menu.

Lauki Koftas in Tomato Gravy

(Bottle Gourd balls in Tomato Gravy)

Ingredients

For Koftas:
2 cups grated lauki
2+2 tbsp gram flour
1/4 tsp turmeric powder
1/2 tsp garam masala
1/2-1 tsp chilli powder
Oil for frying
Salt to taste

For Gravy
1/2 kg tomatoes
1 tbsp ghee
2 tsp coriander powder
1 tsp cumin powder
1/2 tsp turmeric powder
1/2 tsp chilli powder
1/2 tsp garam masala
1/2 tsp sugar, salt to taste
1/2 tbsp chopped coriander leaves

For Koftas:
Mince very fine
2 green chillies
1/2" piece ginger
3 cloves garlic
A little coriander leaves
A few mint leaves

Grind to paste (for Gravy)
1 medium onion
3 cloves garlic
2-3 green chillies
1/2" piece ginger

For Garnish
1/2 cup cream
1 tbsp chopped coriander leaves

Method

1. To grated lauki add turmeric powder and salt, keep aside for 1/2 hour. Just before frying koftas, squeeze gratings. Keep aside the lauki juice for cooking gravy.
2. To squeezed gratings, add minced and dry ingredients (only 2 tbsp gram flour), mix thoroughly, make balls.
3. Heat oil, roll lauki balls in gram flour, deep fry on low heat till golden brown. Drain and set aside.
4. Boil, cool, puree tomatoes.
5. Remove oil from kadai leaving just about 2 tbsp, add 1 tbsp of ghee, fry ground paste till done, add powdered masala and continue frying till oil surfaces.
6. Add tomato puree, sugar, salt and coriander leaves; simmer till blended.
7. Add koftas, continue to cook 1-2 min. more.

To Serve: Pour gravy into a bowl. Beat cream, pour over koftas, garnish with coriander leaves.

Lauki Raitha

(Bottle Gourd in seasoned Curds)

Ingredients

¼ kg lauki	1 tsp cumin seeds
1 small onion, minced	½ tsp chilli powder
1½ cup curds	½ tsp garam masala
1-2 green chillies, minced	Salt to taste
1 tbsp minced coriander leaves	2 tsp ghee

Method

1. Peel and cut lauki into very small pieces. Add just enough water along with salt; cook till soft and all water absorbed.

2. Broil and powder cumin seeds.

3. Heat ghee, fry cooked lauki pieces till quite dry, cool.

4. Beat curds, add minced chillies, onion, ½ tbsp coriander leaves; add lauki, mix thoroughly, pour raitha into a bowl.

5. Garnish with the rest of the masala powders by sprinkling all over the surface along with coriander leaves.

Serve with any pulav.

Note

You can substitute vegetable marrow for bottle gourd.

Lauki Kheer

(Bottle Gourd Payas)

Ingredients

¼ kg lauki	½ tsp vanilla or rose essence
1 litre milk	2 drops green food colour
½ tin condensed milk	1 tbsp chopped cashew nuts
½ cup sugar	and raisins
½ cup sago	2 tsp ghee

Method

1. Peel and grate lauki, steam cook just about 3-5 min. or till it gets soft; remove from fire, cool.

2. Soak sago for an hour or so.

3. Boil milk for a while, add sago; continue to boil till sago is cooked and milk gets quite thick. Beat condensed milk with some hot water (about ½ cup), pour into boiling milk, cook for a while.

4. Now add lauki, food colour, cook 1-2 min. Add essence, mix thoroughly; pour into a bowl.

5. Fry nuts and raisins in ghee; pour into kheer mix.

Serve hot or cold.

Note

Similar preparation can be made using vegetable marrow.

Lauki Parathas
(Bottle Gourd Parathas)

Ingredients

1 cup grated lauki	1 tsp coriander powder
2 cups wheat flour	½ tsp cumin powder
2 tbsp ghee or oil to mix	½ tsp garam masala
Salt to taste	¼ tsp pepper powder
Ghee/oil to make parathas	2 tsp minced coriander leaves
	2 minced green chillies

Method

1. Mix all ingredients using very little water to a soft dough. Cover, set aside 1 hour before using.
2. Take lemon-size balls, roll parathas using flour for dusting.

3. Fry the usual way, using ghee or oil.

Serve hot with vegetable curry or dal.

Note

Parathas can be prepared in a similar way using green papaya, vegetable marrow and radish.

Parangikai Palkootu
(Tender Pumpkin cooked in Milk)

Ingredients

½ kg very tender pumpkin
1-1½ cups milk
1 tsp rice flour
½ tbsp sugar
¼ tsp salt

Garnish
1 tbsp chopped coriander leaves

Seasoning
1 tbsp oil
½ tsp mustard seeds
1 tsp urad dal
2-3 green chillies (small)
1 sprig curry leaf

Method

1. Peel and cut pumpkin into 1″ long pieces. Cut green chillies into 2-3 pieces each.

2. Boil pumpkin in just enough water along with salt. By the time it is cooked, water should have been thoroughly absorbed – *do not overcook.*

3. Add sugar, cook further till sugar melts.

4. Mix rice flour in milk, pour into pumpkin and simmer 2-3 min. till well blended.

5. Season in oil ingredients given, pour into 'kootu'; if thick, add some more milk, mix well.

6. Transfer 'kootu' into a bowl. Garnish with chopped coriander leaves.

Serve hot with puris or rice – an ideal gravy for children with its delicate seasoning. You can reduce chillies, if desired.

Seekumblekai Gojju
(A Sweet-Sour Chutney)

Ingredients

½ kg pumpkin
1 large lemon-size ball of tamarind
1½-2 tbsp powdered jaggery
½ tsp turmeric powder
½ tbsp rice flour
1 tbsp sesame seeds
Salt to taste
1 tsp rasam powder
   or ½ tsp chilli powder

Seasoning

4 tbsp oil
1 tsp mustard seeds
½ tsp fenugreek seeds
¼ tsp asafoetida
1½ tsp urad dal
1 tsp chana dal
4-5 green chillies, slit
2 sprigs curry leaves

Method

1. Dry roast sesame seeds, powder, set aside. Boil tamarind in water, take out thick pulp, set aside.

2. Peel and cut pumpkin into 1 - 1¼" long pieces.

3. Heat oil in a kadai, add seasonings in the order given, adding one by one as each gets done. Fry chilli and curry leaves for a minute, add pumpkin and turmeric powder. Stir fry for 3-5 min. till the vegetable gets soft.

4. Now add some water, tamarind extract, jaggery, rasam or chilli powder, cover and cook till 'gojju' gets quite thick.

5. Mix rice flour with some water, add to 'gojju' along with sesame seed powder. Simmer 2-3 min., remove from fire.

Serve with curd rice – goes well with dosas.

Note

Refrigerated, it will keep for 1-2 weeks also.

Mathan Puli Pachadi

(Pumpkin Sweet, Sour Chutney)

Ingredients

¼ kg pumpkin
1 small ball of tamarind
1 piece of jaggery
¼ tsp turmeric powder
Salt to taste

Grind to paste

3 tbsp coconut gratings
3-4 green chillies
1 tsp mustard seeds
1 tsp rice flour

Seasoning

1 tbsp oil (preferably coconut oil)
1 sprig curry leaf

Method

1. Peel and cut pumpkin into cubes, add turmeric powder, salt and enough water to cook.

2. Take out extract of tamarind, add to pumpkin when it has become soft. Cook further till there is no smell of raw tamarind.

3. Add jaggery, cook till dissolved adding ground paste as well. When jaggery is well blended, remove from fire.

4. Season ingredients in oil as given, pour into 'pachadi', mix well.

Serve as an accompaniment to rice.

Mathan Eriseri

(Pumpkin with Coconut)

Ingredients

¼ kg pumpkin
½ + ¼ cup coconut gratings
½ tsp turmeric powder
Salt to taste

1 tbsp coconut oil
2 red chillies
1 tsp cumin seeds
1-2 sprigs curry leaves

Method

1. Peel and cut pumpkin into cubes; add turmeric powder, salt and enough water to cover pieces; cook till soft.
2. Grind to paste half a cup coconut, cumin seeds and 1 red chilli; add this to cooked pumpkin, simmer 1-2 min.
3. Heat oil, add curry leaves, 1 red chilli (broken into two) and the rest of the coconut; fry till coconut is dark brown in colour, pour into 'eriseri', mix. Remove vessel from fire.

Serve with rice.

Pumpkin – Sweet and Sour
(Pumpkin Dry Curry)

Ingredients

½ kg pumpkin
1 large onion, chopped
½" piece ginger, minced
3-4 green chillies, minced
Salt to taste
1 tbsp chopped coriander leaves

½ tsp turmeric powder
2 tsp coriander powder
1 tsp cumin powder
1½ tsp amchoor
A small piece of jaggery

Seasoning

3-4 tbsp oil
½ tsp mustard seeds
½ tsp cumin seeds
¼ tsp fenugreek seeds

Method

1. Peel and cut pumpkins into small cubes.
2. Heat oil, add seasonings; when done, add onion, ginger and green chillies, fry till onions are browned.
3. Add all dry masalas except amchoor and jaggery, continuing to fry all along.
4. Add pumpkin pieces, stir fry; add salt, sprinkle some water, cook till pumpkin gets soft.

Stuffed Capsicum

Vegetarian Platter – Tandoori Phul, Tandoori Shimla Mirch (Capsicum), Tandoori Aloo

Tava Vegetables

A Vegetable Medley

Cottage Cheese and Peas and Carrots Cooked with Peas

5. Add amchoor and jaggery (powdered), cook 1-2 min. more till ingredients are well blended. Add some chopped coriander leaves, mix and remove from fie.

Serve hot with chapathis.

Pumpkin Khorma

Ingredients

½ kg pumpkin
½ tsp turmeric powder
½ tsp cinnamon
1½ cup curds
1 tsp rice flour
1½ tbsp chopped coriander leaves
   or mint
4 tbsp oil/ghee mixed
Salt to taste

Grind to paste

3 tbsp grated coconut
1″ piece ginger
1 red chilli
1 tsp aniseeds
1 tsp poppy seeds
A few pepper corns (optional)

Seasoning

1 tsp cumin seeds
3 green chillies, slit

Method

1. Peel and cut pumpkin into fairly large pieces. Prick with a needle or fork.
2. Heat half the oil/ghee mixture, fry pumpkin pieces adding turmeric powder and cinnamon. When quite soft, remove from kadai, set aside.
3. Pour rest of the oil into the kadai, add cumin seeds and, when done, the chillies. Stir fry, add ground masala and fry till oil surfaces.
4. Add pumpkin pieces, fry for some time, adding salt as well.
5. Beat curds, mix in rice flour and 1 tbsp coriander leaves, blend, pour into masala, simmer all together for 3-5 min. Remove from fire, pour into a bowl.
6. Garnish with the rest of the coriander leaves, sprinkle a little cinnamon powder, if desired.

Serve hot with puris.

Pumpkin Halwa

Ingredients

2 cups finely grated pumpkin
$1\frac{1}{2} + \frac{1}{2}$ cups milk
$\frac{1}{2}$ cup khova
$2 + \frac{1}{2}$ tbsp ghee
1 cup sugar

1 tbsp almond
1 tbsp cashew nuts
$\frac{1}{2}$ tbsp raisin
2 drops yellow food colour
1 tsp cardamom, powdered
1 tsp rose or almond essence

Method

1. Blanch almonds, grind half of almonds and half of cashew nuts to paste with $\frac{1}{2}$ cup milk, set aside.

2. Cook pumpkin gratings in $1\frac{1}{2}$ cups milk till done; allow the milk to be absorbed fully till mixture gets dry. Remove, cool.

3. Mash cooked pumpkin and khova till well blended; add ground nuts and sugar. Set this on medium heat and cook stirring continuously adding ghee gradually.

4. Cook further till mixture starts to leave sides of vessel. Add food colour, powdered cardamom and essence, mix thoroughly, cook further 1-2 min., remove from fire, pour into a bowl.

5. Fry nuts and raisin in $\frac{1}{2}$ tbsp of ghee, add $\frac{1}{2}$ of it to halwa, mix. Garnish with the rest.

Serve hot.

Note

A similar preparation can be made with bottle gourd or vegetable marrow.

Pumpkin-Nut Pie

Ingredients

For Pastry
    2 cups flour
    ½ cup margarine
      or vanaspathi
    A pinch of salt
    8-9 tsp chilled water
    8″ pie pan
    1 cup cream for serving

For Filling
    2 cups cooked pumpkin
    ¾ cups brown sugar
    ¼-½ tsp sugar
    2 tbsp corn flour
    Pinch of salt
    1 tsp cinnamon powder
    ½ tsp nutmeg powder

For Topping
    1-1½ cups chopped nuts
    4 tbsp brown sugar
    2 tbsp butter

Method

Pastry

1. Sift flour with sugar and salt. Add fat and mix very lightly till mixture resembles bread crumbs.
2. Add water gradually and form a soft dough (add just enough water to hold the dough together to form a ball). Chill dough for 1 hour.
3. Roll dough lightly on a floured board to a 9½″ circle, fit into the pie pan. Prick base gently to remove air pockets. Flute the overhanging dough over edge of pan.
4. Bake blind (without filling) for 10-12 min. till lightly browned.

To make Filling

1. Mash cooked pumpkin thoroughly, add both the sugars, stir till dissolved and blended.
2. Mix corn flour with 2-3 tsp water into a moist paste, add to pumpkin, stir till blended adding cinnamon and nutmeg powders.
3. Turn over mixture into the pan on top of the baked pastry. Sprinkle nuts evenly.

Topping

1. Melt butter, add sugar, stir till dissolved. Pour over nuts covering the entire surface.
2. Bake again for another 10-12 min. or till a skewer passed through comes clean.

To Serve: Cut pie into slices. Beat cream lightly, pour a little over the slices and serve.

Peerkangkai Chutney
(Ridge Gourd Chutney)

Ingredients

2 medium ridge gourds
1½ tsp urad dal
3-4 red chillies
1 small bit of asafoetida

1 tbsp oil
1 small ball of tamarind
2 sprigs curry leaves
Salt to taste

Method

1. Peel and chop gourd, set aside.
2. Fry asafoetida, dal and chillies in half the oil. When dal turns brown, remove from kadai.
3. Pour rest of the oil into kadai, heat, add curry leaves and gourd pieces, fry till soft, remove.
4. Mix together the fried ingredients, fried gourd, tamarind, salt and grind to chutney consistency.

Serve with rice, curd rice or dosas.

Note

This chutney is normally taken along with rice and a raitha. You can also use vegetable marrow instead for this recipe.

Peerkangkai Paruppu

(Ridge Gourd in a mildly spiced Dal)

Ingredients

¼ kg ridge gourd
½ cup moong dal
½ tsp turmeric powder
Juice of ½ lemon
Salt to taste
1 tbsp chopped coriander leaves

Seasoning
1 tbsp oil
½ tsp mustard seeds
A pinch of asafoetida
2-3 green chillies, slit
½" piece ginger, minced
1 sprig curry leaf

Method

1. Peel and cut gourd into small pieces.
2. Cook dal with turmeric powder; when half cooked, add gourd, cook further till done, adding salt. Remove from fire.
3. Heat oil, add seasonings in the order given, pour into dal, add coriander leaves and lemon juice.

Serve with rice.

Turai Tomato

(Ridge Gourd-Tomato Gravy)

Ingredients

½ kg ridge gourd
2 onions, chopped
2 tomatoes
3 green chillies, slit
½ tsp turmeric powder
3 tbsp oil
Salt to taste

Grind to fine paste
½ tbsp mustard seeds
½ tbsp cumin seeds
1 tbsp sesame seeds
2 red chillies
5 cloves garlic

Method

1. Scrape and cut gourd into thick rings, cut tomatoes into fairly large pieces.

183

2. Heat oil, add chillies and onions along with turmeric powder; fry till onions are browned.

3. Add ground masala, fry till oil surfaces; add gourd, continue frying. When slightly soft, add tomatoes, keep frying. If found too dry, sprinkle water occasionally; keep vessel covered while frying.

4. When vegetables are sufficiently fried and have become soft, add salt, enough water, cover and cook till gravy is well blended.

Serve with rice or rotis.

Jhinga-Posto Charchari
(Ridge Gourd-Potato Gravy)

Ingredients

¼ kg ridge gourd
1 large potato
1 tsp chilli powder
½ tsp turmeric powder
A pinch of sugar
Salt to taste

Seasonings
    3 tbsp oil
    ½ kala jeera
    3 green chillies, slit
Grind to paste
    1 tbsp poppy seeds

Method

1. Peel and cut turai into rounds. Peel and cut potatoes into cubes.

2. Heat oil, add kala jeera; when done, add slit chillies and potatoes, fry 2-3 min. Add turai pieces, continue frying adding turmeric and chilli powders. Keep frying till vegetables turn a little soft.

3. Add water, salt and sugar, cook covered till nearly done.

4. Mix poppy seeds paste with some water, add to vegetables and continue to cook till the masala is absorbed and gravy gets dry.

5. Add 1 more tbsp of oil, fry till gravy is browned (if desired).

Serve with rice.

Pudalangai Thair Pachadi

(Snake Gourd Raitha)

Ingredients

¼ kg snake gourd
1½-2 cups curds
½ tbsp chopped coriander leaves
Salt to taste

Seasoning

1 tbsp oil
½ tsp mustard seeds
1 tsp urad dal
2 red chillies, broken
1 sprig curry leaf

Method

1. Scrape and cut snake gourd into very small pieces.

2. Heat oil, add seasonings and when done, add gourd pieces along with salt and fry on low heat till soft. Keep kadai covered now and then while frying – this way the vegetable gets done quickly and with little oil.

3. Remove from fire, cool. Beat curds, add coriander leaves and cooked gourd, mix well.

Serve with any seasoned rice.

Note

This recipe can be prepared with bottle gourd or vegetable marrow also.

Padavalkai Kootu
(Snake Gourd Gravy with Dal and Coconut)

Ingredients

½ kg snake gourd
½ cup moong dal
1 tbsp tamarind pulp
½ tsp turmeric powder
Salt to taste

Seasoning

2 tsp oil
½ tsp mustard seeds
2 sprig curry leaves

Fry in 2 tsp oil

1 tbsp urad dal
¾ tbsp chana dal
½ tbsp coriander seeds
1 tsp poppy seeds
3-4 red chillies
A small piece of asafoetida
4 tbsp grated coconut

Method

1. Fry masala in the order given, removing each one of them when done. Add coconut last, fry till golden brown. Grind all together to paste.

2. Scrape and cut snake gourd into very small pieces, cook with ¼ tsp turmeric powder and salt.

3. Cook dal separate with ¼ tsp turmeric powder.

4. Mix together the cooked dal, gourd, ground paste and tamarind pulp. Add some water if too thick. Simmer 2-3 min. till well blended.

5. Season in oil mustard seeds and curry leaves, add to 'kootu', mix well.

   Serve hot with rice or rotis.

Note

This preparation can be made with ash gourd, bottle gourd and vegetable marrow either separate or a mixture of a piece each.

Stuffed Padaval
(Stuffed Snake Gourd Rolls)

Ingredients

1 medium size tender snake gourd
1 potato, chopped
1 carrot, chopped
1 large onion, chopped
1 small piece of cabbage, chopped
½ cup peas, boiled (optional)
Juice of ½ lemon
Salt to taste
1 tsp garam masala

Mince very fine
2-3 green chillies
½″ piece ginger
A little coriander leaves
A few mint leaves

For frying
½-¾ tbsp flour
A pinch of salt
Oil (about 1 cup)

Method

1. Scrape the snake gourd, wash thoroughly; cut into 2″ long pieces. Scoop out centre (the fibre and seeds) leaving a hollow. Wash once again, leave on a cloth to dry completely.

3. Heat 2 tbsp oil, add minced ingredients except herbs, fry 1-2 min. Add all the chopped vegetables, salt and garam masala, stir fry for about 5 min. Sprinkle some some water, cover and cook.

4. Remove lid, fry vegetables, on low heat, till dry adding minced coriander leaves and mint. Mix thoroughly, remove, cool.

5. Fill the snake gourd pieces with some of the stuffing, seal both ends with flour paste (for this, mix flour with little water to make a thick paste).

6. Deep fry one at a time, drain on paper towel; serve hot.

Note

If snake gourd is not too tender, you could steam cook the pieces (see that they do not break while doing so) and then put in the stuffing.

Vegetable Marrow Soup

Ingredients

¼ kg or 1 large marrow
1 medium onion
  or 1 bunch spring onions
1 large potato
1 tbsp minced dill (*suva bhaji*)
1 tsp pepper
Salt to taste

1-1½ cups milk
2 tbsp butter
  (or) 2 tbsp cream

Method

1. Wash, peel and cut vegetables into medium size pieces, add salt, sufficient water and half of the dill; cook preferably in a pressure cooker.

2. Cool, pass through a mixer. keep aside puree – if too thick, add some water.

3. When about to serve, heat the soup adding pepper. Add boiling milk, allow to simmer 1-2 min.

4. Pour soup into individual bowls, add a dot of butter or a blob of cream and a pinch of dill for garnish.

Serve hot with buttered toast.

Vegetable Marrow – Sweet and Sour

Ingredients

2 medium marrow
2 onions, chopped
1 sprig curry leaf
1 small ball of tamarind
1 small piece of jaggery
½ tsp turmeric powder
2 tbsp oil
Salt to taste

Fry in 1 tsp oil and
grind to paste
  1 tbsp coriander seeds
  1 tsp cumin seeds
  1 tbsp roasted gram
  3-4 red chillies
  4 tbsp grated coconuts

Method

1. Peel and cut marrow into small cubes. Boil tamarind in water, take out extract, set aside.

2. Heat oil, fry onions along with curry leaf and turmeric powder to brown, add marrow, stir fry on low heat till vegetable becomes soft. If necessary, sprinkle some water.

3. When vegetable has cooked, add ground masala, tamarind extract, jaggery, salt and simmer till gravy is blended.

Serve with rice or chapathis.

Vegetable Marrow Puri
(Makes 1 dozen)

Ingredients

1 cup grated marrow	**Powdered masala**
1 cup wheat flour	$\frac{1}{2}$ tsp pepper powder
$\frac{1}{2}$ cup flour	$\frac{1}{2}$ tsp garam masala
3 tsp oil to mix	$\frac{1}{2}$ tsp chilli powder
Oil for frying	$\frac{1}{2}$ tsp cumin powder
	Salt to taste

Method

1. Mix all the ingredients together (except oil for frying), adding very little water, to make a stiff dough. Set aside $\frac{1}{2}$ hour.

2. Roll puris the usual way and deep fry.

Tips ....

On Pressure Cooking

"Most vegetables can be cooked with great success in a pressure cooker. The correct way to cook vegetables is to put them into the smallest quantitiy of water in a covered container, and cook them for the shortest possible time – in this way, they retain not only their vitamin content, but their colour and flavour. When vegetables are cooked in a pressure cooker, this procedure is carried out, and in consequence, vegetables are cooked to perfection.

– 'Marguerite Patten
From the book *Fruit and Vegetable Cookery*

Kitchen Requirements

"Accurate measurements can mean just that little bit of difference between success and failure in cooking, especially in cooking cakes ... Standard measuring spoons and cups are very useful and save a lot of time."

– From *Modern Home Cookery*

Greens

Greens are grown in plenty all over India and there are many varieties of greens. They are *amaranthus, khatta sag, poi sag,* dill *(suva bhaji)*, fenugreek *(methi)*, spinach *(palak)* and *lettuce.* Some of the leaves of vegetables like radish, drumsticks, colocasia, onion, carrot and beet root are also used in cooking. Some of the greens like coriander, curry leaf, mint and dill have been dealt with under the Chapter 'Herbs' while fenugreek and spinach are also under two different chapters. Amaranthus has already been dealt with in the first chapter.

Since Greens have a high content of iron, they are to be definitely included in the daily diet of anaemic people. Carrot leaf juice is also high in iron and carbohydrate and vitamin A. Lettuce, mainly used in salads, is also very rich in vitamin A and has iron and folic acid. Radish leaf juice acts as a curative medicine in urinary problems and mixed with honey is a cure for jaundice.

Greens are rich in vitamins A and C; they also contain folic acid, calcium and iron. They are an inexpensive way of supplying the necessary nutrition to the body. They help in digestion by secreting digestive juices. They provide good roughage. They have innumerable medicinal properties as well. Some of them are good for eyesight and skin while certain others are good for liver, kidney and respiratory problems. Some are laxative while yet others are diuretic. In ayurveda, some of them are even used in curing asthma and bronchitis.

With so much of nutritional value and medicinal properties, greens should be included at least once every alternate day if not every day. One very important point to remember about Greens is that they should be cooked soon after picking or buying as shelf-life reduces their food value and flavour.

Greens cook very easily and require very little seasoning.
Cooked with dal (moong), they have additional nutritive value.
Greens are cooked separately or as a combination of two or
three kinds. Here are many ways of cooking Greens!

Preparations

1. **Keerai Sadam** (Tamil Nadu)
2. **Bussar** (Karnataka)
3. **Masoppu Sar** (Karnataka)
4. **Greens with Moong Dal** (North India)
5. **Greens Ambat** (Karnataka)
6. **Poi sag with Garlic** (West Bengal)
7. **Muli ka sag** (Punjab)
8. **Sarson ka sag** (Punjab)
9. **Onion Leaves with Potatoes** (North India)
10. **Lettuce with Peas** (Western)

Keerai Sadam
(Rice with Greens)

For this rice, use a combination of two to four kinds of Greens. Here it is a combination of amaranthus, fenugreek leaves, drumstick leaves and dill (*suva bhaji*). Spinach can be used instead of drumstick leaves if not available.

Ingredients

1 cup fine rice
2 cups chopped greens
½ cup fresh peas
1 medium carrot, minced
1 large onion, chopped
2 tbsp ghee
½ tsp turmeric powder
1 tsp cumin seeds
Salt to taste

Grind to paste
2-3 green chillies
1″ piece ginger
4 cloves garlic

Broil and powder
2 tsp coriander seeds
3 cloves
1″ piece cinnamon
2 small cardamoms

Method

1. Heat ghee in a pressure cooker, add cumin seeds and, when done, add chopped onion; fry till browned.

2. Add ground paste, fry till ghee surfaces. Now add rice, turmeric powder, greens, vegetables and the powdered masala. Fry 3-5 min. or till vegetables turn soft.

3. Add 2 cups hot water, salt to taste. Cook till done, on low heat without the weight.

Serve hot with raitha – makes a full, nutritious meal by itself!

Bussar
(A Gravy preparation of Dal and Greens)

Ingredients

½ cup tuvar dal (cooked)
4 cups chopped mixed greens
¼ tsp turmeric powder
1 medium onion, chopped
2-3 tbsp coconut gratings
1 small ball of tamarind
1 small piece of jaggery
Salt to taste

Fry in 2 tsp oil, powder
2 tbsp coriander seeds
1 tsp cumin seeds
¼ tsp fenugreek seeds
1 small piece asafoetida
½" piece cinnamon
2-3 red chillies
½ tsp pepper corns

Seasoning

2 tsp oil
1 tsp mustard seeds
½ tsp cumin seeds
2 sprigs curry leaves

Method

1. Cook dal with turmeric powder, mash, set aside.
2. Cook greens separately. When cool, add onion, coconut, 4 tsp of the prepared powder, grind to paste.
3. Extract tamarind water, add salt. Cook for a while, till reduced to less than half the quantity. Add ground greens, mashed dal and jaggery, simmer for sometime adding some water, if necessary.
4. Heat oil, season ingredients given, add to bussar.

Serve hot with rice.

Note

You can use 2-3 kinds of greens for this – a mixture of amaranthus, fenugreek leaves, dill.
The above powder can be used in the preparation of rasam also. Store the rest of the powder after using for bussar.

Masoppu Sar

Ingredients

½ cup tuvar dal
4-5 cups chopped greens
8-10 pods garlic
3 tsp rasam powder
Salt to taste

Grind to paste
½ medium onion
2-3 tbsp grated coconut

Seasoning
1 tbsp ghee
½ tsp mustard seeds
1 tsp cumin seeds
2 red chillies
4-6 pods garlic
½ onion, minced
1 small tomato, minced
2 sprigs curry leaves

Method

1. Boil with some water all ingredients (on the left side) in a pressure cooker. When cool, mash thoroughly adding some more water if necessary to make it of a pouring consistency.

2. Heat ghee, add mustard, cumin seeds and red chilli (broken into 2-3 pieces); when done add onion, garlic and curry leaves. Stir fry till onion turns brown, add tomatoes, fry till done.

3. Pour this seasoning into the greens, stir.

Serve hot with rice.

Note

For this recipe also you can use a mixture of greens.
For rasam powder, follow the recipe of the previous one (Bussar).

Greens with Moong Dal

Ingredients

½ cup moong dal
½ tsp turmeric powder
4 cups chopped mixed greens
1½ tbsp oil
1 tsp cumin seeds
½ chilli or pepper powder
Salt to taste

Chop very fine
½" piece ginger
1 medium onion
3 cloves garlic
3-4 green chillies

Method

1. Wash dal, add 1½ cups water, turmeric powder and set to boil.
2. Halfway through boiling, add greens, ginger, green chillies and salt; simmer till dal is cooked.
3. Heat oil, add cumin seeds; when done, add garlic and onion, fry till browned. Add chilli or pepper powder, stir once, pour into cooked dal-sag mixture, boil 1-2 min. more.

Serve hot with rice or chapathis

Note

1. If desired, 1 chopped tomato may be added in step 3 and fried after the onions are done.
2. If you are serving this for rice, add a little more water and simmer so that it is of a pouring consistency.

Greens Ambat
(Greens with Coconut)

Ingredients

3 cups chopped mixed greens
   (chawlai, suva, methi, palak)
$\frac{1}{2}$ tsp chopped ginger
Salt to taste

Seasoning
2 tsp oil
$\frac{1}{2}$ tsp mustard seeds
1-2 green chillies, chopped (optional)
3 cloves garlic, crushed

For masala
3 tbsp grated coconut
1-2 red chillies
A small ball of tamarind

Method

1. Boil greens with salt and ginger, set aside.

2. Fry in 1 tsp oil the red chillies, add coconut and tamarind; grind to paste.

3. Heat oil, add mustard seeds and, when done, the chillies and garlic; fry till garlic is browned.

4. Add cooked greens, ground paste, mix well, simmer 1-2 min.

Serve with rice or rotis.

Poi sag with Garlic

Ingredients

3 cups chopped poi sag
A pinch of turmeric powder
8-10 cloves garlic, crushed
Salt to taste

Seasoning
$\frac{1}{2}$ tbsp oil
1 tsp cumin seeds
1-2 red chillies
   (broken into 2-3 pieces)

Method

1. Heat oil in a kadai, add cumin seeds and red chillies. When done, add garlic, fry till garlic is browned.

2. Add chopped sag, fry 2-3 min., add salt and turmeric powder. Cook on low heat till done.

Serve with rice and dal.

Note

Khata sag can be prepared in a similar manner.

Muli ka sag
(Leaves of Radish)

Ingredients

2-3 cups chopped muli ka sag
1 large onion, chopped
6-8 flakes garlic, crushed
3-4 green chillies, minced
$\frac{1}{2}$ tsp turmeric powder
Salt to taste

Seasoning
$1\frac{1}{2}$ tbsp oil
$\frac{1}{2}$ tsp mustard seeds
1 tsp cumin seeds
A pinch of asafoetida
Juice of 1 lemon

Method

1. Boil sag with just enough water. When cooked, cool and mash the leaves.
2. Heat oil, add seasonings and when done, the onion, garlic and green chillies. Fry till onion is browned, add cooked sag, turmeric powder and salt. Stir fry for a while till well blended. Add lemon juice, remove from fire.

Serve hot with chapathis.

Note

Leaves of beet root, carrots, turnips can also be prepared the same way.

Sarson ka sag

(Leaves of Mustard plant)

Ingredients

3 cups chopped sag (mustard leaves)
1 cup chopped spinach
2 green chillies
½" piece ginger
1 tbsp tamarind juice
Pinch of sugar
Salt to taste

Seasoning

2 tbsp ghee
6 cloves garlic (optional)
½ tsp turmeric powder
2 red chillies
½ tsp cumin seeds

Method

1. Boil both sags, cool, grind to paste with salt, green chillies and ginger.

2. Heat ghee, add cumin seeds and red chillies; when done, add garlic (whole or minced), fry till browned, adding turmeric powder and sugar.

3. Add ground sag, allow to simmer 1-2 min.; remove, add 2-3 tsp of fresh, white butter befor serving.

Serve hot with *maki ka roti.*

Note

If desired, 1 tbsp *maki ka atta* (corn flour) can be sprinkled while gravy is cooking, in step 3.

Onion Leaves with Potatoes

Ingredients

3-4 medium potatoes
2 bunches spring onions
½ tsp turmeric powder
Salt to taste

Seasoning

1 tbsp oil
1 tsp cumin seeds
1-2 red chillies, broken

Method

1. Wash and cut potatoes (with the skin on) into cubes. Wash and chop onions and onion leaves. Keep all three ingredients separate.

2. Heat oil, add seasonings and, when done, add onions and turmeric powder; stir fry on low flame till onions are browned.

3. Add potatoes, continue to fry till almost done; add onion leaves, stir fry, add salt. Continue to cook till vegetables are soft. Now raise heat and fry 1-2 min. till potatoes are also browned. If necessary, you could add 1 more tbsp oil for this.

Serve hot with phulkas.

Note

Fenugreek leaves can be done in a similar manner.

Lettuce with Peas

Ingredients

1 cup shelled peas	1 tsp sugar
1 head of lettuce	Salt to taste
1 medium onion, minced	Little pepper powder
1 tbsp butter	2 tbsp light cream

Method

1. Break lettuce leaves, wash thoroughly, chop and put in a pan.

2. Add all ingredients to pan except pepper powder and cream; cover and cook till peas are tender; remove from fire.

3. Transfer lettuce onto a serving bowl. Beat cream light, pour into bowl, mix lightly. Sprinkle pepper powder.

Serve with a western meal.

Herbs

In this chapter are included some herbs, out of which three are extensively used in our daily cooking without which our food may not have the same taste and flavour. They are used both in masalas and garnishes. Herbs not only provide nutrition, they make food appetising as well. Western food also uses a number of herbs, but they are not common in India.

1. **Coriander Leaves** *(Hara dania)* – very high content of vitamin A; also has vitamin B_2 and C. Rich in iron, has protein and carbohydrates as well as calcium and phosphorous. No Indian food is complete without the addition of coriander leaves. They add flavour to curries and rasams and chutneys. This ingredient is a must in Indian cooking. Coriander is known as 'cilantro' or 'Chinese parsley', and is used both in Mexican and Chinese cooking.

2. **Curry leaves** (known in Hindi as *Mita Neem*) – like coriander leaves, curry leaf has a very high content of vitamin A. Also has vitamin B, carbohydrate, protein, iron, calcium and phosphorous. Plenty of curry leaves is used in the daily cooking of South Indian food. Also chutneys and chutney powders are prepared which are taken with rice – they are good appetisers. They are considered blood purifiers and help digestion.

3. **Celery** – used in western cooking. Very high content of vitamin A. Also rich in protein, carbohydrate, has iron as well as vitamin C. Both stalks and leaves are used in soups and garnishes.

4. **Dill** (*Suva bhaji*): These are used in plenty in Maharashtra, Gujarat and Karnataka. Western cooking also uses these herbs – for soups and baked dishes along with vegetables.

5. **Mint** is used both in North and South Indian cooking. Very high content of vitamin A; also has iron, protein and carbohydrate. Used in chutneys, masalas and garnishes. Western cooking also uses mint but it looks a little different with a different flavour as well.

6. **Oregano, Thyme, Basil** and **Parsley** are used in western cooking. They are available in their dried form which can keep for a long time. Pizzas, pastas and casseroles use these herbs, specially Italian cooking.

Preparations

CORIANDER LEAVES
1. **Coriander Rice** (North India)
2. **Coriander-Coconut Chutney** (Tamil Nadu-Karnataka)

CURRY LEAVES
3. **Curry Leaf- Garlic Chutney Powder** (Andhra Pradesh)
4. **Karbeva Sar** (Karnataka- Mangalore)
5. **Karuveppilai Kuzhambu** (Tamil Nadu)

DILL
6. **Sabbakki Amavadas** (Karnataka)
7. **Dill-Potato Pancakes** (Western)

MINT
8. **Pudeena Chutney** *(South Indian Style)*
9. **Pudeena Chutney** *(North Indian Style)*

Coriander Rice

Ingredients

1 cup fine rice
½ cup shelled peas (optional)
1 small onion
3 green chillies
3 cloves garlic
½" piece ginger
2 cups picked coriander leaves
Salt to taste

Seasoning
2 tbsp ghee
2 bay leaves
3 cloves
½" piece cinnamon
2 cardamoms

For Garnish
1 medium carrot, finely grated
A few slivered almonds

Method

1. Wash rice, leave on a cloth to dry.

2. Grind all the ingredients on left side except rice and peas. Add enough water to make 2 cups.

3. Heat ghee, add seasonings, and, when done, add rice, fry lightly 1-2 min.

4. Transfer rice onto a rice cooker, add coriander water and peas. Cook till done.

To Serve: Transfer rice onto a plate. Spread evenly, sprinkle grated carrot and slivered almonds. Serve with curds.

Coriander-Coconut Chutney

Ingredients

2 cups picked coriander leaves
1 cup grated coconut
2 tbsp roasted gram
1 cup curds or
    Juice of 1 lemon
Salt to taste

Seasoning
2 tsp oil
½ tsp mustard seeds
1 tsp urad dal
A pinch of asafoetida
2 sprigs curry leaves

Method

1. Grind to chutney consistency the coriander leaves, coconut, gram, salt with about a cup of water.
2. Beat curds smooth, add to chutney or add juice of lemon and mix thoroughly.
3. Season in oil the ingredients given, pour into chutney, mix.

Serve chutney with idli, dosas, vadas or uppumav.

Curry Leaf-Garlic Chutney Powder

Ingredients

2 cups picked curry leaves
4-6 garlic cloves
1 small ball of tamarind
Salt to taste
1 tbsp ghee

$\frac{1}{2}$ tsp coriander seeds
1 tbsp urad dal
$\frac{1}{2}$ tsp cumin seeds
10-12 red chillies

Method

1. Wash leaves, spread on cloth to dry – there should be no water while frying.
2. Heat ghee, fry masalas (given on right side) one at a time, removing from kadai as each is done.
3. When masalas are fried, fry curry leaves on slow heat – they should be fried but not browned. Allow to cool.
4. Grind together tamarind, salt and garlic. When done, add fried ingredients and curry leaves, grind further till all the masalas are powdered and well blended. Remove and bottle.

Serve with rice and ghee or with curd rice.

Note

Good for digestion – when taken with curd rice, removes uneasiness of stomach.

Karbeva Sar
(Curry Leaf Rasam)

Ingredients

Grind to a fine paste
- 4 sprig curry leaves
- 4 tbsp coconut gratings
- 2 green chillies
- A small piece of tamarind
- Salt to taste

Seasoning
- 2 tsp ghee
- $\frac{1}{2}$ tsp mustard seeds
- $\frac{1}{4}$ tsp cumin seeds
- 1 red chilli, broken
- 1 sprig curry leaf
- 1 tbsp chopped coriander leaves

Method

1. To ground paste, add 2 cups water, a pinch of sugar (if desired) and boil for 3-5 min. till it is slightly reduced in quantity; remove from fire.

2. Season ingredients in the order given, pour into rasam.

Serve very hot as an appetiser with a dash of lemon juice (if desired).

Karuveppilai Kuzhambu
(Curry Leaf Gravy)

Ingredients

- 2 cups picked curry leaves
- 1 small ball of tamarind
- Salt to taste

Seasoning
- 4 tbsp oil
- $\frac{1}{2}$ tsp mustard seeds
- 1 tsp urad dal

Fry in 1 tsp oil
- 1 tsp pepper corns
- $\frac{1}{2}$ tsp cumin seeds
- 6 red chillies

Method

1. Wash leaves thoroughly, leave in a colander for water to drain.

2. Take out extract of tamarind – about 1-1$\frac{1}{2}$ cups.

3. Grind to paste fried ingredients along with the rest of the ingredients on left hand side.

4. Heat oil, add mustard seeds and dal; when done, add ground paste, tamarind extract and some more water if too thick.

5. Allow chutney to boil on slow heat for 20-30 min. or till thick chutney consistency. Remove, cool and bottle.

Serve with curd rice or even plain rice.

Note

Very good for digestion – high in iron content.

Sabbakki Amavadas
(Dill Leaf Vadas)

Ingredients

2 cups chana dal
½-1 cup minced dill (sabbakki)
2 medium onions, chopped
Oil for frying

1″ piece ginger
4 green chillies
4 red chillies
2 sprigs curry leaves
Salt to taste

Method

1. Soak dal for 3 hours. Drain all water and grind to a rough paste with all ingredients on right side.

2. To ground batter, add onions and dill, mix.

3. Heat oil in a kadai. Take small lumps of batter, flatten them on the palm of your hand or on a plastic sheet. Gently drop in oil and deep fry to golden brown, turning over once or twice.

Serve hot, with coconut chutney.

Note

The same can be prepared with mint or coriander leaves – omit dill in both cases.

Dill-Potato Pancakes

Ingredients

2 large potatoes
1 cup finely minced dill
1 tsp pepper corns
1-2 tbsp corn flour
Salt to taste
Oil for frying

Method

1. Boil and, while sill warm, peel potatoes and pass through a rice mill or grate.
2. Add salt, pepper, 2 tsp oil and dill, mix to form a smooth dough, adding as much corn flour as required.
3. Take large lemon-sized balls of dough, flatten them to a fairly thick round.
4. Heat a non-stick pan with some oil, place pan cakes on it and fry on fairly high heat, turning over when one side is done.

Serve with tomato ketchup.

Pudeena Chutney *(South Indian Style)*

Ingredients

1 cup picked mint
1 small pellet of tamarind
4 tbsp grated coconut
Salt to taste

2 tsp oil
2-3 red chillies
1 tbsp urad dal

Method

1. Wash leaves, spread on cloth to dry.
2. Heat oil, fry dal and chillies; when done, remove from kadai, fry the mint for while, remove, allow to cool.

3. Grind the fried ingredients with salt, tamarind, coconut and a little water, to a rough paste.

Serve with rice, dosas or idlis.

Note

This chutney can be prepared substituting curry leaves or coriander leaves for mint. For curry leaves, use only half a cup.

Pudeena Chutney *(North Indian Style)*

Ingredients

1 cup picked mint
1 medium onion, minced
3-4 cloves garlic
2-3 green chillies

1 tsp cumin powder
1 tsp coriander powder
½ tsp garam masala
Juice of 1 lemon
Salt to taste

Method

Grind together all ingredients to a fine paste. Add lemon juice and mix.

Note

You could make a raitha with this chutney. Beat 1 cup curds smooth with a little salt, add chutney, mix. Omit lemon juice.

Serve with rotis.

Jack fruit

It is a common Indian fruit and vegetable, extensively grown in Kerala and coastal Karnataka. In the North, raw jack fruit is more relished, made into pickles and chutneys. In the South, specially Kerala, the fruit has a pride of place and is served on festive occasions. Raw jack fruit is also used as a vegetable in various preparations.

Raw jack fruit is high in carbohydrates, has vitamin A, protein, potassium and fibre. As a fruit also it is very high in carbohydrate as well as protein.

Preparations

1. **Palakkai Curry** (Tamil Nadu)
2. **Palakkai-Thengaipal Kootu** (Kerala)
3. **Jack fruit Seed Dry Curry** (Karnataka)
4. **Kathal Masala** (Uttar Pradesh)
5. **Jack fruit Cutlet** (Bihar)

Palakkai Curry
(Jack fruit Coconut Dry Curry)

Ingredients

½ kg raw jack fruit
½ cup tuvar dal
½ cup turmeric powder
2 tbsp grated coconut
A pinch of sugar
Salt to taste

Seasoning

1 tbsp til oil
½ tsp mustard seeds
1 tsp urad dal
1 tsp chana dal
1-2 red chillies
2 sprigs curry leaves

Method

1. Remove the thick outer skin of the jack fruit with a sharp knife, cut into small pieces along with the seeds. Add turmeric powder and enough water and cook. When nearly done, add salt, cook till pieces are soft.

2. Boil dal with enough water to cook. When done, dal should be soft and not mushy.

3. Heat oil, add seasonings in the order given; when curry leaves are done, add cooked tuvar dal, stir fry; add cooked jack fruit, fry 1-2 min. longer. Add grated coconut, sprinkle a pinch of sugar, mix, remove.

Serve with rice and rasam.

Note

While cutting the jack fruit, use some oil on your hands; otherwise the sticky substance that oozes out will make it difficult for cutting.

Palakkai-Thengaipal Kootu

(Jack fruit Gravy with Coconut Milk)

Ingredients

½ kg raw jack fruit
1½ cups coconut gratings
1 onion, chopped
2-3 green chillies, slit
Juice of ½ lemon
Salt to taste

Seasoning
3 tbsp oil/ghee
½ tsp mustard seeds
A pinch of asafoetida
2 sprigs curry leaves
½ tsp turmeric powder
½ tsp chilli powder
1 tbsp chopped coriander leaves

Method

1. Add 1 cup boiling water to coconut gratings, extract thick milk by squeezing, set aside. Add 2 more cups of boiling water; when cool, pass through a liquidiser, strain, take out the 'thin milk'. Keep both separate.

2. Remove the thick outer skin of jack fruit, cut into very small pieces along with the seeds.

3. Heat oil, add mustard seeds and asafoetida, then the curry leaves, green chillies and onion; fry till the onion turns brown. Add jack fruit pieces, fry on low heat for 3-5 min. till they get soft.

4. Add turmeric and chilli powders, stir 1-2 min., add 'thin' coconut milk, cover and cook. When jack fruit pieces are done, add salt, cover and cook for some more time.

5. Add first milk, the chopped coriander leaves and sugar, simmer for 2-3 min. more. Remove from fire, add lemon juice and mix.

Serve hot with rice.

Jack fruit Seed Dry Curry

Ingredients

25-30 jack fruit seeds
3 green chillies
2 tbsp grated coconut
A pinch of sugar
Juice of ½ lemon
1 tbsp chopped coriander leaves
Salt to taste

Seasoning

3 tsp til oil
½ tsp mustard seeds
1 tsp chana dal
1 tsp urad dal
2 sprigs curry leaves
1 tbsp ground nut

Method

1. Boil, peel and pound coarsely the seeds along with chillies and salt.

2. Heat oil, add seasonings; when done, add ground nut, stir till browned lightly (on low heat).

3. Add pounded jack fruit seeds, continue to fry for a couple of minutes longer.

4. Now add coconut, sugar and chopped coriander leaves, mix thoroughly, remove from fire. Sprinkle lemon juice, mix once again.

Serve hot with rice as an accompaniment.

Note

1. If desired, a little fresh garam masala can be sprinkled on the pieces and served as a tea time snack. See recipe for garam masala next page.

2. Boiled, peeled and pounded jack fruit seeds can be used in the preparation of vegetable gravies like 'kootu'.

Kathal Masala

(Jack fruit Garam Masala Gravy)

Ingredients

2 cups tender jack fruit pieces
1 large onion, chopped
1½ cups curds
½ cup oil
1-2 bay leaves
½ tsp turmeric powder
1 tsp chilli powder
2 tbsp chopped coriander leaves
Salt to taste

Grind to a paste
6 cloves garlic
1" piece ginger
2 green chillies (optional)

Dry roast and powder (garam masala)
3 cloves
2 small cardamoms
1" piece cinnamon
2 tsp coriander seeds
½ tsp cumin seeds

Method

1. Pressure cook jack fruit pieces with some salt, till soft, set aside.

2. Heat oil, add bay leaves and chopped onion, fry till onion turns brown.

3. Add ginger-garlic paste, stir fry 1-2 min.; add chilli powder, turmeric powder and jack fruit pieces, continue frying for sometime, adding garam masala powder. When masalas are well mixed with jack fruit pieces, add curds beaten smooth.

4. Add half the chopped coriander leaves, cover and simmer for sometime for gravy to form. Add some water if too thick.

5. Remove from fire, garnish with the rest of the coriander leaves

Serve hot with peas pulav or parathas.

Jack fruit Cutlet

Ingredients

½ kg jack fruit
½ cup chana dal
6 cloves garlic
1″ piece ginger
3-4 green chillies
1 onion, chopped
1 tbsp chopped mint
1 tbsp chopped coriander leaves

Seasoning

2 tsp coriander powder
1 tsp garam masala
½-1 tsp chilli powder (optional)
A pinch of aniseeds (crushed)
Salt to taste
Oil for frying
A little gram flour

Method

1. Soak dal for 2-3 hours. Pressure cook jack fruit and dal along with salt; remove from cooker, cool.

2. Grind jack fruit and dal to a slightly rough paste with garlic, ginger and green chillies and onion.

3. To ground paste, add all seasonings (except oil and gram flour) along with chopped herbs. Form the mixture into a smooth dough.

4. Break portions of dough (the size of a large lemon), form into a cutlet; roll in gram flour.

5. Heat oil in a frying pan, shallow fry cutlets, turning over once, till golden brown.

Serve with pudeena chutney.

Knol-khol

Belongs to the cabbage family. Vastly cultivated all over India, has the same nutritive value. Some of the recipes of cabbage and cauliflower can be interchanged with knol-khol. Here are two ways of cooking this vegetable.

Preparations

1. **Knol-khol Coconut Dry Curry** (South India)
2. **Knol-khol Tomato Gravy** (North India)

Knol-khol Coconut Dry Curry

Ingredients

3 medium knol-khol
4 tbsp tuvar dal
2 green chillies, slit
2 tbsp grated coconut
½ tsp turmeric powder
Salt to taste

Seasoning

1 tbsp sesame seed oil
½ tsp mustard seeds
1 tsp urad dal
1 red chilli, broken
2 sprigs curry leaves
1 tbsp chopped coriander leaves

Method

1. Pare knol-khol, cut into medium size cubes. Add enough water, ¼ tsp turmeric powder, salt and cook till soft. Cook dal separate with just enough water and ¼ tsp turmeric powder till it is just done.

2. Heat oil, add seasonings (except coriander leaves) and, when done, add green chillies and cooked dal, stir fry; add cooked vegetable and coconut, fry 1-2 min. adding chopped coriander leaves. Mix well.

Serve with rice and sambar.

Note

Knol-khol can be used as a vegetable for sambar.

Knol-khol Tomato Gravy

Ingredients

2 medium knol-khol
3 medium tomatoes
1 onion, chopped
4 green chillies, slit
$\frac{1}{2}''$ piece ginger, minced
1 tbsp chopped coriander leaves
3 tbsp oil
$\frac{1}{2}$ tsp cumin seeds

Powdered masala
$\frac{1}{4}$ tsp turmeric powder
$\frac{1}{2}$ tsp chilli powder
$\frac{1}{2}$ tsp garam masala
2 tsp coriander powder
1 tsp cumin powder
1 tsp gram flour

Method

1. Pare and cut knol-khol into medium size pieces.
2. Boil tomatoes till soft. Discard water, cool, peel skin and mash tomatoes, set aside puree.
3. Heat oil, add cumin seeds and, when done, the green chillies, ginger and onion; fry till onion turns brown.
4. Add dry masalas one at a time, frying all the time, add tomato puree. Continue to fry for some time.
5. Add knol-khol pieces, stir fry for 1-2 min. Sprinkle some water, cover and cook on low heat till vegetable turns soft. Add salt, cook for some more time adding coriander leaves till gravy is well blended.

Serve hot with phulkas.

Cooking Terms used in recipes

Basting	When frying keep dropping the oil on to the food being fried and allow it to cook.
Batter	Mix flour and liquid to form a smooth consistency which can be poured into a pan or dropped into hot oil - as for pancakes or bhajjias.
Blanch	Cover fruit or Vegetable with water, steam or boil till skin is soft, cool; peel off skin.
Blend	Combine ingredients till mixture is smooth.
Broil	Roasting ingredients dry on low heat till browned.
Chop	To cut into small pieces.
Combine	Mixing together two or more ingredients.
Croutons	Bread cubes fried or toasted till crisp.
Deep fry	Frying in a Kadai with a lot of oil or ghee.
Dice	Cut into small pieces, particularly for salad.
Dough	A mixture of flour with a liquid generally water kneaded into a smooth ball which should be possible to roll - as for puris or chapathis.
Drain	Removing all the liquid using a strainer.
Garlic flake	One individual piece in a whole garlic.
Gravy	A thickish liquid in a curry.
Liquidise	To pass cooked (or raw) ingredients in an electric mixer to get a semi-liquid mixture.
Mince	Chop very fine.
Marinate	To allow food to soak in a seasoned liquid, particularly vinegar or curds.
Pare	To peel off outer skin of fruits and vegetables.
Puree	Rubbing vegetable or fruit through a sieve to form a thick smooth sauce.
Shallow fry	Frying food in a shallow pan with little oil or ghee.
Saute	To fry using little oil till golden.
Slivers	Long thin pieces, particularly those of almonds.

Lady's Finger

(Bhendi, also known as Okra)

Extensively grown all over India and a commonly used vegetable. Has vitamin A, carbohydrate, protein and salts.

Mucilage, which is a sticky substance in lady's finger, is used for treatment of dysentery and gastric ulcer. It also acts as an expectorant in cases of asthma, emphysema and bronchitis.

According to old folk's tale, lady's finger is supposed to be good for the brain!

Here are five ways of preparing lady's finger though the most common, simple and delicious way is 'deep fried bhendi'.

Preparations

1. **Vendakkai Curry and Thair Pachadi** (Tamil Nadu)
2. **Bendekai Gojju** (Karnataka)
3. **Bhendi Fry** (North India)
4. **Bhendi Masala Gravy** (North India)
5. **Stuffed Bhendi** (Maharashtra-Gujarat)

Vendakkai Curry and Thair Pachadi

(Lady's finger Fry/Raitha)

Ingredients

½ kg lady's finger
2-3 tbsp oil
1 sprig curry leaf
Salt to taste

½ tsp mustard seeds
1 tsp urad dal
2 red chillies, broken
¼ tsp turmeric powder

Method

1. Wash, wipe dry each lady's finger, cut into fairy thin rounds.

2. Heat oil, add seasonings and, when done, the curry leaf and vegetable; stir fry for 1-2 min. Add salt, cover, lower heat and allow to cook for 3-5 min.

3. When done, remove cover, raise the heat and fry adding some more oil if you desire it very crisp.

Serve with rice.

Note

This can be made into Thair Pachadi (Raitha) by frying the pieces very crisp. Beat 1 cup curds and little salt; cool the fried lady's finger and add to curds, mix.

Bendekai Gojju
(Lady's finger Sweet and Sour Chutney)

Ingredients

¼ kg lady's finger
6-8 green chillies, chopped
2 sprigs curry leaves
1 small ball of tamarind
1 small piece of jaggery
½ tsp turmeric powder
2 tbsp oil
Salt to taste

Dry roast and powder
½ tbsp sesame seeds
½ tsp cumin seeds
¼ tsp fenugreek seeds

Seasoning
½ tsp mustard seeds
1 tsp urad dal
1 tsp chana dal

Method

1. Wash, wipe and cut lady's finger into small pieces (¼").

2. Boil tamarind in water, take out extract, set aside.

3. Heat oil, add seasonings and, when done, add chopped chillies, curry leaves and vegetable; fry on low heat for 2-3 min. till vegetable gets soft, adding turmeric powder while frying.

4. Add tamarind extract, jaggery and salt; allow to simmer for a while – till well blended and of chutney consistency.

5. Add prepared powder, mix thoroughly, remove from fire.

Serve with rice or chapathis or dosas.

Note

Refrigerated, it will keep for a week or so.

Bhendi Fry

Ingredients

¼ kg lady's finger
2 tbsp oil
A pinch of asafoetida
½ tsp cumin seeds
½ tsp mustard seeds
¼ tsp turmeric powder
½ tsp chilli powder
Salt to taste

Mince fine
1 medium onion
2-3 green chillies
3 cloves garlic (optional)
½" piece ginger
A little coriander leaves

Method

1. Wash, wipe and cut bhendi into thick slices.

2. Heat oil, add seasonings (mustard seeds, cumin seeds and asafoetida). When done, add minced ingredients (except coriander leaves), stir fry for 1-2 min. adding turmeric and chilli powders. Continue to fry on medium heat till bhendi gets slightly soft. Add salt, cover, reduce heat and allow to cook for a while.

3. Remove the cover when done, fry a little longer – adding some more oil if you desire it crisp. Remove from fire.

Serve as an accompaniment with rice or rotis.

Bhendi Masala Gravy

Ingredients

¼ kg bhendi
2 tomatoes
1 onion, chopped
2-3 green chillies, slit
2 tbsp chopped coriander leaves
3-4 tbsp oil

Seasoning
1 tsp cumin seeds
¼ tsp turmeric powder
½-1 tsp chilli powder
½ tsp garam masala
2 tsp coriander powder
Salt to taste

Method

1. Wash, wipe and cut bhendi into 2″ long pieces – if small cut into 2 halves. Heat half the oil, fry bhendi till golden brown.

2. Boil tomatoes in water till skin shrivels. Discard water, cool, peel skin and mash, set aside.

3. Heat rest of the oil, add cumin seeds; when done, add green chillies and onion, fry till onion turns brown.

4. Add all the dry masalas one by one (except salt), continue to fry till oil surfaces.

5. Add tomato puree, half the chopped coriander leaves; simmer for a while till well blended, adding salt.

6. Now put in the fried bhendi, rest of the coriander leaves and, on low heat, cook for some more time; remove from fire.

Serve hot with parathas.

Stuffed Bhendi
(Stuffed Lady's finger)

Ingredients

125 gm lady's finger
  (small, tender)
2 tbsp curds
1½ tbsp chopped coriander leaves
2-3 tbsp oil
½ tsp mustard seeds
A pinch of asafoetida
2 sprigs curry leaves

Grind to paste
3 green chillies
½" piece ginger
1 small onion
1 tsp coriander powder
½ tsp cumin powder
¼ tsp turmeric powder
Salt to taste

Method

1. Wash, wipe dry and slit lady's finger one side only after cutting away the top.

2. Mix ground paste with curds and chopped coriander leaves, stuff lady's finger with this very carefully.

3. Heat oil (preferably in a non-stick pan) and, when hot, season with mustard seeds, asafoetida and curry leaves.

4. Place the stuffed bhendi in the fry pan, lower heat, cover and allow to cook for 3-5 min.

5. Remove cover, turn vegetable carefully over, fry the other side also. If required some more oil can be added in case the vegetable sticks to the pan. Fry to a golden brown.

Serve hot with rice or rotis.

Mango (Raw)

Grown in plenty all over India, both in raw and fruit forms, they are extensively consumed. The fruit is just delicious, hence the name 'King of fruits'. In the raw form, mangoes have a high content of carbohydrate, traces of iron and protein as well as vitamins A and C.

Raw mangoes can be prepared either in daily cooking or as preserves in the form of pickles and chutneys. Since this book deals with vegetables only, preparations given here are of raw mangoes in various ways of daily cooking. Pickles and chutneys made from raw mangoes are not covered here, as that would take a separate volume.

Preparations

1. **Mangai Sadam** (Tamil Nadu)
2. **Mangai Pachadi** (Tamil Nadu)
3. **Mango Dal** (Karnataka)
4. **Mango Curry** (Kerala)
5. **Mango-Coconut Chutney/Pachadi** (South India-Kerala)
6. **Kachi-Kerry-nu Shak** (Gujarat)
7. **Mango-Mint Cooler**

Mangai Sadam

Ingredients

1-1½ cups rice
1 medium mango, grated
3-4 green chillies, slit
½ tsp turmeric powder
½ tsp chilli powder (optional)
Salt to taste
A little extra oil

Seasoning
2 tbsp oil
½ tsp mustard seeds
1 tsp urad dal
1 tsp chana dal
1 red chilli, broken
A pinch of asafoetida
2 sprigs curry leaves

Method

1. Cook rice so that each grain is separate preferably in a rice cooker. When done, spread on a plate to cool, sprinkle some oil, set aside.

2. Heat oil, add seasonings one at a time; when curry leaves are done, add green chillies and grated mango, stir fry 1-2 min.

3. Add turmeric powder, chilli powder and salt, fry a while longer till oil surfaces. Remove from fire, cool.

4. Mix the prepared chutney with the rice using only the tips of your fingers very lightly.

Serve with ginger pachadi.

Mangai Pachadi
(Mango-Jaggery Chutney)

Ingredients

1 medium mango
1 lemon size jaggery
2-3 green chillies, cut
¼ tsp turmeric powder
1-2 tsp rice flour

Seasoning
2 tsp oil
½ tsp mustard seeds
1 sprig curry leaf
A pinch of asafoetida
Salt to taste

226

Method

1. Wash and cut mango into fairly big pieces, add sufficient water, turmeric powder and salt, bring to a boil.

2. When pieces are cooked, add jaggery, cook till it is dissolved.

3. Add a little water to rice flour, mix, pour into mango and simmer till thick.

4. Season in oil the ingredients given, add to pachadi, mix, remove from fire.

Note

This chutney is specially prepared in Tamil Nadu on New Year's day. 1 tsp of dried or fresh neem flowers are fried in oil and added to pachadi on that day.

Mango Dal
(Dal seasoned with Mango)

Ingredients

½ cup tuvar or moong dal
1 medium mango, minced
3 green chillies, slit
1 tbsp oil/ghee
¼ tsp turmeric powder
2 cloves garlic, crushed (optional)
2 sprigs curry leaves

Grind to paste
2-3 tbsp coconut gratings
½" piece ginger
1 tbsp chopped coriander leaves

Seasoning
½ tsp mustard seeds
¼ tsp cumin seeds
1 red chilli, broken
A pinch of asafoetida

Method

1. Boil dal with sufficient water and turmeric powder. When half done, add mango pieces and green chillies, simmer till dal is cooked.

2. Heat oil, add seasonings and, when done, add curry leaves and garlic; fry till browned.

3. Add ground paste, stir fry till oil surfaces. Add cooked dal, cook 1-2 min. more.

Serve with rice or rotis.

Note

If desired, 1 chopped onion may be added in step 2.

Mango Curry
(A spicy Chutney, Kerala style)

Ingredients

2 medium mangoes
1 large onion, chopped
A pinch of turmeric powder
A piece of jaggery
3 tbsp oil
2 sprigs curry leaves
Salt to taste

Grind to paste

2 tbsp coriander seeds
4-5 red chillies
$\frac{1}{2}$ tsp cumin seeds
4-6 cloves garlic
$\frac{1}{2}''$ piece ginger

Method

1. Peel and cut mango into medium size pieces.
2. Heat oil, add curry leaves and onion; fry till browned; adding turmeric powder and ground masala, continue to fry till oil surfaces.
3. Add mango pieces, fry till they turn soft.
4. Add jaggery, salt and cook till chutney consistency, sprinkling some water if necessary.

Note

Will keep for about a week or so.

Mango-Coconut Chutney/Pachadi

Ingredients

1 medium mango, chopped
1 tbsp coriander leaves
Salt to taste

Seasoning

1 tbsp oil
½ tsp mustard seeds
2 sprigs curry leaves

Grind to paste

½ cup coconut gratings
4-5 green chillies
1-1½ tsp mustard seeds
3 cloves garlic (optional)
 or a pinch of asafoetida

For Raitha

1-1½ cups curds

Method

1. Mix together chopped mango, coriander leaves, salt and ground masala. Season in oil ingredients given, add to chutney, mix.

   For Pachadi: Beat curds smooth, add to the above chutney. A pinch of sugar may be added if desired; mix all together.

Serve as an accompaniment.

Kachi-Kerry-nu Shak

(Mango Chutney Gujarati Style)

Ingredients

1 large raw mango
1 large lemon size ball of jaggery
¼ tsp turmeric powder
½-1 tsp chilli powder
½ tsp garam masala (optional)
Salt to taste

Seasoning

2 tbsp oil
½ tsp mustard seeds
A pinch of asafoetida
1-2 red chillies, broken
1 sprig curry leaf

Method

1. Wash, peel and cut mango into thin slices.
2. Heat oil, add seasonings one at a time; when curry leaves are done, add mango slices and fry adding turmeric and chilli powders.

3. Continue to fry till mangoes turn soft; add jaggery and salt, cover and allow to cook.

4. When jaggery has melted and chutney becomes thick add garam masala, mix, remove.

Serve with chapathis or short eats.

Mango-Mint Cooler

Ingredients

2-3 mangoes, sliced
A handful of mint
A large piece of ginger, sliced
1 tsp cumin seeds
1 tsp pepper corns
A pinch of salt
2-3 drops of green food colour
Sugar, about 1-1$\frac{1}{2}$ cup

Method

1. Boil all the ingredients (except the last two) with 2-3 cups water, cool, mash; pass through sieve and take out as much juice as you can – about 1-1$\frac{1}{2}$ cups.

2. Take an equal amount of sugar to that of the juice. Add some water, boil to a one-third consistency. Cool thoroughly, add food colour.

3. Mix cooled juice, sugar syrup, cool further and bottle.

Note

A very refreshing drink for summer.

Onion

Grown extensively all over India, onions form the most important vegetable in our daily cooking, specially in the preparation of pulavs, curries and chutneys, as well as the most important seasoning agent. Besides adding flavour to food, onions have high medicinal properties and therefore it is advisable to take onions in our daily diet, especially in the raw form, in salads and raithas.

Onion has a high content of carbohydrates, some protein and traces of vitamins and iron, and has sodium, potassium and calcium.

Raw onions prevent colds. Boiled and pureed in milk, it gives one a good night's rest. Has antiseptic properties as well. Onions are used both as a preventive and a curative medicine for stomach ailments. Regular use of onions is helpful in preventing diarrhoea and dysentery. Fresh onion juice with ginger and honey is an effective cure for bronchitis.

Preparations

1. **Vengaya Kara Kuzhambu** (Tamil Nadu)
2. **Erulli Gojju** (Karnataka)
3. **Theeyal** (Kerala)
4. **Khandha Besan** (Maharashtra)
5. **Onion Pulav with Coconut Milk**
6. **Pyaj Kachumber/Raitha** (North India)
7. **Brown Onion Soup** (Western)
8. **Onion-Potato/Egg Casserole** (Western)

Vengaya Kara Kuzhambu

(Onion, Garlic hot Gravy)

Ingredients

100 gm small (red) onions
(about 1 cup)
1 pod garlic (1 full)
1 lemon-size ball of tamarind
$\frac{1}{2}$ tsp turmeric powder
$2\frac{1}{2}$ tbsp oil
Salt to taste

Fry in 1 tsp oil
3 tbsp coriander seeds
6-8 red chillies
$\frac{1}{2}$ tsp fenugreek seeds
1 tsp aniseeds
$1\frac{1}{2}$ tsp urad dal
Seasoning
$\frac{1}{2}$ tsp mustard seeds
2 sprigs curry leaves

Method

1. Wash and peel onions and garlic.

2. In 2 tbsp oil, fry onions and garlic to a brown. Remove 5-6 onions, 4-5 cloves of garlic, cool and grind this along with fried masala ingredients. Set aside.

3. Boil tamarind in water, take out extract. Add sufficient water if too thick, add this to fried onions and garlic along with turmeric powder, salt and 1 sprig curry leaf; set to boil.

4. When sufficiently boiled (will have reduced to about half the quantity), add ground masala (mixed with some water, if too thick). Simmer for 2-3 min. or till gravy is blended.

4. Heat 1 tsp oil, fry mustard seeds and curry leaves, add to 'kuzhambu'.

Serve hot with rice.

Erulli Gojju
(Onion Sweet-Sour Chutney)

Ingredients

6 medium onions, chopped
8-10 green chillies, cut
2 sprig curry leaves
½ tsp turmeric powder
A large lemon-size ball of tamarind
A small piece of jaggery
Salt to taste

Seasoning

3 tbsp sesame seed oil
½ tsp mustard seeds
¼ tsp asafoetida
¼ tsp fenugreek seeds
1 tsp urad dal
1 tsp chana dal
½-1 tsp chilli powder (optional)

Method

1. Boil tamarind in water, extract pulp, set aside.

2. Heat oil, add seasonings in the order given (except chilli powder); when dals are browned, add onions, green chillies, and curry leaves; add turmeric powder, fry till onions are browned.

3. Add tamarind extract, jaggery, chilli powder if desired, and salt. Cook till oil surfaces, remove from fire.

Serve with rice or rava dosas.

Tips ....   **To extract Coconut Milk**

To grated coconut add boiling water (as specified in recipe), leave aside 10-15 min. or till cool. Then squeeze gratings, or pass through a liquidiser, and take out 'thick' (*first*) milk. Strain and set this aside.

Then add some more boiling water to gratings, cool, pass through a liquidiser to get maximum amount of 'milk'; strain the resultant liquid, set aside this (*second*) or 'thin' milk. Discard gratings.

Theeyal
(Onion in Coconut-Tamarind Gravy)

Ingredients

¼ kg small (red) onions
2 tbsp oil
¼ tsp turmeric powder
2 sprigs curry leaves
1 lemon size ball of tamarind
Salt to taste

Fry in 1 tsp oil to brown and grind

1 tbsp coriander seeds
3 red chillies
½ cup coconut gratings
3-4 small onions

Seasoning

1 tsp mustard seeds
1 red chilli, broken

Method

1. Extract tamarind pulp by boiling in water; add some water, turmeric powder, salt, 2 sprigs curry leaves and set to boil till the quantity is reduced to about half.

2. Heat oil, add mustard seeds and red chilli; add onions, curry leaves and fry till browned and soft. Add this to boiling tamarind water, cook for some more time.

3. Now add ground masala, a little water if too thick and simmer 1-2 min., remove from fire.

Note

If desired, a small piece of jaggery can be added in step 3.

Serve with rice.

Khandha Besan

(Known popularly as Bombay Chutney)

Ingredients

¼ kg onions, peeled and sliced
3 green chillies, slit
½ tsp turmeric powder
½-1 tsp chilli powder
1½-2 tbsp gram flour
Salt to taste

Seasoning

2 tbsp oil
½ tsp mustard seeds
2 sprigs curry leaves
2 tbsp chopped coriander leaves

Method

1. Heat oil, add mustard, and when done, add onions, chillies and curry leaves along with turmeric powder; fry till onions are soft and browned.

2. Add 1½-2 cups water to gram flour, mix thoroughly so that no lumps are formed. Add chilli powder, salt and half the chopped coriander leaves; add this to onions, simmer on low heat, stirring often.

3. When gravy is well blended, add rest of coriander leaves, mix, remove from fire.

Serve with puris or rava dosas.

Note

If desired, 1-2 tomatoes can be chopped and added in step 1 after onions are browned.

Onion Pulav with Coconut Milk

Ingredients

1 cup fine rice	**Seasoning**
1 cup peeled pearl onions	2 bay leaves
3 green chillies, slit	3 cloves
6 cloves garlic	2 cardamoms
1″ piece ginger	2 1″ stick cinnamon
1 tbsp chopped coriander leaves	$\frac{1}{4}$ tsp pepper corns
6 tbsp grated coconut	Salt to taste
3 tbsp ghee	**For Garnish**
	2 tbsp chopped coriander leaves

Method

1. Grind coconut, ginger, garlic and coriander leaves to paste. Add 2 cups hot water, cool, squeeze ground paste, strain and take out coconut masala milk. You should have 2 cups. Discard gratings.

2. Wash rice, leave on a cloth to dry.

3. Heat half the ghee, add onions, fry on low heat till they turn soft and light pink in colour; remove from kadai, set aside.

4. Heat rest of the ghee, add seasonings; when done, add green chillies, fry, add rice, fry 2-3 min.

5. Add coconut masala milk, salt and cook till done, preferably in a rice cooker.

6. Mix fried onions, half the chopped coriander leaves, transfer to a rice plate, garnish with the rest.

Serve hot with a vegetable curry.

Pyaj Kachumber/Raitha

Ingredients

For Kachumber

    1 large onion, minced
    2 green chillies, minced
    1 tbsp minced coriander leaves

For Raitha

    1-1½ cup curds (not sour)
    A pinch of sugar

½ tsp chilli powder
A pinch of pepper powder
Juice of ½ lemon
Salt to taste

Method

1. **Kachumber:**

   Mix together all the ingredients in a salad bowl, serve chilled.

   Raitha:

   Beat curds smooth, add sugar, pour into kachumber, mix thoroughly, serve.

   If desired, a large pinch of broiled, powdered cumin seeds may be sprinkled on raitha. Omit lemon juice.

Brown Onion Soup

Ingredients

    2 large onions
    1 medium potato
    2 tbsp butter
    1 bay leaf
    1″ piece cinnamon
    3 cloves
    A few pepper corns

For white sauce

    1 tbsp butter
    1 tbsp flour
    1½ cups milk
    Salt to taste
    A large pinch of mixed herbs

Method

1. Cut onions into thin slices, grate potato.

2. Melt 2 tbsp butter, add spices; when done, add onions, fry till light brown in colour adding potato gratings. Stir fry for 1-2 min. longer.

3. Add 3-4 cups water, salt, cook; cool, discard bay leaf, and spices (except pepper), puree, set aside.

4. *To prepare white sauce:* Melt 1 tbsp butter on very low heat, add flour, fry till it turns light brown; remove from fire, add milk gradually mixing all the while so that there are no lumps. Put back on fire, cook to a thin custard consistency.

5. To white sauce, gradually add onion puree, stirring all the while; simmer for 1-2 min. till blended, adding herbs.

Serve very hot with toast.

Onion-Potato/Egg Casserole

Ingredients

4 onions, thickly sliced	**For sauce**
2 tbsp butter	4 tbsp butter
3 large potatoes, boiled	3 tbsp flour
or 3 eggs, hard boiled	3 cups milk
A large pinch of herbs	1-1½ cups grated cheese
½ tsp pepper powder	½ tsp pepper powder
Salt to taste	A pinch of mustard powder

Method

1. Slice potatoes thick or slice eggs, keep separate.

2. Melt butter, fry sliced onions till light pink in colour, sprinkle a pinch of salt and pepper.

3. *Prepare cheese sauce:* Melt butter on low heat, fry flour to a light pink colour, remove pan from fire, add milk gradually stirring all the while see that no lumps are formed. Put back on fire, cook to custard consistency (on low heat). Add seasonings, grated cheese and herbs, mix thoroughly. This is the cheese sauce.

4. Grease a casserole dish thoroughly. Spread at the bottom of the dish half of the fried onions; cover onion layer with potato or egg slices. Sprinkle some salt and pepper powder on slices.

5. Cover this layer with the rest of the onions, even out surface.

6. Pour cheese sauce over onion layer, shake vessel gently for sauce to spread. Bake in a hot oven for 12-15 min. or till top is golden brown.

Serve hot with garlic toast.

Papaya

A delicious fruit, grown in most parts of our country. Has a high content of carbohydrates and vitamin A. Has calcium and proteins as well, besides some medicinal properties. It is used in the raw form as a vegetable – here are four ways of cooking raw papaya. Most preparations using bottle gourd and vegetable marrow can be substituted for raw papaya.

Preparations

1. **Green Papaya Curry** (Gujarat)
2. **Green Papaya and Green Gram Gravy**
3. **Pappali Kootu** (Kerala)
4. **Papaya Paratha** (North India)

Green Papaya Curry

Ingredients

1 small raw papaya
3-4 green chillies
1 tbsp chopped coriander leaves
$\frac{1}{2}$ tsp turmeric powder
1 tbsp gram flour
Salt to taste
A sprig of curry leaves

Seasoning
$1\frac{1}{2}$ tbsp oil
A pinch of asafoetida
$\frac{1}{4}$ tsp fenugreek seeds
$\frac{1}{2}$ tsp mustard seeds
$\frac{1}{2}$ tsp cumin seeds

Method

1. Cut papaya into thin slices, chillies into thick rounds.
2. Heat oil, add seasonings in the order given; when done, add papaya slices and turmeric powder, fry 1-2 min. Add salt, little water, cover and cook on low heat.
3. When vegetable has turned soft and dry, sprinkle gram flour and half the coriander leaves, cover and cook for a while longer. When gram flour has cooked, remove from fire. Sprinkle rest of the coriander leaves, mix.

Serve with rice or chapathis.

Green Papaya and Green Gram Gravy

Ingredients

1 small raw papaya
$\frac{1}{2}$ cup green gram
$\frac{1}{2}$ tsp turmeric powder
1 large onion, chopped
1 large tomato, chopped
1 tbsp chopped coriander leaves
2 sprigs curry leaves
Juice of 1 lemon
2 tbsp oil
Salt to taste

Grind to paste
4 tbsp grated coconut
A few pepper corns
1 tsp cumin seeds
3-4 green chillies
1" piece ginger
5-6 cloves garlic
A pinch of garam masala

Method

1. Cut papaya into cubes, cook with some salt, set aside. Soak green grams for 2-3 hours, boil with a pinch of turmeric powder. Keep separate.
2. Heat oil, add curry leaves and onion; fry till browned adding $\frac{1}{4}$ tsp turmeric powder.
3. Add ground paste and tomatoes, stir fry till oil surfaces.
4. Add cooked vegetable, dal and some salt (if necessary), simmer 2-3 min. adding some water if mixture is too thick.
5. Remove vegetable from fire, add chopped coriander leaves and lime juice, mix thoroughly.

Serve with rotis.

Pappali Kootu

(Green Papaya with Coconut and ground nuts)

Ingredients

1 green papaya
1 onion, chopped
$\frac{1}{2}$ tsp turmeric powder
2 tbsp ground nuts, roasted
1 tbsp chopped coriander leaves
2 tbsp tamarind water
Salt to taste

Fry in 2 tsp oil and grind to paste
2 tsp coriander seeds
$\frac{1}{2}$ tsp urad dal
$\frac{1}{2}$ tsp cumin seeds
2 red chillies
3 tbsp grated coconut

Seasoning

1 tbsp oil
$\frac{1}{2}$ tsp mustard seeds
2 slit green chillies
1 sprig curry leaf

Method

1. Wash, peel and cut papaya into small cubes, add turmeric powder, little salt and cook till tender.
2. Add tamarind water, cook 1-2 min. longer, add ground paste, mix, simmer for a while.

3. Heat oil, add seasonings and, when done, add chopped onion, fry till browned. Add this to papaya along with coriander leaves, mix thoroughly.

4. Powder roughly the roasted ground nuts, add to 'kootu', mix.

Green Papaya Paratha

Ingredients

For filling
1 small raw papaya, 2-3 cups grated
2-3 green chillies, minced
$\frac{1}{2}$" piece ginger, minced
1 tbsp chopped coriander leaves
Salt to taste
Oil for frying

For dough
3 cups wheat flour
3 tsp oil to mix
A pinch of salt
Water to mix

Method

1. Mix together ingredients for dough, gradually add water, knead to form a smooth dough, cover, set aside for at least $\frac{1}{2}$ hour.

2. Heat $\frac{1}{2}$ tbsp oil, add all ingredients for filling, fry for a little while, cook till dry. Remove from fire, cool.

3. Take lemon size balls of dough, form into a 'cup' using some oil or flour; fill 'cup' with a little papaya mixture, close, pat into shape, roll into a circular paratha using some oil or flour.

4. Heat tava, fry parathas as usual, using some oil while frying – fry both sides golden brown.

Serve hot with mint or coriander chutney.

Peas

Peas are a favourites vegetable; though not always available. It is seasonal, grown only in winter, specially in Northern India and colder places of the South. Both fresh and dried peas make excellent dishes.

Fresh peas have a high content of protein, carbohydrate, vitamins A, B_1, B_2 and traces of C as well as traces of iron.

Some popular and some unusual recipes of peas are given here.

Preparations

1. **Mutter Pulav** (North India)
2. **Mutter-Paneer** (Punjab)
3. **Spicy Peas Parathas** (North India)
4. **Masala Bath** (Maharashtra)
5. **Green Peas in Coconut Gravy** (South India)
6. **Pattani Sundal** (Tamil Nadu)
7. **Mutter Ghanta** (West Bengal)
8. **Green Peas Soup** (Western)
9. **Spaghetti-Peas** (Western)
10. **Peas in Potato Cups** (Western)

Mutter Pulav
(Peas Pulav)

Ingredients

2 cups basmati rice
1 cup shelled peas
1 medium onion, finely sliced
4 tbsp ghee
Salt to taste

For Garnish

A few almonds, slivered
1 tbsp chopped coriander leaves

Seasoning

2 bay leaves
3-4 cloves
3 big cardamoms
2 ½" pieces cinnamon
2 slit green chillies
½" minced ginger

Method

1. Wash rice, leave on a cloth to dry.

2. Heat 2 tbsp ghee and fry sliced onion, crisp and brown, remove, set aside.

3. Fry slivered almonds, keep aside.

4. Pour 2 tbsp more of ghee, add seasonings and, when spices are done, add ginger and green chillies, fry 1 min., add rice, stir fry for 2-3 min., add peas, salt, 2½ cups water and cook till done (preferably in a rice cooker).

To Serve: Transfer rice onto a rice plate, even out surface, mix in fried onion and almonds, sprinkle coriander leaves.

Serve pulav with vegetable kurma.

Note

You could use 1 cup coconut milk mixed with 1½ cups water instead of 2½ cups water. Coconut milk gives a delicious taste and flavour.

Mutter-Paneer
(Peas-Paneer Gravy)

Ingredients

250 gm paneer, cubed
1-1½ tbsp flour
2 cups shelled peas, boiled
2 tomatoes, chopped
¼-½ cup cream (for garnish)
½ cup ghee
A large pinch of saffron
1 cup hot milk
Salt to taste
2 tbsp chopped coriander leaves

1-2 green chillies, slit (optional)
1-2 bay leaves
1 tsp ginger-garlic paste
2 medium onions, (ground
 separately or grated)
2 tsp coriander powder
1 tsp cumin powder
1 tsp garam masala
1½-2 tsp chilli powder
½ tsp turmeric powder

Method

1. Heat half the ghee, roll paneer cubes in flour, fry to golden brown. Soak saffron in hot milk, put fried paneer into this, leave aside.

2. Pour rest of the ghee into kadai, add bay leaves and green chillies (if you are using), fry 1 min. Now, add ginger-garlic paste, fry on low heat till oil surfaces, add ground onion, continue to fry.

3. When onion has browned, add rest of the powdered ingredients one by one, continuing to fry all the time. If it appears dry, sprinkle a little water. When ghee surfaces, add chopped tomatoes, continue to fry till masalas are blended. Add boiled peas, cook 3-5 min.

4. Add paneer cubes along with the milk it has soaked in and cook for a while longer. When gravy is sufficiently thick, remove.

To Serve: Pour gravy into a bowl. Beat cream smooth, put a little into gravy, mix. Pour the rest over the curry, sprinkle coriander leaves and serve hot with puris or parathas.

To make paneer:

1½ litre milk, juice of 1 large lemon

Boil milk and, while still on fire, add lemon juice gradually till milk starts to curdle. Boil for 1-2 min. and remove from fire. When cool, strain through muslin cloth, keep aside the whey. Take out the paneer, knead into a smooth dough, wrap it in a thick cloth, place a weight on top and leave aside for an hour or so. When paneer dough has flattened out, remove weight, cut into cubes. You will get 250-265 gm of paneer (roughly). Alternatively, you could purchase ¼ kg paneer in the market.

Note

1. For this recipe, you could substitute potatoes (3 medium ones) instead of paneer. Peel and cut potatoes into small cubes, fry in oil to golden, set aside. Follow the rest of the recipe as before, substituting potato for paneer. For this, omit milk and saffron.

2. Whey, left over from paneer may be used for cooking gravy.

Spicy Peas Parathas

Ingredients

For dough

3 cups wheat flour
3 tsp oil or vanaspathi
   (for mixing)
½ tsp salt
Oil or vanaspathi for frying

For Filling

1 cup peas, boiled
2 green chillies, minced
½" piece ginger, minced
2 tbsp chopped coriander leaves
Salt to taste

Roast and powder

1½ tsp coriander seeds
½ tsp cumin seeds
2 cloves
¼" piece cinnamon
6-8 pepper corns
1 red chilli
1 tsp aniseeds

Method

1. Mix together flour, salt, vanaspathi/oil; knead to a soft dough, cover, set aside.
2. Mash boiled peas, keep aside.
3. Heat 2 tbsp oil, add minced ingredients, fry 3-5 min. and when fried, add mashed peas, roasted and powdered masala along with salt, fry 1 min. more. Remove, set aside to cool.
5. Take a large lemon size ball of dough, make a cup (using oil while doing so). Put some of the filling in, close cup, pat into a round.

6. Roll each round carefully on a floured board, dusting with flour into a paratha.

7. Put the paratha on a tava (skillet) on medium heat, cook both sides using ghee or oil till brown and dark spots appear on surface.

Serve very hot with a mild raitha or just plain curds.

Masala Bath
(Rice and Peas cooked with Goda Masala)

Ingredients

$1\frac{1}{2}$ cups fine rice
1 cup shelled peas
3 tbsp refined oil
$\frac{1}{4}$ tsp turmeric powder
1 tbsp ghee
Juice of 1 lemon

Seasoning
$\frac{1}{2}$ tsp mustard seeds
$\frac{1}{2}$ tsp cumin seeds
A pinch of asafoetida
3 green chillies, slit
2 sprigs curry leaves
Salt to taste

For Goda masala
$\frac{1}{2}$ tbsp sesame seeds
2 tbsp grated copra
$\frac{1}{2}$ tbsp coriander seeds
$\frac{1}{2}$ tsp cumin seeds
2 cloves
$\frac{1}{2}''$ piece cinnamon
1 bay leaf
1 small piece of asafoetida

For Garnish
1 tbsp chopped coriander leaves
1 tbsp fresh grated coconut

Method

1. Dry roast sesame seeds and copra gratings, each separate, remove from kadai. Add 2 tsp oil to kadai, fry the rest one at a time separately, remove each when done. Mix all together, cool and powder.

2. Wash rice, leave on cloth to dry.

3. After frying masalas, add rest of the oil to kadai, add seasonings; when done, add rice, turmeric powder, Goda masala, continue to fry for a couple of minutes more, adding the peas also.

4. Now add $3\frac{1}{2}$ cups water, salt and cook till done, preferably in a rice cooker. Add ghee, mix and leave till serving time.

To Serve: Transfer rice on to a plate, sprinkle lemon juice, mix. Garnish with grated coconut and chopped coriander leaves.

Serve with plain tuvar dal or kadhi.

Green Peas in Coconut Gravy

Ingredients

2 cups boiled peas
1 cup coconut gratings
1 tsp poppy seeds, broiled
1 tbsp chopped coriander leaves
3 tbsp ghee
Salt to taste

For Garnish

1 few chopped and fried
   cashew nuts (optional)

Grind to paste

1 medium onion
3 green chillies
5-6 cloves garlic (optional)
1" piece ginger
5-6 cashew nuts
$\frac{1}{2}$ tsp garam masala
$\frac{1}{2}$ tsp turmeric powder
$\frac{1}{2}$ tsp chilli powder

Method

1. Grind coconut and poppy seeds to a very fine paste, set aside.
2. Heat ghee, add ground masala paste and fry on low heat till ghee surfaces.
3. Add boiled peas, salt and simmer 1-2 min.
4. Mix 2 cups boiling water to coconut paste, add half of the coriander leaves and pour into peas, simmer for some time. If the gravy is not thick, mix $\frac{1}{2}$ tbsp rice flour in a little water, pour into peas, cook till blended.

Serve hot (garnished with the rest of coriander leaves) with puris or pulav.

Pattani Sundal
(Peas-Coconut Dry Curry)

Ingredients

2 cups boiled peas
1″ piece ginger
3 green chillies
2 tbsp grated coconut
1 tbsp chopped coriander leaves
Salt to taste

Seasoning
2 tbsp til oil
1 tsp mustard seeds
2 tsp urad dal
A piece of asafoetida
2 sprigs curry leaves

Method

1. Cut chillies into 2-3 pieces each, chop ginger.

2. Heat oil, add seasonings and when dal turns brown, add curry leaves, ginger and chillies. Fry ½ min., add boiled peas, salt and cook till dry – if there is any water, allow it to get absorbed.

3. Add grated coconut, chopped coriander leaves and, if desired, 1 tsp of lemon juice; mix thoroughly.

Serve as a cocktail snack.

Mutter Ghanta
(Peas in Milk Gravy)

Ingredients

1 cup shelled peas
2 potatoes, cubed
1½-2 cups milk
1 tsp flour
Pinch of sugar
Salt to taste

Garnish
1 tbsp coconut gratings (optional)
1 tbsp chopped coriander leaves

¼ tsp turmeric powder
½ tsp chilli powder
Seasoning
1½ tbsp ghee
1 bay leaf
2 cloves
½ tsp cumin seeds

Method

1. Heat ghee, add bay leaf, cloves and cumin seeds. When done, add potatoes, stir fry on low heat keeping it covered in-between frying. Add peas along with turmeric and chilli powders. Fry a while longer, add salt. Sprinkle some water, cover and cook till done.

2. Mix flour with milk and sugar, add to vegetable and cook till a thick gravy is formed. Remove from fire.

3. Garnish with coconut and coriander leaves.

Serve with hot puris   it is a mildly spiced gravy.

Green Peas Soup

Ingredients

2 cups shelled peas	**For white sauce**
1 small onion, minced	2 tbsp butter
4 sprigs mint	1 tbsp flour
A big pinch of dried herbs	1½ cups milk
Salt to taste	1 tsp pepper powder
A pinch of curry powder (optional)	**For Garnish**
½ cup thick cream (optional)	½ tbsp chopped mint

Method

1. Boil peas with all ingredients on the left side except curry powder and cream. Cool, pass through a liquidiser, set aside puree.

2. *Prepare white sauce:* Melt butter, add flour, fry till it turns to a light pink, add milk gradually, stirring all the while so that no lumps are formed. Add pepper and curry powder.

3. Gradually add peas puree to white sauce adding some milk if too thick. Add some salt, if necessary. Keep soup hot till serving time.

To Serve: Beat cream smooth. Pour hot soup into bowl, add a swirl of cream to each bowl, garnish with a pinch of chopped mint.

Serve with toasted bread.

Spaghetti-Peas

Ingredients

2 cups boiled spaghetti
1 cup boiled peas
2 tbsp butter
$1-1\frac{1}{2}$ tbsp bread crumbs
1 cup grated cheese
Salt to taste

For white sauce
3 tbsp butter
2 tbsp flour
3-4 cups milk
A large pinch of herbs
1 tsp pepper powder
Salt to taste

Method

1. Leave cooked spaghetti in cold water till required.
2. Make white sauce as in the above recipe. Follow step 2. Add pepper powder, salt and herbs, mix well.
3. Drain out the cold water from spaghetti, add to white sauce along with cooked peas and $\frac{3}{4}$ cup of cheese. Add some salt if required.
4. Grease a casserole dish, pour the above mixture into it; even out surface, sprinkle with remaining cheese and bread crumbs. Dot with butter.
5. Bake at 190°C (for about 20-25 min.) till the cheese has melted and light brown layer has formed on top.

Serve as a main dish with soup.

Peas in Potato Cups

Ingredients

6 medium potatoes
3-4 tbsp corn flour
1 cup boiled peas
1 small onion, minced
$\frac{1}{2}$ cup grated cheese
2 tbsp thick cream
A little tomato sauce for garnish

2 tbsp butter
2 tbsp minced fresh herbs
  – dill or parsley
  or 1 tsp dry herbs
1 tsp pepper powder
Salt to taste

Method

1. Boil potatoes, peel skin and, while still warm, mash thoroughly with a masher or fork. Sprinkle some salt, pepper powder, herbs and add enough corn flour to hold the dough. Mix all together and form a soft dough.
2. Melt 1 tbsp butter, add minced onion and fry on low heat till they turn pink.
3. Add boiled peas and seasonings (on right side), stir fry for 1-2 min., add grated cheese, mix, remove from fire.
4. Beat cream light, add to cooked peas, mix thoroughly, set aside.
5. Divide potato dough into 6 balls. Take each ball, work into a 'cup'. Make all 6 cups thus.
6. Grease a muffin tray thoroughly; place 'potato cups' in each muffin mould, brush the inside of the potato cups with some melted butter.
7. Place the muffin tray in a hot oven and bake at 190°C for 10-12 min. or till the 'cups' are lightly browned. Take out the tray, place individual potato cups on a serving plate.
8. Fill each 'cup' with the cheese filling, dot with tomato sauce, serve immediately.

Note

1. The above recipe can be served with a North Indian meal also. Substitute Indian masala, chopped green chillies, garam masala powder and minced coriander leaves. You could substitute paneer for cheese, omit cream. Method will be the same.

Peas-Potato Salad:

Instead of serving potato cups plain, they could be placed along with a salad.

Slice 2 firm tomatoes, grate 1-2 carrots and have some lettuce leaves ready. On a salad plate, make a bed of lettuce, arrange tomato slices all around, sprinkle grated carrots.

Place potato cups all around plate on the tomato slices. Sprinkle lemon juice and salt on the vegetables, serve immediately.

Serve cold with a pasta dish.

Pineapple

A delicious, tropical fruit and, like the papaya, the raw pineapple can be used as a vegetable. Jams and chutneys can be prepared (bottled as well). Pineapple slices (fruit) served with cream is a delicacy.

Has carbohydrates as well as vitamin A and potassium. Here are three ways of using raw pineapple which is just about to ripen (do not use pineapple which has ripened).

Preparations

1. **Pineapple-Coconut Milk Stew** (Kerala)
2. **Pineapple Gojju** (Karnataka)
3. **Pineapple Rasam** (Tamil Nadu)

Pineapple-Coconut Milk Stew

Ingredients

1 small pineapple
1 cup grated coconut
3 green chillies, slit
2 tsp rice flour
½-1 tbsp sugar (to taste)
Salt to taste

Seasoning
1 tbsp ghee
3 cloves
1″ piece cinnamon
3 cardamoms
1 bay leaf
A pinch of pepper powder

Method

1. Cut the thick outer skin of the pineapple with a sharp knife. Remove the 'eyes' by using a fine scoop or knife. Cut the pineapple into slices, cut slices into small pieces. If the centre is too hard, discard. Otherwise, chop that also.

2. To coconut gratings, add 1 cup boiling water, cool, squeeze to take out 'thick' milk, set aside. Add 1½-2 cups boiling water, cool. Pass through a liquidiser, take out 'thin' milk, discard gratings, set the second milk also aside.

3. Heat ghee, add seasonings given on the right side except pepper and, when done, add pineapple pieces, stir fry on low heat till sufficiently soft.

4. Mix rice flour with the second milk, add to pineapple, add salt and simmer till pineapple is cooked and soft.

5. Add thick milk, pepper; simmer 1-2 min., remove from fire.

Serve hot with puris.

Pineapple Gojju

(Chutney, Karnataka style)

Ingredients

1 medium pineapple
½ tsp turmeric powder
1 tbsp tamarind juice (optional)
1 small piece of jaggery (optional)
2 tbsp oil
2 sprigs curry leaves
½ tsp mustard seeds
Salt to taste

Dry roast separately:
2 tbsp copra gratings
½ tsp sesame seeds

Fry in 2 tsp oil
½ tsp chana dal
½ tsp urad dal
1-2 red chillies
A pinch of asafoetida
A pinch each of mustard,
cumin and fenugreek seeds

Method

1. Pare and cut pineapple into small pieces as in the previous recipe.

2. Dry roast sesame seeds and copra gratings, remove from kadai. Heat 2 tsp oil, fry the rest of the ingredients, one at a time, continuing to fry all along. Mix all together and powder.

3. Heat oil, add mustard and, when done, the curry leaves and pineapple pieces along with turmeric powder; fry till pieces turn soft. Add some water, salt; cover and cook till tender (on low heat).

4. Add tamarind and jaggery according to the sourness of fruit, if required. Cook for some more time.

5. Add prepared powder, simmer 1-2 min. more, remove when chutney consistency has formed.

Serve with rice or dosas.

Note

Refrigerated, it will keep for over a week.

Pineapple Rasam

Ingredients

½ of a small pineapple
2 tbsp tuvar dal, boiled
½ tsp turmeric powder
1 tbsp chopped coriander leaves
2 sprigs curry leaves
Salt to taste

Seasoning

1 tsp mustard seeds
1 sprig curry leaf

**Fry in 1 tsp oil and
grind to paste**
1 tsp chana dal
½ tsp urad dal
½ tsp cumin seeds
A pinch of asafoetida
10 pepper corns

Method

1. Cut pineapple as in the first recipe; take out a few slices. Chop slices, add some water, squeeze and extract as much juice as you can – about 1-1½ cups. Add 1 cup hot water to mashed dal, churn, set aside.

2. To pineapple juice, add turmeric powder, salt, curry leaf, boil 1-2 min.

3. To ground paste, add 1 cup water; add this to boiling pineapple juice; boil further 2-3 min.

4. When sufficiently boiled, add churned dal, simmer for a while.

5. Season in oil, mustard seeds and curry leaf, pour into rasam; add chopped coriander leaves, remove.

Serve very hot with rice or as an appetiser.

Vegetable Biryani

Banana Kababs

Fried Potatoes with Coconut Chutney

Puris with Cooked Potatoes

Assorted Vegetables

Potato

Potatoes are grown all over the world and, in some European countries, they form the staple food/diet. They are equally popular in our country too; there are numerous varieties of potatoes, varying in size, shape and even colour.

Potato is rich in carbohydrates, has proteins, vitamins and traces of iron as well as copper. The carbohydrate in potato supplies energy and heat. Potatoes should be cooked as far as possible with their jackets on as these contain the minerals and vitamins.

Since potatoes are both common and a favourite vegetable, there are innumerable ways of making them. Compiled here are only one recipe each from a region/state. There are many more ways of cooking potatoes. Being popular in western countries, there is quite a range of western preparations, of which a few have been given here.

Preparations

1. **Potato Podimas** (Tamil Nadu)
2. **Potato Sagale** (Karnataka- Mangalore)
3. **Potato Moilee** (Kerala)
4. **Potato Roast** (Andhra Pradesh/Tamil Nadu/Karnataka)
5. **Alu-Baigan Tharkari** (Orissa)
6. **Alu-Baigan Jhol** (West Bengal)
7. **Garlic Potatoes** (Bihar)
8. **Alu ka Tehri** (Uttar Pradesh)

9. **Alu Parathas** (Punjab)
10. **Batata nu Shak** (Gujarat)
11. **Batata Vada** (Maharashtra)
12. **Potato Khorma –** *Moglai Style*
13. **Green Potatoes –** *Parsi Style*
14. **Alu Tikkies** (North India/Western)
15. **Potato Rabdi** (North India)
16. **Potato Soup** (Western)
17. **Potato Croquette** (Western)
18. **Potato Pie** (Western)
19. **Baked Potatoes** (Western)
20. **Potato Cold Salad** (Western)

Potato Podimas
(Delicately seasoned Potatoes)

Ingredients

¼ kg potatoes (3-4 medium size)
3-4 green chillies
2 sprigs curry leaves
1 tbsp chopped coriander leaves
Juice of ½ lemon
Salt to taste

Seasoning
1½ tbsp oil
½ tsp mustard seeds
1 tsp urad dal
1 tsp chana dal
A pinch of asafoetida

Method

1. Boil, peel and break potato into medium size pieces. Cut chillies into 2-3 pieces each.

2. Heat oil, add seasonings and when dals turn golden brown, add chillies and curry leaves. Stir fry, add potato pieces, salt; fry 1-2 min. more.

3. When potatoes are lightly browned, add chopped coriander leaves, lemon juice and mix thoroughly.

Serve with rice and onion sambar.

Note

If desired, 1 onion, chopped, can be fried with chillies in step 2, along with a pinch of turmeric powder. Add potatoes when onion turns brown. This is a very popular potato preparation common to all the Southern states.

Serve with puris.

Potato Sagale

(Potatoes cooked with tamarind)

Ingredients

¼ kg potatoes
1 onion, thickly sliced
¼ tsp turmeric powder
2 tbsp coconut gratings
2 tbsp tamarind pulp
Salt to taste

**Fry in 1 tsp oil and
grind to paste**
1 tbsp coriander seeds
½ tbsp urad dal
3 red chillies
½ methi seeds

Seasoning

2 tbsp oil
½ tsp mustard seeds
1 sprig curry leaf

Method

1. Boil, peel and break potatoes into fairly large pieces.

2. Grind fried ingredients with coconut, set aside.

3. Heat oil, add mustard seeds; when done, add curry leaves and onion along with turmeric powder. Fry till onion turns brown.

4. Add potatoes, continue to fry till they are slightly browned.

5. Add ground paste and salt, stir fry 1-2 min. Add tamarind pulp, stir and cook till masalas are well blended. (If you want more gravy, add some water, cook 1-2 min. more.)

Serve hot with rice or rotis.

Potato Moilee

(Potatoes in Coconut Milk Gravy)

Ingredients

4 medium potatoes
½ shelled peas (optional)
1 cup grated coconut
A pinch of turmeric powder
½-1 tsp chilli powder (optional)
Juice of 1 lemon
Salt to taste

3 tbsp ghee/oil
1 onion, chopped
4 cloves garlic, minced
½" piece ginger, minced
3 green chillies, slit
2 sprigs curry leaves
1 tbsp chopped coriander leaves

Method

1. Add ½ cup boiling water to grated coconut, cool; squeeze gratings and extract 'thick' milk, set aside. add 1½ cups of boiling water to gratings once more, cool. Pass through a liquidiser, strain the resultant liquid (second milk), set aside. Discard gratings.

2. Boil, peel and cut potatoes into fairly large pieces. Boil peas with some salt, set aside both.

3. Heat ghee/oil, add curry leaves and onion along with turmeric powder; stir fry till onion turns a light pink colour.

4. Add minced ginger, garlic and green chillies, stir fry. Add potato pieces and chilli powder, fry 2-3 min. till potatoes are slightly roasted. Add second coconut milk, peas and salt; cover and cook on low heat for some time.

5. Now add first milk, half of the chopped coriander leaves, mix, boil once, remove from fire.

6. Before serving, add lemon juice, mix. Pour moilee into a bowl, garnish with the rest of the coriander leaves.

Serve hot with pulav or puri.

Potato Roast

(A simple way of preparing potatoes, common to all Southern states)

Ingredients

½ kg potatoes
½ tsp turmeric powder
1½-2 tsp chilli powder
4 tbsp oil
Salt to taste

Seasoning

Pinch of asafoetida
½ tsp mustard seeds
1 tsp urad dal
1 red chilli, broken into two
A big pinch of asafoetida
1 sprig curry leaf

Method

1. Boil and peel potatoes, break them into medium size pieces.

2. Heat oil, add seasonings; when dal has turned brown, add curry leaf, then the potatoes. Add turmeric, chilli powders and salt, mix thoroughly and continue to fry alternately on 'sim' and high till they are nicely roasted and browned. If you want it very crisp, add some more oil while roasting.

Serve very hot with onion sambar – a delicacy in the South – both served on festive occasions.

Note

A similar preparation can be made with colocasia and yam – both very popular in the South.

Alu-Baigan Tharkari
(Potato-Brinjal Gravy)

Ingredients

½ kg potatoes
¼ kg brinjal
2 + 1 onions
4 tbsp oil
1 tbsp ghee
½ tsp turmeric powder
2 bay leaves
Salt to taste

Grind to a fine paste

2 tbsp coriander seeds
½ tbsp cumin seeds
3 red chillies
¼ tsp pepper corns
3 cloves
1″ cinnamon
2 large cardamoms

Method

1. Wash and cut potatoes into fairly large pieces. Cut brinjals also into big pieces; keep both separate. Chop 2 onions, slice the third.

2. Heat oil, add bay leaves and chopped onion, fry till onion turns brown. Add potatoes, turmeric powder, continue to fry on low heat till they turn somewhat soft and brown.

3. Add brinjals, continuing to fry, keeping vessel covered in- between frying.

4. When vegetables have turned sufficiently tender, add ground masala and stir fry on low heat; sprinkle water so that the masalas do not get singed. Fry for some time more.

5. Add salt, water, cover and cook till done.

6. When about to serve, heat ghee, add sliced onions, fry till dark brown, add to tharkari, mix, pour into a serving bowl.

Serve hot with plain rice or puris.

Note

This is a common preparation in West Bengal and Orissa.

Alu-Baigan Jhol

(Potato, Brinjal and Tomato Gravy)

Ingredients

4 medium potatoes
2 medium brinjals
2 tomatoes
1 large onion, sliced
1 tbsp tamarind extract
1 tsp turmeric powder
Salt to taste

Grind to a very fine paste
1$\frac{1}{2}$ tbsp coriander seeds
1 tsp cumin seeds
3 red chillies
2 tsp mustard seeds
6-8 cloves garlic

Seasoning
3-4 tbsp oil
2 bay leaves

Method

1. Cut all the vegetables into fairly large pieces – keep each separate.
2. Heat oil, add bay leaves and onions along with turmeric powder, fry till browned.
3. Add potatoes, fry (on low heat) till quite soft, keeping vessel covered in-between frying.
4. Add brinjals, continue to fry; add tomatoes, fry for some more time all the vegetables, sprinkling some water to prevent it getting burnt. Reduce heat, cover and allow to cook till vegetables are nearly done.
5. Add ground paste, tamarind pulp and salt, some more water if necessary; simmer for some time more.

Serve hot with rice.

Garlic Potatoes

Ingredients

2 large potatoes
8-10 cloves garlic
2-3 red chillies
$\frac{1}{2}$ tsp turmeric powder
Salt to taste

Seasoning
3-4 tbsp oil
$\frac{1}{2}$ tsp cumin seeds

Method

1. Wash and cut potatoes into thick slices with the skin on (like French fries).
2. Grind the ingredients on the left side (except potatoes) to a fine paste with a little water. Smear this on potato slices.
3. Heat oil, add cumin seeds and, when done, add potato slices and stir fry, turning over and over again all the time till potatoes are soft and browned. Keep covered and cook on 'sim' while frying. When done, if you need them very crisp and roasted, remove cover, add some more oil and fry on high flame, stirring all the while, till dark brown.

Serve hot with phulkas.

Alu ka Tehri
(Potato Pulav)

Ingredients

1 cup fine (basmati) rice	**Grind to a fine paste**
2 medium potatoes	3 cloves garlic
1 medium onion, sliced	1" piece ginger
2 tsp coriander powder	1 medium onion
$\frac{1}{2}$-1 tsp chilli powder	$\frac{1}{4}$ tsp turmeric powder
$\frac{1}{2}$-1 tsp garam masala	**Seasoning**
4 tbsp ghee	1 tsp cumin seeds
Salt to taste	

Method

1. Wash rice, spread on a cloth to dry; wash and cut potatoes into medium size pieces.
2. Heat half the ghee, fry sliced onions to dark brown and crisp, set aside for garnish.
3. Add potatoes, fry to a golden brown, remove.
4. Add rest of the ghee, add cumin seeds and when done, add ground masala along with chilli and coriander powders and fry till oil surfaces.

5. Add rice, garam masala, stir fry. Add potatoes, $2\frac{1}{2}$ cups water and salt. Cook till done, preferably in a rice cooker.

Serve garnished with fried onion.

Alu Parathas

Ingredients

For the Parathas
3 cups wheat flour
3 tsp ghee or vanaspathi
Salt to taste
Oil for frying

For Filling
2 medium potatoes
1-2 green chillies
A few mint leaves
A little coriander leaves
1 tsp coriander-cumin seed powder
$\frac{1}{2}$ tsp chilli powder (optional)
A pinch of amchoor

Method

1. Mix the flour with 3 tsp ghee, salt and enough water to form a soft dough; cover and set aside.
2. Boil, peel and mash potatoes.
3. Mince green chillies, mint and coriander leaves.
4. Mix mashed potatoes, minced ingredients and add the powdered masalas (on right side) with some salt; set aside.
5. Take a large lump of dough and, with greased hand, form a cup. Put some of the filling inside, close the cup and pat into a round. Very carefully roll into a circle on a floured board, dusting with flour.
6. Transfer paratha carefully onto a tava and, on medium heat, cook both sides. Then apply ghee and cook further till browned and crisp.

Serve very hot with pickles or chutney.

Batata nu Shak

(Potatoes in Curd Gravy)

Ingredients

¼ kg potatoes
½ cup curds (sour)
Pinch of sugar
2 tbsp oil
Pinch of asafoetida
2 sprigs curry leaves
Salt to taste

Powdered masalas

1 tsp coriander-cumin seed powder
½ tsp garam masala
½ tsp chilli powder
½ tsp turmeric powder

Grind to a fine paste

1 medium onion
3 green chillies
½" piece ginger
3 cloves garlic

Dry roast and powder

½ tbsp ground nuts
½ tbsp roasted gram
½ tbsp grated coconut

For Garnish

1 tbsp chopped coriander leaves

Method

1. Boil, peel and cut potatoes into large cubes.

2. Heat oil, add asafoetida and curry leaves; when done, add ground paste and stir fry till oil surfaces.

3. Add powdered masalas (on left side) one by one, stirring all the while; add salt, fry 1-2 min. more, add potato cubes and fry till they are evenly coated with the masala.

4. Beat curds smooth, add sugar, pour into potatoes. Cook over low heat till almost dry. Now add roasted and powdered ingredients, stir for some time; remove from fire.

Serve garnished with chopped coriander leaves as an accompaniment to rice or with rotis.

Batata Vada

Ingredients

2 large potatoes
2-3 green chillies, minced
$\frac{1}{2}''$ piece ginger, minced
1 tbsp chopped coriander leaves
1 tbsp ground nut, powdered (optional)
1 tbsp grated coconut
Juice of $\frac{1}{2}$ lemon
$\frac{1}{2}$ tsp sugar
Salt to taste

For Batter

1 cup gram flour
A pinch of turmeric powder
A pinch of asafoetida powder
$\frac{1}{2}$ tsp chilli powder
A pinch of baking soda
Salt to taste
Oil for frying

Method

1. Boil, peel and mash potatoes roughly, roast and powder ground nuts.

2. Mix potatoes, ground nut powder and all the other ingredients to form a smooth dough. Make small balls of dough, set aside till required.

3. Mix in a bowl all the batter ingredients with some water to form a thick batter, adding 2 tsp hot oil.

4. Heat oil, dip potato balls in gram flour batter and deep fry.

Serve sizzling hot with coconut chutney or tomato ketchup – an excellent tea time snack.

Note

If desired, 1 large onion can be chopped and fried to a golden brown colour and added to potatoes in step 2.

Potato Khorma – *Moglai Style*

Ingredients

½ kg small potatoes
2 large onions, sliced
1 cup curds
1 tsp sugar
½ tsp turmeric powder
¾ cup oil
2 bay leaves
3-4 green chillies, slit
A pinch of saffron
½ cup hot milk
Salt to taste

For Garnish

A few fried nuts
1 tbsp chopped coriander leaves
½ cup cream

Grind to paste

1″ piece ginger
6 cloves garlic
3-4 tbsp coconut gratings
6-8 cashew nuts or almonds
½ tsp chopped mint
1 tsp chopped coriander leaves

Dry roast and powder

3 cloves
2 small cardamoms
1 tsp poppy seeds
½ tsp shahjeera (optional)
3-4 red chillies

Method

1. Boil, peel and prick potatoes with a sharp needle, keep aside. If large ones are used, cut into fairly big pieces. Soak saffron in ½ cup hot milk.

2. Heat ⅓ of the oil, fry onions to a light reddish brown colour, remove from kadai.

3. Pour ⅓ more of the oil, fry potatoes, carefully turning over all the while – see that they do not break. Sprinkle some salt while frying. Fry till browned, set aside.

4. Pour rest of the oil, season with bay leaves and green chillies; add ground masala along with turmeric powder; fry for a while.

5. Now add powdered masala, continue to fry till oil surfaces.

6. Add 1-1½ cups water, saffron along with milk; cover and cook on 'sim' till gravy is formed.

7. Beat curds smooth along with sugar, pour into gravy, cover and cook some time, adding fried potatoes and onions. Simmer for 3-5 min., remove from fire.

To Serve: Pour khorma into a bowl. Beat cream lightly, pour over khorma. Garnish with fried nuts and chopped coriander leaves.

Served with pulav or puris.

Green Potatoes – *Parsi Style*
(With or without eggs)

Ingredients

½ kg potatoes
¼ boiled peas
6 hard boiled eggs (optional)
1 large onion, chopped
Juice of 1 lemon
4 tbsp oil
Salt to taste
½-1 tsp chilli powder

Seasoning

2 bay leaves
2 cloves
2 cardamoms
½" piece cinnamon

Garnish

½ cup cream (optional)
A little chopped coriander leaves

Grind to a fine paste

4-5 green chillies
1" piece ginger
5-6 cloves garlic
4 tbsp chopped coriander leaves
1 tbsp chopped mint
4-5 cashew nuts
1 tsp aniseeds
1 tsp poppy seeds
½ tsp garam masala

Method

1. Boil, peel and cut potatoes into fairly large pieces.
2. Heat half of the oil, fry potatoes, sprinkling some salt (on low heat) till browned, remove from kadai; keep aside.
3. Heat rest of the oil, add bay leaves, seasonings and chopped onions, fry till browned.
4. Add ground paste, continue to fry till oil surfaces adding chilli powder; sprinkle some water if too dry.

5. Add fried potatoes, a little water if necessary along with some salt. Cover and cook on low heat till potatoes are well blended with gravy. Remove from fire, pour potato curry into a serving bowl.

6. *a)* Beat cream smooth, pour over potatoes, garnish with coriander leaves and sprinkle lemon juice.

   b) If you are using eggs, shell the hard boiled egg, cut carefully lengthwise into two. Fry these halves in a little oil till lightly browned. Arrange fried eggs on the sides of the bowl, garnish as before.

Alu Tikkies

Ingredients

½ kg potatoes
4 green chillies, minced
2 medium onions, chopped
1 tbsp chopped coriander leaves
1 tsp chopped mint leaves
2 slices of bread
Oil for frying
Salt to taste

2 tsp coriander powder
1 tsp cumin seed powder
½ tsp chilli powder
A pinch of garam masala
½ tsp amchoor
   or 2 tsp lemon juice
1 tbsp flour
½-1 cup bread crumbs

Method

1. Boil, peel and mash potatoes while still warm

2. Heat 2 tbsp oil, add chillies and onion, fry to a light brown colour.

3. Add all the powdered masalas, stir fry, add potato dough, salt, minced herbs and lemon juice. Mix all together, remove from fire, transfer to a plate, allow to cool.

4. Soak bread slices in water, squeeze dry, add to potato dough, mix thoroughly.

5. Take out small balls of dough, flatten on the palm of your hand; make alu tikkis thus.

6. Mix together flour in 1 cup water to a thin paste.

7. When about to serve, dip tikkis in flour paste, roll in bread crumbs and shallow fry, preferably in a non-stick pan.

Serve sizzling hot with any chutney.

Note

Potato cutlets can be served with western meals also. For this, omit all the masala ingredients – use only chilli, pepper powders and minced dill or parsley. Use lemon juice. Method will be the same.

Serve with ketchup.

Potato Rabdi
(Alu Kheer)

Ingredients

1 large potato	12 cashew nuts or almonds
8 cups milk	5-6 cardamoms
A large pinch of kesar	A few drops almond essence
1 cup sugar	

Method

1. Wash, peel and grate potato on a very fine grater – there should be about 1 cup of gratings. Wash the gratings in cold water 2-3 times to remove all starch. Soak kesar in very hot milk (about $\frac{1}{4}$ cup).
2. Grate 8 of the nuts fine, chop the rest, keep both separate. Powder cardamoms.
3. Boil milk and, while boiling, add potato gratings. Continue to boil on low heat for some time. Add grated nuts and sugar.
4. Boil briskly for some time – keep stirring all the while. When sufficiently thick (rabdi or custard consistency), add powdered cardamom, almond essence, mix thoroughly, remove from fire.
5. Pour rabdi into a bowl, garnish with chopped nuts.

Serve hot or cold.

Potato Soup

Ingredients

2 medium potatoes
1 medium onion
1 small piece celery
    or $\frac{1}{2}$ tsp celery seeds
1 tbsp butter

1 cup milk
1 tsp pepper powder
Salt to taste
A big pinch of herbs
Grated cheese for garnish

Method

1. Grate potatoes, chop onions and celery.
2. Melt butter, add onions; fry to a light pink colour. Add grated potatoes and celery pieces; fry 2-3 min. or till lightly done. Add enough water to cover the vegetables. Cover pan with lid and cook till vegetables have turned soft. Remove from fire; cool.
3. Pass vegetables through a liquidiser, set aside puree.
4. A little before serving, heat milk, add puree gradually; add salt and pepper, boil 1-2 min., remove.
5. Pour hot soup into bowls, add a little grated cheese.

Serve with garlic toast.

Potato Croquette

Ingredients

1 cup mashed potatoes
1 minced onion
1 egg, beaten
Bread crumbs
Oil for frying

Seasoning
1 tsp pepper powder
$\frac{1}{2}$ tsp mustard powder
$\frac{1}{2}$-1 tsp chilli powder
1 tsp dried herbs
Salt to taste

Method

1. To mashed potatoes (while still warm), add all seasonings; make a soft dough.
2. Make small balls of dough, keep aside.

3. When about to serve, dip balls in egg, roll in bread crumbs; deep fry to a golden brown. Leave on absorbent paper to drain.

Serve hot with tomato ketchup either as a tea time snack or at dinner.

Potato Pie

Ingredients

½ kg potatoes	½ tbsp pepper powder
½ cup shelled peas	Salt to taste
1 small carrot	2 tbsp butter
A few cauliflower florets	2 tbsp refined oil
2 tsp fresh, minced herbs	4 tbsp bread crumbs
(dill or parsley)	½ cup grated cheese
1 medium onion, minced	1 tbsp tomato ketchup

Method

1. Boil, peel and mash potatoes while still warm, with a pinch of salt, pepper powder and 1 tbsp butter.
2. Chop carrots and cauliflower; cook with peas and some salt.
3. Heat oil, fry onions till translucent, add cooked vegetables, stir fry. Add pepper powder, salt, herbs, tomato ketchup and some of the cheese, mix thoroughly, remove from fire.
4. Grease a pie dish thoroughly with some oil, sprinkle ¾ bread crumbs over the entire surface. On this, spread the potato dough, even out the surface. Top the potato with vegetable mixture, spread evenly. Cover this with the rest of the cheese. Melt the remaining butter, pour over cheese, sprinkle bread crumbs very lightly on this.
5. Bake in a moderate oven for 20-30 min. or till top is browned and cheese has melted.

Serve hot as a main dish with soup and buttered bread.

Baked Potatoes

Ingredients

4 large potatoes
½ small onion, minced
½ small carrot, grated fine
1 tbsp minced dill or parsley
1 cup thick curds (not sour)
2 tbsp finely grated cheese
1-2 tbsp butter

Seasoning

½ tsp chilli powder
1 tsp pepper powder
2 minced green chillies
Pinch of sugar
Salt to taste

Note

If you are serving a fully western meal, substitute sour cream for curds. Also, instead of green chillies, chop a small piece of capsicum. Substitute mustard powder for chilli powder.

Method

1. Boil potatoes in their jackets. When cold, cut each potato into 2 halves. Carefully scoop out the centre portion leaving ¼″ thickness on sides.
2. Mix all the ingredients except butter into a smooth paste.
3. Brush the outsides of the potatoes with melted butter. Carefully fill each potato centre with the prepared mixture, spread evenly. Brush the tops with butter.
4. Place stuffed potatoes on a tray and grill in an oven for 5-7 min. or till browned.

Serve hot with soup and toasted butter.

Note

If curds is watery, hang it in a clean muslin cloth for ½-1 hour or till all the water is drained. Beat smooth, then add the other ingredients.

Potato Cold Salad

Ingredients

1 large potato
½ cup shelled peas
1 medium onion, minced
1 egg, hard boiled
1 tbsp minced parsley or dill

Dressing
1 tbsp water
1 tbsp butter
½ tbsp vinegar (white)
A pinch of salt
¼ tsp pepper powder
A dash of lemon juice

Method

1. Boil potato, peel when cooled, cut into cubes. Boil peas with a little salt. Shell, chop or dice the egg. Mix all these, set aside.

2. Heat water, adding butter, pepper powder and salt. When butter has melted, add vinegar, mix, remove from fire. Pour this over potato-egg mixture, allow to cool.

3. In a salad bowl, combine potatoes, minced onion, part of the herbs and lemon juice, mix thoroughly; sprinkle rest of the herbs on top; leave in the refrigerator, covered.

Serve chilled. If desired, a few bread croutons (fried crisp) can be mixed when serving.

Radish

Known from ancient times, radish is cultivated all over the world and in India too. Both the tap root and the leaves are used in cooking – comes in two colours – white and pink.

Has carbohydrates, vitamins B, C and salts. Has high medicinal value, too.

Eaten raw in salads with salt, pepper and lemon juice, is good for piles, constipation and jaundice – helps in digestion. Radish juice mixed with salt and honey is a cure for whooping cough and bronchitis. Leaves also are of a high medicinal value.

Radish contains a volatile oil which has a carminative action.

Preparations

1. **Mullangi Kosamalli** (Tamil Nadu)
2. **Radish Foogath** (Tamil Nadu)
3. **Radish with Moong Dal**
4. **Muli Rotis** (Punjab)
5. **Muli Kadhi** (Gujarat)

Mullangi Kosamalli

(A salad preparation)

Ingredients

1 large radish
1-2 green chillies
Juice of ½ lemon
Little chopped coriander leaves
Salt to taste

Seasoning

1 tsp oil
¼ tsp mustard seeds
1 spring curry leaf
A pinch of turmeric powder

Method

1. Scrape, wash and cut radish into ½" long thin pieces – for this cut into circles, each circle cut lengthwise. Cut chilli into 2-3 pieces.

2. Heat oil, add mustard seeds; when done the curry leaves, chilli pieces and turmeric powder; stir, pour into the vessel containing radish slices.

3. Mix together with radish salt, lemon juice and coriander leaves.

Serve chilled.

Note

In the South, radish sambar is very popular and quite a delicious preparation – for this refer to 'Drumstick' (see sambar), substitute ½ kg radish for drumstick (cut radish into circles).

Radish Foogath
(A spicy dry curry)

Ingredients

3 medium radish
1 medium onion, chopped
2 tbsp gram flour
1 tbsp chopped coriander leaves
3 slit green chillies
$\frac{1}{4}$ tsp turmeric powder
$\frac{1}{2}$ tbsp oil
Salt to taste

Grind to paste
2 tbsp coconut gratings
$\frac{1}{2}$" piece ginger
3 cloves garlic

Seasoning
$1\frac{1}{2}$ tbsp oil
$\frac{1}{2}$ tsp mustard seeds
2 cloves
$\frac{1}{2}$" piece cinnamon
1 spring curry leaf

Method

1. Scrape and cut radish into quarters.
2. Fry gram flour in $\frac{1}{2}$ tbsp oil to golden brown, set aside.
3. Heat rest of the oil, add seasonings and when done , add curry leaves, slit chillies and onions along with turmeric powder. Fry till onions turn brown.
4. Add radish, fry 1-2 min. on low heat; then add ground paste, stir fry for a while. Now add salt, sprinkle some water, cover and cook till radish has turned soft.
4. Add fried gram flour, fry till vegetable is almost dry. Sprinkle chopped coriander leaves, mix and remove. If desired a little lemon juice may be sprinkled.

Serve with rotis.

Tips ....   **For Koftas**

Squeeze gratings of vegetables (bottle gourd, vegetable marrow, or radish), stir fry on low heat to remove moisture; then add rest of the ingredients as recipe requires.

Radish with Moong Dal

Ingredients

1 large radish
½ cup moong dal
½ tsp turmeric powder
2 tbsp chopped coriander leaves
½ tbsp oil/ghee
Juice of ½ lemon
¼ tsp sugar
Salt to taste

Grind to paste
4 cloves garlic
3-4 green chillies
1" piece ginger

Seasoning
½ tsp mustard seeds
½ tsp cumin seeds
A pinch of asafoetida
1 red chilli, broken
2 sprigs curry leaves

Method

1. Boil dal with enough water and turmeric powder on low heat – do not allow dal to get mushy.

2. Scrape radish, cut into thin semi-circles, add to dal along with ground paste and salt. Cook till radish turns soft.

3. Heat oil, season in ghee/oil the ingredients given in the same order. When done, pour into dal. Add sugar, coriander leaves, simmer once, remove from fire. Add lemon juice.

Note

If desired, 1 onion, chopped may be fried in 1 tbsp oil to golden brown, and added to dal in step 3.

Muli Rotis

Ingredients

2 cups wheat flour
1 cup finely grated radish
   (about 2 medium radish)
3 tsp oil for mixing
1 tbsp minced coriander leaves

$\frac{1}{2}$ tsp chilli powder
$\frac{1}{2}$ tsp turmeric powder
$\frac{1}{2}$ tsp coriander powder
$\frac{1}{2}$ tsp cumin powder
Salt to taste
A little ghee

Method

1. Mix together all the ingredients (except ghee) to form a soft dough. Add very little water as radish will exude water when mixed with salt and turmeric powder. Leave the dough for 5-8 min. and make rotis – do not keep dough very long (if you must, then refrigerate the dough).

2. Roll out rotis, slightly thicker than for normal chapathis. Cook on medium heat both sides till brown spots appear. Now apply some ghee and cook again both sides till it gets crisp.

Serve hot with dal or raitha.

Note

An alternate way of making muli rotis is to make the dough separate and filling separately. Just before making rotis, squeeze gratings, add all masalas, make cups out of the dough, put in the filling and roll out parathas; shallow fry.

Muli Kadhi

(Radish in Butter Milk Gravy)

Ingredients

¼ kg muli
   (about 3 medium size)
A pinch of turmeric powder
2 tbsp gram flour
1 cup curds
½ tsp sugar
½-1 tsp chilli powder
Salt to taste

Mince fine

3 green chillies
½" piece ginger
4-5 cloves garlic
Little coriander leaves

Seasoning

2 tbsp oil
½ tsp mustard seeds
A pinch of asafoetida
2 sprigs curry leaves

Method

1. Scrape and cut radish into quarters.

2. Heat oil, add seasonings; when mustard seeds are done, add curry leaves, minced ingredients (except coriander leaves), stir fry on low heat adding radish slices. Add turmeric powder and stir for 2-3 min. more, sprinkle some water and cook till soft.

3. Beat curds smooth, add chilli powder, sugar, salt and gram flour, mix thoroughly adding 1½-2 cups water. There should be no lumps – mixture should be smooth. Pour this onto radish and simmer on low heat till kadhi is slightly thick. Add coriander leaves, mix.

Serve hot with rice.

Spinach

Very largely cultivated all over the world as in India, it is a popular 'green', highly nutritive. Has a very high content of vitamin A; also rich in carbohydrates, protein and iron and has folic acid and amino acids. It is the cheapest form of protein, its yield equal to that of eggs, meat and other costly vegetables. Eating fresh spinach daily supplies the required amount of iron, vitamin A and folic acid to the body. Regular use of spinach is a sure cure for anaemia, and it is specially recommended for pregnant mothers.

Most of the preparations given in 'Amaranthus' and 'Greens' can be prepared with spinach also, expecially the South Indian gravies and curries. These, therefore, have not been mentioned separately in this chapter. A few recipes of fenugreek (*methi*) can also be substituted for spinach.

Preparations

1. **Palak-Methi Pulav** (North India)
2. **Palak-Chana** (North India)
3. **Palak-Paneer** (Punjab)
4. **Sindhi Palak**
5. **Palak-Methi Parathas**
6. **Spicy Spinach Soup**
7. **Spinach Florentine** (Western)
8. **Spaghetti Spinach** (Italian)
9. **Spinach Cups**
10. **Spinach-Cheese Cutlets**

Palak-Methi Pulav
(Spinach-Fenugreek Leaf Rice)

Ingredients

1½ cups fine rice
2 cups chopped palak
½ cup chopped methi
½ cup peas, boiled (optional)
½ cup soft, fresh paneer
  (optional)
2 tbsp flour
1 onion, sliced thin
4 tbsp ghee
A little pepper powder
Salt to taste

Grind to paste
  3-4 green chillies
  6 cloves garlic
  1″ piece ginger
  1 small onion

Seasoning
  2 bay leaves
  3 cloves
  2 ½″ cinnamon bits
  3 small cardamoms
  6 pepper corns

For garnish

A few fried nuts (optional)

Method

1. Wash rice, leave on a cloth to dry.
2. Cook palak and methi with very little water. Cool and pass through a liquidiser.
3. Heat ½ of the ghee, fry sliced onions to dark brown, remove, set aside for garnish.
4. Crumble paneer, add a pinch of salt, little pepper and a pinch of garam masala. Make small balls, roll in a little flour, deep fry, set aside.
5. Pour rest of the ghee into cooker, add seasonings and, when done, add ground paste and fry; add palak puree, fry till ghee surfaces.
6. Add rice, stir fry for a couple of minutes.
7. Add 3 cups boiling water, salt, cover and cook till done (preferably in a rice cooker).
8. When about to serve, remove lid of cooker, mix in boiled peas, ¾ of the fried paneer balls. Transfer rice onto a rice plate, even out surface.

   Garnish with the rest of the paneer balls, fried nuts and onions.

Serve hot with curds – it is a complete meal in itself.

Palak-Chana

(Spinach Gravy with Kabuli Chana)

Ingredients

1 cup Kabuli chana
4 cups chopped spinach
1 cup chopped methi
1 large onion
1″ piece ginger
6 cloves garlic
4-5 green chillies
3-4 tbsp oil/ghee

Dry Masalas

1 tsp chilli powder
½ tsp turmeric powder
2 tsp coriander powder
1 tsp cumin seed powder
1 tsp garam masala
Salt to taste
½ cup thick tamarind pulp

Method

1. Soak chana overnight with ½ tsp baking soda. Next day, wash thoroughly and pressure cook with some water till soft. Remove lid, add salt, cook a little more so that the extra water gets absorbed.

2. Cook palak and methi with a little salt; cool. Add all the ingredients on right side, except oil and chana, and pass through a liquidiser; set aside puree.

3. Heat oil, add spinach puree and fry for 2-3 min. Add all the dry masalas one by one, continuing to fry all the time, till oil surfaces.

4. Now add cooked chana, tamarind pulp and some water (if necessary). Simmer till gravy is blended.

To Serve: Pour gravy into a bowl, garnish with sliced raw onion or some curds beaten smooth. Serve with nan or parathas.

Palak Paneer
(Spinach with Cottage Cheese)

Ingredients

4 cups chopped palak
1 cup chopped methi
100-150 gm paneer
4 tbsp ghee/oil
$\frac{1}{2}$ tsp turmeric powder
2 tsp flour
$\frac{1}{2}$-1 cup cream (as required)
Salt to taste
A little ($\frac{1}{2}$ cup) hot milk

Grind to paste
1 small onion
1 medium tomato
1″ piece ginger
6 cloves garlic
3-4 green chillies

Powdered Masalas
1 tsp coriander powder
$\frac{1}{2}$ tsp cumin powder
$\frac{1}{2}$-1 tsp chilli powder
$\frac{1}{2}$-1 tsp garam masala

Method

1. Boil palak and methi with a little salt, cool; pass through a liquidiser, set aside puree.

2. Cut paneer into cubes; roll in flour, deep fry in some ghee; soak in hot milk to which $\frac{1}{2}$ tsp turmeric powder has been added.

3. After frying paneer, pour rest of the ghee into kadai, add ground paste, fry for 3-5 min. on very low heat. Gradually add powdered masalas one by one, continuing to fry all the while till ghee surfaces.

4. Add pureed palak, stir fry till done on low heat. Add paneer cubes along with the milk it was soaked in; simmer 1-2 min.

To Serve: Pour palak-paneer into a serving bowl. Beat cream smooth, pour over gravy.

Serve hot with puris.

Sindhi Palak
(Spinach, Vegetables and Dal Gravy)

Ingredients

3-4 cups chopped spinach
½ cup chopped dill
4 tbsp chana dal
1 small carrot
1 medium potato
1 small tomato
1 medium onion
1 small brinjal
1 tbsp thick tamarind pulp
Salt to taste

Mince fine
5 cloves garlic
1″ piece ginger
4 green chillies
Powdered Masalas
1 tsp coriander powder
1 tsp cumin powder
½ tsp turmeric powder
½-1 tsp chilli powder
2 tbsp oil
1 tbsp ghee
½-1 tsp garam masala

Method

1. Wash and chop all vegetables; soak chana dal for 2-3 hours.

2. Heat 2 tbsp oil in a pressure cooker, add minced ingredients, fry 1 min., add chopped vegetables, fry 3-4 min. till they turn soft. Add chopped spinach and dill, continue to fry for a while.

3. Strain water from dal, add dal to cooker, fry. Add all the dry masalas one by one except garam masala. Fry for some time. Add some water, salt, close cooker and pressure cook till the vegetables are tender.

4. Remove lid of cooker, add tamarind pulp and mash thoroughly, simmer 1-2 min. more till well blended.

5. Just before serving, heat ghee, fry garam masala, pour into cooker, mix.

Serve with phulkas or rice.

Note

If desired, some cream can be poured over the gravy.

Palak-Methi Parathas
(Spinach-Fenugreek Leaf Parathas)

Ingredients

2½ cups wheat flour
½ cup gram flour
3 tsp oil for mixing
Oil for frying

3 cups chopped palak
1 cup chopped methi
3 green chillies
½" piece ginger
3 cloves garlic
½ tsp aniseed
Salt to taste

Method

1. Boil palak and methi, cool. Grind to a paste with all the ingredients given on right side along with salt.

2. Mix wheat flour, gram flour, 3 tsp oil and the ground palak; form a smooth dough adding very little water (if necessary). Cover dough, set aside.

3. Divide dough into large lemon-size balls, roll into a thick circle, smear circles with some oil, fold into a triangle, roll triangle into parathas.

4. Heat tava, put the paratha on it and cook on low heat till done. When brown spots start to appear, raise the heat, then fry adding some oil till crisp. Turn over, fry the other side.

Serve hot with raitha or chutney.

Spicy Spinach Soup
(Soup Indian Style)

Ingredients

3 cups chopped spinach
1 large potato, grated
1 medium onion, minced
2 cloves garlic, minced
¼" piece ginger, minced
1 tbsp chopped coriander leaves
A little cream for serving

2 tbsp ghee
A pinch of cumin seeds
1 tsp pepper powder
½ tsp nutmeg powder
A pinch of garam masala
Salt to taste
1½ cups milk

Method

1. Heat ghee, add cumin seeds; when done, add minced ingredients; fry. Add grated potatoes, chopped spinach, fry for a while longer.
2. Add pepper powder, salt, nutmeg powder, garam masala, 2-3 cups water and cook till vegetables are done (preferably in a pressure cooker – if so add less water). Remove from fire, cool, pass through a liquidiser.
3. Add some water to puree (if too thick), add milk and simmer on low heat till soup consistency.

To Serve: Pour soup in individual soup bowls. Beat cream smooth, add a dollop to each bowl. Garnish with a pinch of coriander leaves, placed on the cream.

Spinach Florentine
(Egg/Cheese baked on a Spinach base)

Ingredients

8 cups chopped spinach
1 onion, minced
1 cup cream
4 eggs (optional)
1-2 cups grated cheese
1 tbsp butter
1 tsp pepper powder
Salt to taste

For White Sauce
4 tbsp butter
4 tbsp flour
3 cups milk
1-1½ tsp pepper powder
A large pinch of nutmeg
Little salt

Method

1. Boil and cool spinach, pass through a liquidiser, set aside puree.
2. Melt 1 tbsp butter, add minced onion, stir fry on low heat till light pink in colour. Add spinach puree, salt and pepper powder. mix thoroughly, remove from fire.
3. **Prepare White Sauce:** Melt butter on low heat, add flour, stir fry till it turns pink in colour. Gradually add milk (see that no lumps are formed) – this can be done by removing the pan from fire. When all the milk has been added, put back pan on fire, simmer on low heat continuously stirring till custard consistency. Add seasonings, mix, remove from fire.

4. Add white sauce to spinach puree. Beat cream light, add to this along with ¾ of the cheese. Mix all together thoroughly, pour into a greased dish, shake dish to even out surface.

5. Separate yellows from whites of eggs, beat yellow thick and creamy, adding pepper powder and salt. Beat white stiff, pour into yellow, mix both together.

6. Pour eggs onto spinach layer, sprinkle ¼ cup cheese on top.

7. Set the dish in a pan containing water, leave this in the oven to bake at 190°C or till eggs are done.

Serve hot with toast.

Note

If you do not desire eggs, omit. Sprinkle 1 cup of extra cheese on top of spinach layer to cover and bake as before.

Spaghetti Spinach

Ingredients

8 cups chopped spinach	3 tbsp butter
100 gm spaghetti	3 tbsp flour
1½-2 cups grated cheese	2½-3 cups milk
1 onion, minced	2 tsp corn flour
2 cloves garlic, crushed	2 tsp pepper powder
1 tbsp butter (extra)	Salt to taste
Little bread crumbs	2 tsp minced fresh herbs or dried (oregano, parsley)

Method

1. Boil spinach with very little water – alternatively, steam cook, cool; pass through a liquidiser, set aside puree.

2. Boil some water, add 1 tsp oil, some salt and cook spaghetti till soft. Remove from fire, discard water and leave spaghetti on a plate to cool sprinkling some oil so that it does not get sticky.

3. Melt butter, add onion and garlic, fry on low heat till translucent; add flour, stir fry till lightly browned.

4. Add spinach puree along with salt, pepper powder and herbs, fry 1-2 min.

5. Mix milk with corn flour, gradually add to spinach, stirring all the while. Simmer mixture for 2-3 min., remove from fire. This is spinach sauce.

6. Grease a casserole dish. Mix together spinach sauce, spaghetti, ¾ of the cheese, pour into dish, shake vessel to spread evenly.

7. Sprinkle rest of the cheese on top along with bread crumbs, dot with butter.

8. Bake in a moderate oven for ½ hour or till top is browned.

Serve hot as a main dish.

Spinach Cups

Ingredients

1 cup spinach puree (seasoned)
1 dozen slices of bread
A little extra butter
1 cup grated cheese
1 dozen muffin cups

Method

1. Prepare spinach puree as in previous recipe. Follow steps 1, 3 and 4 only. The spinach puree should be **thick**. Add ½ cup grated cheese, mix thoroughly, set aside.

2. Grease muffin cups (or small aluminium baking cups) with butter. Discard edges of slices, press slice into the cup. Brush the inside of the slices with butter, bake in a hot oven at 200°C (400°F) for 10-12 min. or till crisp. Prepare all cups thus, set aside.

3. When about to serve, fill bread cups with the spinach-cheese sauce. Sprinkle some more cheese on top and grill in a hot oven till cheese melts for 5-8 min. (220°C- 400°F).

Serve hot with tomato or carrot soup.

Spinach-Cheese Cutlets

Ingredients

$\frac{1}{2}$ cup thick spinach puree (see previous recipe)
$1\frac{1}{2}$-2 cups bread crumbs
1 tsp each pepper and mustard (powdered fresh)
A little salt (to taste)
2 tbsp grated cheese
1 egg (optional) or 1 tsp flour mixed with $\frac{1}{2}$ cup water
Oil for frying
Extra bread crumbs (for frying)

Method

1. Mix all ingredients (except the last three) to form a smooth dough. If you are using egg, mix egg with all the other ingredients.
2. Take out small balls of dough, pat into a cutlet, set aside.
3. When about to serve, dip cutlets in flour paste, roll in bread crumbs, shallow fry.

Note

1. If you are using eggs, there is no need to roll in flour paste.

2. If you require a North Indian flavour, add minced chillies, chilli and garam masala powders (to taste) to the dough.

Sweet Potato

Sweet potato is cultivated all over India. Its pink tubers are full of carbohydrate (starch). Vitamin C is found in its fresh milky juice. It is prepared like a gruel and taken in place of rice by the poor. It is also taken in a simple form by boiling the tubers with jaggery.

Preparations

1. **Sweet Potato-Coconut Dry Curry** (Tamil Nadu)
2. **Sweet Potato with Garlic** (Andhra Pradesh)
3. **Sweet Potato Paratha** (North India)
4. **Sweet Potato Casserole** (Western)

Sweet Potato-Coconut Dry Curry

Ingredients

2 large sweet potatoes
1-2 green chillies, cut
2 tbsp grated coconut
A small piece of jaggery (optional)
Salt to taste

Seasoning
1 tbsp oil
½ tsp mustard seeds
½" piece ginger
1 red chilli, broken
1 sprig curry leaf

Method

1. Boil sweet potatoes in their jackets. If desired peel, otherwise keep the skin on and cut into small pieces, while still warm.
2. Heat oil, add seasonings; when done, add green chillies, stir fry. Add sweet potato pieces, grated coconut, salt and jaggery; fry 1-2 min. more; remove from fire.

Serve hot with rice and rasam or sambar.

Sweet Potato with Garlic

Ingredients

3 medium sweet potatoes
1 large onion, chopped
3 cloves garlic, minced
¼ tsp turmeric powder
Salt to taste
½-1 cup milk
1 tbsp chopped coriander leaves

Seasoning
1½ tbsp oil
½ tsp mustard seeds
½ tsp cumin seeds
2-3 red chillies, crushed
or 1 tsp chilli powder
1 sprig curry leaf

Method

1. Wash and cut sweet potatoes into medium size cubes. Add very little water, some salt and cook till they become soft – do not over cook
2. Heat oil, add seasonings and when done, add garlic and onion along with turmeric powder. Fry till onions turn brown, add cooked sweet potatoes, some more salt if necessary, little water. Cover and cook till blended.

3. Add milk, chopped coriander leaves, mix, simmer 1-2 min. more. Remove from fire.

Serve with rice or rotis.

Sweet Potato Paratha

Ingredients

1 cup boiled, mashed sweet potato
2 cups wheat flour
1 tbsp lemon juice
Salt to taste
Oil for frying

Mince fine
4 green chillies
½" piece ginger
Little coriander leaves
A few mint leaves

Powdered Masalas
2 tsp coriander-cumin powder
1 tsp amchoor
½ tsp garam masala

Method

1. Mix together the flour with a pinch of salt, 2 tsp oil and make a very stiff dough, using very little water.

2. To mashed sweet potato add all ingredients on right side, along with lemon juice and some salt, make a soft dough, break off small balls, keep aside.

3. When about to serve, make parathas thus: Take a small portion of the dough, make it into a cup using oil for doing so. Place a ball of sweet potato inside the cup, close, flatten on a floured board and roll lightly into a paratha (do not use force while rolling or the filling may spill out).

4. Transfer parathas onto a tava, on medium heat, cook on both sides. Then apply ghee, raise the heat, and cook further till browned and crisp.

Serve very hot with a hot chutney for dinner.

Sweet Potato Casserole

Ingredients

2 large sweet potatoes
1 cup brown sugar (mixed with a pinch of nutmeg)
3 tbsp butter
3/4-1 cup bread crumbs

Method

1. Boil sweet potatoes in their jackets, plunge in cold water. When cool, discard skin, cut into 1/4" thick slices.
2. Grease a rectangular oven-proof dish, cover the base with half the slices. Sprinkle brown sugar on the entire surface. Dot with 1 tbsp butter.
3. Cover the sugar layer with the rest of the slices, cover this with the bread crumbs. Melt two tbsp butter; pour over crumbs.
4. Bake in a moderate oven (350°F- 180°C) till browned on top.

Serve with cream or custard for dessert.

Tomato

Tomato is a very popular vegetable/fruit extensively cultivated both in India and in Western countries. It is eaten in the raw as well as cooked form, raw tomatoes of course being more nutritious.

Tomatoes have a high content of vitamin A and C as well as sulphur and salts like potassium. An ideal fruit/vegetable for a diabetic. They have plenty of medicinal properties as well. They act as an antiseptic in the intestines and prevent formation of gas. A glass of tomato juice every morning is a cure for liver ailments as well as constipation. Besides, the juice with glucose acts as a good tonic, specially for children. They are also used in cosmetics, as face-packs.

Many delicious preparations can be made from tomatoes. In most North Indian cooking (curries), they form the base with garlic and onion. Any number of chutneys, sauces and pickles can be prepared from tomatoes. In western cooking, specially Italian, tomato sauce/paste forms the basis for most preparations.

Here are fifteen different ways of cooking tomatoes, each from a different region of our country.

"For torpid liver, eat tomatoes which contain vegetable calomel and then sip water freely between meals; due to high sulphur contents in it, it cures torpidity of the liver, rheumatism, skin diseases and asthma." – *Quote from Dr. C. S. Carr, U.S.A.*

Preparations

1. **Tomato Biriyani**
2. **Tomato Kurma** (Tamil Nadu/Andhra Pradesh)
3. **Stuffed Tomatoes:** *a) North Indian Style - Fried*
   b) Western Style - Baked
4. **Tomato Raitha and Pachadi** (North Indian/South India)
5. **Tomato Kuzhambu** (Tamil Nadu)
6. **Tomato Rasam** (Karnataka/Mangalore)
7. **Tomato Stew** (Kerala)
8. **Tomato Pitla** (Maharashtra)
9. **Tomato Khatta** (Orissa)
10. **Tomato Raisin Chutney** (West Bengal)
11. **Tomato Kasaundi** (North India)
12. **Tomato Soup with Coconut Milk Sauce** (Indian Style)
13. **Fresh Tomato Sauce baked with Pasta/Eggs** (Italian)
14. **Tomato Aspic Salad**
15. **Tomato Flowers** (Western)

Tomato Biriyani

Ingredients

2 cups rice
$\frac{1}{2}$ kg tomato
A large pinch of saffron
   or $\frac{1}{4}$ tsp turmeric powder
4 + 2 tbsp ghee
Salt to taste

Seasoning and Garnishing

2 bay leaves
1 sliced onion
1-1$\frac{1}{2}$ tbsp almond or
   cashew nuts, cut into slivers
1 tbsp raisins
A few small cardamoms
2 tbsp chopped coriander leaves

Broil and Powder

2 tsp poppy seeds
1 tsp aniseeds
2 $\frac{1}{2}$" piece cinnamon
4-6 cloves,
4-6 red chillies

Grind to paste

1 medium onion
1" piece ginger, sliced
6 cloves garlic

Method

1. Cook rice, preferably in a rice cooker with saffron or turmeric powder and a little salt; each grain should be separate.

2. Plunge tomatoes into boiling water, cook 3-5 min., cool, peel skin, mash thoroughly to form a puree, set aside.

3. Heat 2 tbsp ghee, fry raisins, cashew nuts and cardamom, remove from kadai. Fry bay leaf and sliced onion, fry till onion is brown, remove; keep all these aside for garnish.

4. Add 2 more tbsp ghee, add ground masala, fry till ghee surfaces. Add powdered masala, stir fry.

5. Now add tomato puree, salt and keep stirring till fried, add 1 tbsp chopped coriander leaves, mix, remove from fire.

6. Grease a large casserole dish with some ghee, transfer $\frac{1}{2}$ of the cooked rice into it, spread evenly. Pour the tomato curry over this. Sprinkle just a few nuts and raisins and fried onions, mix them into the curry. Even out surface, transfer rest of the rice onto the curry layer. Sprinkle some ghee on top, cover and bake at 400°F (190°C) in a hot oven for 15-20 min.

7. When ready to serve, remove lid of casserole dish, sprinkle rest of the nuts, fried onions and coriander leaves.

Note

Alternative way to make biriyani: After rice is cooked, transfer onto a plate, sprinkle some hot ghee all over. Now add the tomato curry and mix it, using only the tips of your fingers, very lightly. When rice and curry have mixed properly, transfer biriyani onto a serving plate, garnish with fried onions, nuts and raisins.

Serve hot with raitha.

Tomato Kurma

Ingredients

6-8 medium tomatoes
1 onion, chopped
3 green chillies, slit
1-2 tbsp chopped coriander leaves
1-1½ cup curds
1 tsp sugar
½ tsp turmeric powder
½ tsp chilli powder (optional)
½-1 tsp garam masala
2 tbsp oil
2 tbsp ghee
Salt to taste

Grind to paste

1 medium onion
1″ piece ginger
5 cloves garlic
1 tsp poppy seeds
4 tbsp coconut gratings
A little coriander leaves

Seasoning

2 bay leaves
3 cloves
½″ piece cinnamon
1-2 cardamoms
5-6 pepper corns

Method

1. Wash and cut tomatoes into eight pieces if large, or 4 pieces if small.

2. Heat a mixture of ghee and oil, add seasonings and, when done, add chillies and onion; fry till onion is browned. Add ground paste, fry 2-3 min. Now add powdered masalas. Continue frying till oil surfaces.

3. Add tomatoes, fry for some time, sprinkling some water if necessary. Cover vessel and allow to cook on 'sim' till tomatoes have turned soft.

4. Beat curds smooth, adding sugar, half of the chopped coriander leaves and garam masala, mix and pour into cooked tomatoes, simmer just once and remove from fire.

5. Pour into a serving bowl, sprinkle rest of the chopped coriander leaves.

Serve hot with puris or pulav.

Stuffed Tomatoes – *North Indian Style – Fried*

Ingredients

6 large tomatoes
½ cup masoor dal
1 large potato
Oil for frying
A little flour
Salt to taste

½ tsp turmeric powder
½ tsp chilli powder
1 tsp garam masala
A pinch of pepper powder
Mince very fine
1 medium onion
½″ piece ginger
A little coriander leaves

Method

1. Select firm, ripe, red tomatoes. Cut out the tops and scoop out as much pulp as possible. Smear the insides with some salt, set aside.

2. Boil dal with turmeric powder and just enough water (do not over cook or allow to go mushy), set aside. Boil, peel and mash potato, mix both together. Heat 2 tbsp oil, add minced ingredients, fry till onions are lightly browned; add dal-potato mash, continue to fry adding chilli, pepper, garam masala powders and salt. Mix thoroughly, fry for another 2 min., remove, cool.

4. Just before filling, invert tomatoes to remove any juice; shake well, fill with potato-dal mixture, press a little bread crumbs on top of this.

5. Pour a little oil in a non-stick pan (preferably), place tomatoes cut side down, reduce heat, cover pan with lid and cook 2-5 min. or till tomatoes have turned soft. When one side is browned, carefully turn and fry the other side also, till tomatoes have become soft.

Serve hot as a side dish for a meal.

Note

1. The scooped out pulp can be prepared into a sauce – see recipe on the next page. If desired, boiled peas can be substituted for dal.

Stuffed Tomatoes – *Western Style – Baked*

Ingredients

6 large tomatoes
1 cup cooked rice
½ cup boiled peas
½-1 cup grated cheese
4 tbsp butter
Little bread crumbs
Salt to taste
Sauce

Mince very fine
    1 large onion
    1 small capsicum
    Little parsley or dill
Seasoning
    1 tsp pepper powder
    1 tsp white mustard powder

Method

1. Follow the above recipe for preparing tomatoes for stuffing. Keep aside pulp for sauce.
2. Melt 2 tbsp butter, add onion, fry till transparent; add capsicum, fry for a while adding herbs. Cover and cook capsicum till soft.
3. Add rice, peas, seasonings, mix thoroughly. Add ½ the cheese, herbs, mix once again.
4. Just before filing, invert and shake tomatoes to remove all juice. Fill with rice-peas mixture.
5. Press a few bread crumbs on top of the filling, put a little melted butter on top of crumbs.
6. Brush tomatoes on the outside with some melted butter and set it in a greased oven-proof dish. Pour the sauce over, sprinkle cheese.

7. Bake the tomatoes at 350°F (170°C) for some time (20-30 min.) or till tomatoes get soft.

To make sauce: In 1 tbsp oil, fry 1 minced onion till pink in colour. Add tomato pulp (set aside) along with ½ tsp chilli powder, 1 tsp sugar, pinch of pepper powder and some salt. Mix 2 tsp flour with ¼ cup (optional) water, add to tomatoes and simmer until sauce-like consistency.

Tomato Raitha and Pachadi

Ingredients

3 tomatoes, chopped
1-1½ cup curds
1 green chilli, minced
1 tbsp chopped coriander leaves
Salt to taste

For Pachadi only
2 tsp oil
½ tsp mustard seeds
1 sprig curry leaf

Method

For Raitha:

Beat curds smooth, add all the ingredients, mix thoroughly. If desired, 1 small onion, minced fine, can be added to raitha.

For Pachadi:

Mix all the ingredients as before except green chilli. Heat oil, add mustard seeds and when done, the curry leaf and chilli, stir fry, pour into curd-tomato mixture, mix.

Serve with pulav/seasoned rice.

Tomato Kuzhhambu
(Tomato-Coconut Gravy)

Ingredients

¼ tomatoes, chopped
1 medium onion, chopped
¼ tsp turmeric powder
2 tbsp oil
1 tbsp chopped coriander leaves
Salt to taste

Fry in 2 tsp oil
1 tbsp coriander seeds
1 tsp cumin seeds
1½ tbsp chana dal
2-3 red chillies
2 tbsp coconut gratings

Seasoning

¼ tsp mustard seeds
½ tsp urad dal
1 sprig curry leaf

Method

1. Fry in 1 tbsp oil the chopped onion to brown, add fried ingredients, chopped tomatoes; grind to paste.

2. To ground masala, add 1-2 cups water, turmeric powder and salt, mix thoroughly.

3. Heat 1 tbsp oil, add seasonings and, when done, add ground mixture and chopped coriander leaves and simmer for some time on 'sim' till gravy is thick.

Serve hot with rice with some ghee sprinkled on rice.

Tips ....   **Tomato Puree**

Cover tomatoes with water, 1" above the level of the vegetable, boil briskly for 8-10 min. (till the skin shrivels); remove from fire, discard water, cool. Peel skin and mash or puree as recipe states.

Tomato Rasam

Ingredients

2 large tomatoes, chopped
¼ cup tuvar dal
½ tsp turmeric powder
2 tbsp grated coconut
1 tbsp tamarind pulp
1 tbsp chopped coriander leaves
Salt to taste

Fry in 2 tsp ghee

¼ tsp fenugreek seeds
½ tsp cumin seeds
2 tsp coriander seeds
2 red chillies
A pinch of asafoetida
1 sprig curry leaf

Seasoning

2 tsp ghee
½ tsp mustard seeds
1 sprig curry leaf

Method

1. Boil tuvar dal with a pinch of turmeric powder, mash thoroughly, add some water (about 1-1½ cups), mix, set aside.

2. To chopped tomatoes add 4 cups water, tamarind pulp, salt, pinch of turmeric powder and curry leaf. Boil for 10-12 min. or till reduced to half.

3. To fried ingredients add grated coconut, grind to a very fine paste, add water, about one cup, if it is too thick.

4. Add this ground paste and dal with half the chopped coriander leaves to boiling tamarind water and simmer for some more time till you get the required consistency.

5. Fry in ghee the mustard seeds and curry leaf, pour into rasam, garnish with the rest of the coriander leaves.

Serve very hot with rice or as an appetiser. (For this, add a little more water and a little salt. Rasam should be thin.)

Tomato Stew

(Tomatoes in Coconut Milk Gravy)

Ingredients

½ kg tomatoes, cut into fours
1 large onion, chopped
3 green chillies, split
2 tbsp chopped coriander leaves
1½ cups grated coconut
2 tsp rice flour
Salt to taste

Seasoning

3 tbsp ghee
1 tsp cumin seeds
2 sprigs curry leaves
½ tsp turmeric powder
1 tsp ginger-garlic paste

Method

1. Add 1 cup boiling water to grated coconut; when sufficiently cool, squeeze gratings to extract 'thick milk', set this aside. To gratings add 1 cup more boiling water; when cool, pass through a liquidiser; squeeze the resultant liquid, take out 'thin milk', discard gratings.

2. Heat ghee, add cumin seeds; when done, add curry leaves, chillies and onion; fry till onion turns lightly brown.

3. Add ginger-garlic paste, turmeric powder, stir fry 2-3 min. Add tomatoes, fry for a while and when tomatoes are sufficiently soft add 'thin milk' mixed with rice flour, cover and cook till done. Add half the chopped coriander leaves.

4. When about to serve, heat the gravy, add 'thick milk', simmer just once, remove from fire (do not boil after adding 'thick milk'). Garnish with rest of the coriander leaves.

Serve hot with puri or pulav.

Tomato Pitla

Ingredients

½ kg tomatoes
4-5 green chillies
2 tbsp oil
1½ tbsp gram flour
1 tbsp chopped coriander leaves
Salt to taste

Seasoning
½ tsp mustard seeds
½ tsp cumin seeds
¼ tsp fenugreek seeds
A pinch of asafoetida
½ tsp turmeric powder

Method

1. Wash and cut tomatoes into fairly large pieces. Cut chillies into 2-3 pieces each.

2. Heat oil, add seasonings; when done, add chillies and tomatoes, stir fry (on low heat) till they turn quite soft.

3. Mix gram flour with 1½-2 cups water, salt, half of the chopped coriander leaves; pour into kadai, cover with a lid and simmer till a thick gravy is formed.

4. Garnish with rest of the coriander leaves.

Serve hot with rotis.

Tomato Khatta
(Sweet-Hot-Sour Chutney)

Ingredients

½ kg tomatoes, chopped
1 large onion, chopped
½ tsp turmeric powder
3 tbsp oil
1 tbsp sugar
Salt to taste

Seasoning
1 tsp cumin seeds
3-4 red chillies
Fry in 1 tsp ghee and powder
2 tsp cumin seeds

Method

1. Heat oil, add seasonings and when done, add onion and fry till browned, adding turmeric powder.

2. Add tomatoes, continue to fry on low heat till they have become soft. Add salt and sugar, very little water, cover vessel and allow to simmer for 5-7 min. or till tomatoes have cooked to chutney consistency.

3. Add fried cumin powder, mix and remove from fire.

Serve hot with puris.

Note

Refrigerated, will keep for a week.

Tomato Raisin Chutney

Ingredients

1 cup chopped tomatoes
½ cup sugar
Juice of 1 lemon
½" piece ginger, cut into thin slivers
Salt to taste
1 tbsp raisins

Method

1. In a thick bottomed saucepan put all the ingredients together (except lemon juice) and simmer on low heat till tomatoes are cooked and form a chutney consistency.

2. Cool, add lemon juice, mix thoroughly, bottle.

Note

Refrigerated, it will keep about two weeks.

Tomato Kasaundi

Ingredients

1 kg firm, ripe tomatoes
1 cup oil
1 tsp turmeric powder
1 tbsp chilli powder
1 tbsp sugar
1 cup vinegar
½-1 tbsp salt (or to taste)

Grind to fine paste

12 cloves garlic
½″ piece ginger
6 green chillies
½ tsp fenugreek seeds
2 tsp mustard seeds

Seasoning

1 tsp mustard seeds
½ tsp asafoetida
¼ tsp fenugreek seeds
6 green chillies, slit
6 cloves garlic, minced
½″ piece ginger, minced
2 sprigs curry leaves

Method

1. Wash, wipe and cut tomatoes into medium pieces.
2. Grind ingredients in vinegar, set aside.
3. Heat oil, add seasonings, one by one. When fenugreek seeds are browned add slit chillies, minced garlic and ginger and curry leaves; stir fry. Add ground masala and continue to fry, adding chilli and turmeric powders till oil surfaces.
4. Add tomatoes, fry for a while. Add salt, sugar, vinegar (if any left) and simmer mixture till chutney consistency.
5. Cool and bottle.

Serve with bread or chapathis.

Note

Refrigerated, it will keep for about a month.

Tomato Soup with Coconut Milk Sauce
(Indian Style)

Ingredients

¼ kg tomatoes, chopped

1 onion, chopped

½" piece ginger, minced

3 cloves garlic, minced

1 tbsp minced coriander leaves

2 tbsp ghee

4 tbsp grated coconut

1 tbsp flour

A pinch of nutmeg

1 tsp pepper powder

Salt to taste

Method

1. Add 2 cups boiling water to coconut gratings. When sufficiently cool, squeeze gratings or pass through a liquidiser. Strain the resultant liquid and keep aside the coconut milk.

2. Heat 1 tbsp ghee, add ginger, garlic, onion and fry till onion turns light pink in colour. Add tomatoes, stir fry for a while. Then add some water (about 1-1½ cups), cover vessel and allow to cook on 'sim', adding salt; remove, cool.

3. Pass cooked tomato through a liquidiser, strain the pulp, discard seeds and skin, take out the thick juice.

4. To the juice, add pepper powder and nutmeg, boil briskly 1-2 min., set aside.

5. Heat 1 tbsp of ghee, add flour and fry on low heat till it turns light brown. Gradually add coconut milk, stirring all the while. Now cook on medium heat till it gets a custard consistency (coconut milk sauce).

6. Gradually pour the coconut milk sauce into tomato soup, stirring all the time.

7. When about to serve, heat soup, pour into individual bowls, garnish with a pinch of coriander leaves.

Fresh Tomato Sauce baked with Pasta/Eggs

Ingredients

For Sauce

1 kg tomatoes, chopped
$\frac{1}{4}$ kg onion, chopped
6-8 cloves garlic, minced
1 capsicum, small, minced
1 carrot, small, grated
1 stalk celery, minced
    or 1 tsp celery seeds
Little chopped parsley, minced
    or dill, minced

$\frac{1}{2}$-1 cup grated cheese
3 tbsp oil
1 tbsp sugar
$\frac{1}{2}$ tsp oregano
1 tsp pepper powder
Salt to taste

For Pasta

150 gm spaghetti
    (or macaroni) or 6 eggs
2 tbsp butter
1 cup bread crumbs
A pinch of salt, pepper, herbs

Method

To make Sauce

1. Heat 2 tbsp oil, add garlic and onions, fry till light pink. Add celery, carrot, capsicum, stir fry for 2-3 min. Add tomatoes, continue to fry for a while longer. Add seasonings, some water, simmer for 8-10 min. or till a thick consistency. Remove, cool. Pass cooked tomato through liquidiser, discard seeds and peel, keep aside the sauce.

2. Boil plenty of water, add some salt and 1 tsp oil; add pasta, cook till soft. Remove from fire, discard water.

3. Mix prepared sauce with pasta, add some cheese, seasonings, herbs, mix. Pour this into a well-greased casserole dish, shake so that it spreads evenly.

4. Cover top of pasta and sauce with the rest of the cheese, dot with butter and bake in a hot oven (400°F/210°C) for 20-30 min. till butter melts.

Tomato Sauce with Eggs

1. Mix 2 tbsp flour with $\frac{1}{4}$ cup water, add to tomato sauce (from step 1). Simmer for 3-5 min. till sauce gets very thick. Pour this hot sauce onto a greased flat casserole dish.

313

2. Allow sauce to cool a bit. Make slight depressions in 6 places. Break an egg in each depression. Sprinkle some cheese ($\frac{1}{2}$ cup), on top of the sauce, cover the dish and keep it in a moderate oven till eggs are done (about 20-30 min.).

Serve hot as a main dish for a western menu.

Note

The eggs can be cooked in a non-stick pan. Instead of a casserole dish, use a non-stick fry pan. Follow steps 1 and 2 in **Method**. Instead of keeping it in the oven, cook eggs on gas on 'sim' in the fry pan itself, covering the pan with a tight-fitting lid.

Tomato Aspic Salad

Ingredients

For the Mould
2 cups tomato juice
2 tbsp gelatine
1 small onion, minced (optional)
A small piece of celery, minced
$\frac{1}{2}$ small carrot, grated fine
1 tsp minced basil or parsley
$\frac{1}{2}$ tsp pepper powder
$\frac{1}{2}$ tsp lemon juice
2 tsp sugar
Salt to taste
A fluted mould
A large salad plate

For Salad
A few lettuce leaves
1 small cucumber
2 large tomatoes
A piece of cabbage
1 large carrot

For Dressing
2 tbsp lemon juice
1 tsp sugar
$\frac{1}{2}$ tsp pepper powder
2 tbsp olive oil
Salt to taste
A pinch of herbs

Method

1. Soak gelatine in hot water ($\frac{1}{4}$ cup), set aside.
2. To tomato juice, add all the minced and grated vegetables, simmer 3-5 min., remove from fire; when cooled, strain the mixture.
3. To the resultant liquid, add softened gelatine, seasonings, herbs, mix thoroughly, pour into the mould (rinsed in cold water). Set in a refrigerator.

4. ***Prepare vegetables for the salad:*** wash lettuce leaves, wipe with a piece of cloth, set aside. Wash the other vegetables. Peel and slice cucumber and slice tomatoes, grate carrot, cut cabbage into thin strips. Keep each of the vegetables separate.

5. Mix together ingredients for dressing, leave in the refrigerator till serving time.

To set the salad plate

Spread lettuce leaves all around the plate. Arrange tomato and cucumber each in a circle leaving the centre free for the mould. Sprinkle grated carrot and cabbage strips all over the vegetables.

Remove mould from the refrigerator, hold it under the tap for 1-2 min. for gelatine to loosen. Carefully turn the mould upside down right in the centre of the plate. Shake gently for aspic to loosen, then remove the mould, leaving the jelly free. Remove dressing from the refrigerator, shake bottle, pour dressing over vegetables – be careful not to pour it over the jelly. Serve immediately.

Makes an attractive centre-spread for your table!

Tomato Flowers
(A boiled salad)

Ingredients

6-8 firm, ripe tomatoes	Juice of 1 lemon
1 small potato, carrot,	$\frac{1}{2}$-1 tsp pepper powder
capsicum and onion, each	1 tsp white mustard
$\frac{1}{2}$ cup peas	1 tsp sugar
1 tsp minced herbs	Salt to taste
$\frac{1}{2}$ cup parmesan cheese	A few chopped walnuts
or Amul cheese	
1 cup cream	

Method

1. Wash tomatoes; with a sharp knife cut each tomato into fours, then each piece into two. Each tomato is therefore cut into eight, half way through to the base. Scoop out all the pulp, wash tomatoes carefully in water, removing all seeds, shake well; sprinkle some salt and pepper on each, set aside.

2. Peel potato and carrot, cut into very small cubes, add peas, a little salt and boil in just enough water – *do not over cook the vegetables.*

3. Mince onion and capsicum. When the vegetables are sufficiently cooled, add minced onion, capsicum, herbs and seasonings.

4. Beat cream light, add to vegetables along with cheese and a little of the walnut, blend to form a smooth mixture.

5. Stuff some of this carefully into the tomatoes. Stick a piece of walnut on top of the filling. Garnish with some parsley. Serve chilled.

Note

The same salad can be served with North Indian food. Change the seasonings and herbs. To boiled vegetables, add minced green chilli, a pinch of garam masala, chopped coriander leaves. For parmesan cheese, substitute soft paneer, crumbled.

Vegetables

Recipes with mixed vegetables – a combination of two or more – have been compiled under the letter 'V'. Mixed vegetable preparations are not only tasty but also nutritious, as each vegetable has its own nutritive property and, therefore, a combination of vegetables will provide different nutrients to the body. Most of the preparations are common to all regions. Hence, no specific region is mentioned against the recipes. They have been broadly categorised into four different styles of cooking.

Preparations

WESTERN STYLE

1. **Cream of Vegetable Soup**
2. **Vegetable Exotica**
3. **Vegetable Au-gratin**
4. **Vegetable Medley**
5. **Vegetable Gourmet**

CHINESE STYLE

6. **Vegetable Noodles**
7. **Vegetables – Sweet and Sour**
8. **Vegetable Pancakes**

NORTH INDIAN STYLE

9. **Vegetable Rice**
10. **Vegetable-Paneer Casserole**

11. **Moglai Vegetable**

12. **Kadai Vegetable**

13. **Dum Vegetables**

14. **Vegetable Kachumber**

SOUTH INDIAN STYLE

15. **Vegetable Biriyani**

16. **Vegetable Kurma**

17. **Vegetable Stew with Milk**

18. **Aviyal**

19. **Vegetable Kootu**

20. **Vegetable Navratan**

Cream of Vegetable Soup

Ingredients

1 each (small) of the following vegetables:
  potato, carrot, tomato, onion and capsicum (optional)
A small piece each of cabbage and celery (optional)
A few florets of cauliflower, $\frac{1}{2}$ cup peas
Half of a small vegetable marrow
A few sprigs of parsley or dill
$1\frac{1}{2}$ tbsp butter
$1\frac{1}{2}$-2 cups milk
$\frac{1}{2}$ tsp pepper corns
Salt to taste
A large pinch of nutmeg or mace (optional)
A little grated cheese for garnish

Method

1. Chop all vegetables. Leaving aside onion, herbs and capsicum, put all the rest together in a pressure pan, add salt, pepper corns and enough water to cover vegetables and pressure cook.

2. When cool, take out a little of the cooked vegetable for garnish. Pass the rest through a liquidiser, strain, set aside puree.

3. Melt butter, fry onion to a light pink colour, add capsicum and herbs; fry till capsicum is soft.

4. .Add vegetable puree to pan and simmer 2-3 min., adding a little water if soup is too thick. Keep soup hot till serving time.

5. When about to serve, boil milk, pour into soup, add nutmeg, little more pepper powder if desired, simmer, remove from fire.

To Serve: Pour soup into individual bowls, garnish each bowl with 1 tbsp of cooked vegetable (kept by), sprinkle some cheese, serve at once.

Vegetable Exotica

(A moulded Salad on a platter of Vegetables with French-Honey dressing)

Ingredients

For the Mould
1 packet lemon jelly
1 medium carrot, grated fine
1 tbsp grated cucumber
   or 1 tbsp minced celery
1 tbsp minced spring onion leaves
1 tsp minced spring onion
½ tsp pepper powder
Salt to taste

For Dressing
4 tbsp olive oil
   or refined oil
1 tbsp lime juice
   or white vinegar
1 tbsp honey
2 tsp sugar
1 tsp pepper powder
½ tsp white mustard (optional)
1 tsp minced herbs
Salt to taste

For Salad
1 small cucumber
2 medium tomatoes
2 medium carrots
1 small piece cabbage
A few lettuce leaves

A fluted mould
A large salad plate

Method

1. Make jelly following instructions on the packet. Mix together all other ingredients (on left side). When jelly is about to set, whisk this into jelly thoroughly.

2. Wash the fluted mould in very cold water, rub some oil on the insides of the mould; pour the jelly-vegetable mixture into it, cover mould tight and set it in the refrigerator.

3. Combine all dressing ingredients in a jar or bottle, shake thoroughly and leave this also in the refrigerator.

3. Prepare vegetables for salad: wash all vegetables thoroughly; shake lettuce leaves (to rid of the excess water) and dab them with a paper napkin; leave aside. Peel and cut cucumber into thin slices. Peel carrots, cut one into slices, grate the other. Cut tomatoes into slices. Shred cabbage.

   Arrange the plate thus: Keep lettuce leaves all around plate, like a border. On the leaves, arrange cucumber, carrot and tomato slices alternately. Leave the centre of the plate free for the jelly. Sprinkle the grated carrot and cabbage on the slices. Leave the plate in the refrigerator, covered.

When about to serve, hold jelly mould under a running tap for 1-2 min. for jelly to loosen, run a knife through on each side. Holding the jelly upside down in the centre of the salad plate, remove mould, leaving jelly free. Shake dressing ingredients thoroughly, sprinkle over vegetable (take care not to sprinkle over the jelly) and serve at once.

Makes a delightful centre piece.

Note

If desired, 4 small tomatoes can be made into flowers (see recipe under tomatoes) and the salad decorated.

Instead of lemon juice for dressing, you can use pineapple or orange juice.

Vegetable Au-gratin
(Mixed Vegetables baked in Cheese Sauce)

Ingredients

4 cups cubed, mixed vegetables (carrot, potato and French beans, shelled peas)
$1\frac{1}{2}$ cup grated cheese
4 tbsp butter
3 tbsp flour
$3-3\frac{1}{2}$ cups milk
$\frac{1}{2}$ cup light cream (optional)
$\frac{1}{2}$-1 tsp mixed, fresh herbs (minced) or dry herbs (parsley or dill)
2 tsp pepper powder
Salt to taste
Little bread crumbs (about $1\frac{1}{2}$-2 tbsp)

Method

1. Boil vegetables with some salt and just enough water – see that it does not over cook. Or, you could steam cook the vegetables using a vegetable 'steamer'.

2. *Prepare White Sauce:* Melt 3 tbsp butter on low heat, add flour, fry till light pink in colour. Add milk gradually, seeing to it that no lumps are formed. Simmer on low heat till mixture gets thick.

3. Remove from fire, add ¾ of grated cheese, minced herbs, beat cream, add to sauce along with seasonings. This is cheese sauce.

4. To cheese sauce, add cooked vegetables and mix thoroughly; pour this mixture into a casserole dish, well greased.

5. Sprinkle top with the rest of the cheese and bread crumbs, dot with butter and bake at 400°F for 20-30 min. or till top is browned.

Serve as a main dish with soup and toast.

Note

If desired, 1 cup cooked macaroni shells can be added in step 4 to vegetables.

Vegetable Medley
(Vegetable-Cheese balls in Tomato Sauce)

Ingredients

1 each potato, carrot (large)
  onion and capsicum (medium)
A small piece of cabbage
A few cauliflower florets
½ cup shelled peas
2 tsp minced herbs
  (fresh or dry)
½ cup grated cheese
1-2 slices bread, crumbled
3 tbsp oil
1 tsp pepper powder
1 tsp curry powder
1 tsp chilli powder (optional)
Salt to taste
Little cream for garnish

For sauce
1 kg tomatoes
1 onion (large)
1 medium carrot
½ tsp minced herbs
1 tsp pepper powder
1 tsp sugar
Salt to taste
2 tsp flour

For batter (mix together)
¼ cup flour
1 cup water
Pinch of salt
  (or 1 egg, beaten)

Bread crumbs
Oil for frying

Method

1. Chop all vegetables fine, keep onion and capsicum separate.

2. Heat oil, fry onion till light brown, add capsicum, fry for a while. Add chopped vegetables, continue to fry adding salt, pepper powder, chilli powder; sprinkle some water, cover and cook on low heat till vegetables are tender. Remove from fire, cool.

3. To cooked vegetables, add herbs, cheese and crumbled bread and make soft dough, adding 1 more slice of bread if necessary. Make lemon-size balls, set aside.

4. Mix together flour, salt and water to a thin paste. Dip vegetable balls in this, roll in bread crumbs and deep fry. Alternately, dip balls in beaten egg, roll in crumbs, deep fry. Set aside.

To make Sauce:

1. Chop onions, carrot and tomatoes. Add minced herbs, salt, pepper powder and water, pressure cook. Pass vegetables through a liquidiser, discard peels and skin.

2. To sauce add sugar, some more salt if necessary, little pepper powder, a pinch of herbs. Mix flour in $\frac{1}{2}$ cup water to a smooth paste, add to sauce. Allow to simmer 3-5 min. or till quite thick (sauce consistency).

3. When about to serve, pour hot sauce into a bowl, drop vegetable balls into it. Beat cream light, pour over balls, sprinkle a pinch of herbs, if desired.

Serve with fried rice or boiled noodles.

Vegetable Gourmet

(Eggs or Cheese cooked on a layer of mixed vegetable sauce)

Ingredients

2 medium onions, chopped

2 medium tomatoes, chopped

1 capsicum, chopped

1 potato, chopped fine

1 carrot, grated

4 eggs

    or 1-1½ cups grated cheese

Salt to taste

4 tbsp oil

4 tbsp tomato sauce

1 tsp pepper powder

½-1 tsp chilli powder

2 tsp minced, fresh

    or dry herbs (oregano,

    parsley, dill)

Method

1. Heat oil, add onions, fry till lightly browned. Add capsicum and tomatoes, continue to fry till they turn a little soft. Now add potato and carrot, fry for a while. Add salt, sprinkle a little water, cover and cook till vegetables are tender.

2. Add all the seasonings, mix thoroughly, remove from fire.

3. Add ¾ cup of the cheese, herbs, tomato sauce, mix again till vegetables and the rest are well blended. Transfer this onto a greased oven-proof circular dish, even out the surface.

4. Make 4 depressions on the surface of the vegetables, equidistant from one another. Break an egg in a cup (to make sure it is fresh), pour the egg into the depression. Pour the rest of the eggs also in a similar way.

5. Sprinkle some salt and pepper powder on top of the egg. Sprinkle rest of the cheese all over the vegetable layer (do not sprinkle on the eggs). Cover dish and leave it in a moderate oven for 30-40 min. or till eggs are set. Remove lid and serve at once.

Serve either at dinner or at breakfast with toasted, buttered bread slices.

Note

If you do not with to use eggs, substitute ½ more cup of cheese. Instead of the eggs, sprinkle cheese completely on the vegetable layer, cover and bake/cook as before.

You can make this in a non-stick fry pan itself right from step 1. Do not transfer vegetables into an oven-proof dish. Instead, continue to work steps 4 and 5, cover pan with a tight lid and cook on 'sim' till eggs are set.

Vegetable Noodles

Ingredients

A small bunch of spring
    onions with leaves
5-6 cloves garlic
A small piece of cabbage
A handful of beans
A few florets of cauliflower
½ cup shelled peas
1 each potato, capsicum
    and carrot
2 cups boiled noodles
6 tbsp refined oil

Seasoning

¼-½ cup vinegar
3-4 tbsp tomato sauce
2 tsp soya sauce
1-2 tsp chilli sauce

Raitha

2 tsp sugar
1 tsp ajinomoto
1 tbsp corn flour
¼ cup water
Salt to taste

Method

1. Cut onion leaves into 1″ pieces; slit the spring onions into two, mince garlic.

2. Cut florets of cauliflower into small pieces.

3. Cut the rest of the vegetables into thin strips; keep each separate.

4. Heat oil, add minced garlic, brown. Add onions, fry to a light brown. Add one vegetable at a time, continuing to fry all the while, adding onions leaves last.

5. When vegetables have become sufficiently tender, add peas, salt, sprinkle some water, cover and cook on low heat till done.

6. Add vinegar, soya sauce, tomato sauce, chilli sauce, sugar, ajinomoto, cooked noodles and mix thoroughly.

7. Add water to corn flour, make into a paste, pour into noodles, simmer 2-3 min. till everything is well blended. Remove from fire.

Serve with soup – makes a complete meal.

Vegetables – Sweet and Sour

Ingredients

2 medium carrots
2 capsicums (medium)
1 medium onion
½ small cauliflower
½ small cucumber (4″ piece)
A bunch of spring onions
A small piece of cabbage
4 tbsp oil
Salt to taste

Seasonings

¾-1 cup vinegar
3 tbsp sugar
1 tsp chilli powder
1 tsp pepper powder
½ tsp ajinomoto
2 tbsp tomato sauce
4 tbsp corn flour
3 cups water

Method

1. Wash, scrape and cut carrots into rounds. Break cauliflower into medium size florets. Cut cabbage into chunks, cucumber into medium size pieces. Cut spring onions into four, onions into thick slices, capsicum into strips. Cut onion leaves into 1″ strips. Keep each of these vegetables, separate.

2. Cook carrots, cauliflower, cucumber and cabbage with just enough water and a little salt – they should be tender but not too soft. Alternatively, the vegetables can be steam cooked with a little salt sprinkled over them in a steamer.

3. Heat oil, fry onions on high flame till pink; add capsicum, fry till soft. Add steamed vegetables along with little salt, pepper powder and ajinomoto; stir for 1-2 min.

4. Mix corn flour with water to a smooth paste, add chilli powder, tomato sauce, vinegar, sugar and mix thoroughly. Pour this into vegetables, cook for another 3-5 min. or till quite thick (sauce consistency), remove from fire.

Serve hot with fried rice.

Vegetable Pancakes

Ingredients

For batter – without eggs
Sieve together
    1 cup flour
    $\frac{1}{2}$ tsp baking powder
    $\frac{1}{2}$ tsp salt
Mix together
    1 cup warm milk
    1 tbsp refined oil

Ingredients

For batter – with eggs
    Mix all together, beat thoroughly, set aside:
    1 cup flour
    Pinch of salt
    1 cup milk
    1 egg well beaten

Ingredients

For filling

1-1$\frac{1}{2}$ cups cooked, mixed vegetables (potato, carrot, cauliflower, peas)	$\frac{1}{2}$-1 tsp pepper powder
	$\frac{1}{2}$ tsp ajinomoto
1 medium onion, chopped	Salt to taste
2 tbsp tomato sauce	2 tbsp refined oil
1 tbsp soya sauce	
1 tsp chilli sauce	

Method

For Pancakes (without eggs)

1. Mix the sieved flour with milk-oil mixture, beat thoroughly. Leave aside for $\frac{1}{2}$ hour at least.

2. When about to make pancakes, add $\frac{1}{4}$-$\frac{1}{2}$ cup water and beat batter thoroughly once again so that it is of pouring consistency.

3. Grease a non-stick pan (preferably), pour a ladle of batter, quickly turn pan around so that the batter spreads (like a dosa). Pour a little oil on sides and on top, cover pan and cook till lightly browned. Turn over, cook the other side also. Make 6 pancakes thus, set aside.

For Pancakes (with eggs)

Follow the same method as before.

Method

For Filling

Note

It is better to prepare the filling earlier, so that as soon as the pancakes are ready, they can be served.

Heat oil, fry onion to brown, add cooked vegetables, stir fry; add all the sauces, and seasoning, mix thoroughly; remove from fire.

To Serve: Fill about 2 tbsp or so of the filling in the centre of the pancake, fold 1/3 over vegetable, fold the second half over the first, quickly turn over (so that the seam side is at the bottom). Transfer pancakes onto a plate and serve sizzling hot with a dab of tomato ketchup or chilli sauce.

Note

Pancakes can be prepared both for Western and North Indian menu. For these, all you have to do is to change the seasonings and sauce.

Western Style: Use pepper powder, a little curry powder or chilli powder and a tsp of dry or fresh herbs. Serve with cheese sauce or grated cheese sprinkled on top.

North Indian Style: Fry chopped green chillies along with onion. Add chilli powder, a pinch of garam masala and chopped coriander leaves. Serve pancakes with dania or pudeena chutney.

(For both the methods, drop soya sauce, chilli sauce and ajinomoto.)

Vegetable Rice

Ingredients

1½ cups rice
1 large onion, chopped
2 slit green chillies
1 small capsicum
1 medium carrot
½ small cauliflower
A handful of French beans
½ cup shelled peas
1 cup chopped fenugreek leaves
2 tbsp chopped coriander leaves

1 tbsp ginger-garlic paste
2 tbsp oil
1 tbsp ghee
Juice of 1 lemon
Salt to taste

Seasoning

2 bay leaves
2 cloves
½" piece cinnamon
2 cardamom
6-8 pepper corns
¼ tsp turmeric powder

Method

1. Wash rice and leave on a muslin cloth to dry.

2. Wash and cut all vegetables into very tiny pieces (as in Chinese Fried Rice).

3. Heat oil and ghee, add seasonings, fry till done.

4. Add onion, slit chillies and continue to fry till onion turns brown. Add ginger-garlic paste, stir fry till oil surfaces.

5. Now add all the vegetables in the order given, continuing to fry all the while. When fenugreek leaves are fried, add rice and fry 2-3 min. along with turmeric powder.

6. Add 4 cups water, salt, half of the chopped coriander leaves and lemon juice. Cover and cook till done (preferably in a rice cooker).

Serve hot with the rest of the coriander leaves sprinkled; if desired, a few fried nuts can also be sprinkled. Serve with any raitha.

Vegetable-Paneer Casserole

Ingredients

12 slices bread
1 large each capsicum, onion
  and tomato
1 medium potato and
  carrot
1 small cauliflower
$\frac{1}{2}$ cup shelled peas
3-4 green chillies, minced
1 tbsp minced coriander leaves
3 tbsp tomato sauce

1 cup crumbled paneer (fresh)
1-1$\frac{1}{2}$ cups milk
$\frac{1}{2}$ tsp chilli powder
$\frac{1}{2}$ tsp pepper powder
$\frac{1}{2}$ tsp garam masala
3 + 2 tbsp oil
  (refined oil or vanaspathi)
Salt to taste
A large casserole dish

Method

1. Grease the casserole dish with some refined oil. Discard crusts of bread, soak each slice in milk and line the casserole dish, covering the bottom of the dish. Set aside.

2. Chop all vegetables fine, steam cook with some salt, potatoes, carrots, cauliflower and peas.

3. Heat oil, add chillies and onion, fry till onion is lightly browned, add capsicum, fry till they turn soft, add tomatoes, continue to fry till done.

4. Add steamed vegetables and all the dry masalas one by one, continuing to fry all the while.

5. Now add crumbled paneer, chopped coriander leaves, some salt (if necessary), mix thoroughly adding tomato sauce.

6. Pour this vegetable filling on to the bread, covering the entire area. Crumble 2-3 slices of bread (after removing crusts) into fine, soft crumbs. Sprinkle this on top of vegetables.

7. Warm 2 tbsp oil/vanaspathi, pour over the entire bread crumb surface.

8. Bake at 190°C for 20-30 min. or till top is browned and crisp.

Serve at a buffet dinner.

Moglai Vegetable

Ingredients

2 each potatoes and carrots
A handful of beans
1 small cauliflower
1 cup peas, shelled
½ small vegetable marrow
A few double beans, shelled
3 large onions, chopped
½ cup almonds
A few raisins
1 cup curd (not sour)
4 tbsp ghee + 1 tbsp
1 cup hot milk
2 bay leaves
2-3 slit green chillies (optional)
A large pinch of saffron
½ cup milk
Salt to taste

Grind to paste
6 cloves garlic
1″ piece ginger
3-4 red chillies
½ tsp turmeric powder

Powder very fine
1 tbsp coriander seeds
3-4 cloves
2½″ cinnamon pieces
2 large cardamoms
6-8 pepper corns

Garnish
A few slivered almonds
A few raisins – fried
    in ghee (1 tbsp)
1 tbsp chopped coriander leaves

Method

1. Wash, peel potato and carrot, string beans, cut cauliflower into florets – cut all vegetables into small pieces (like cubes), steam cook sprinkling some salt, set aside. *Do not over cook.*

2. Soak, blanch and grind almonds to a very fine paste, add some water, mix, set aside. Soak kesar in some hot milk.

3. Heat 2 tbsp ghee, fry onions to brown; remove, cool and grind to paste.

4. Heat rest of the ghee, add bay leaves and green chillies, add ground paste and stir fry on low heat till ghee surfaces.

5. Beat curds smooth, mix onion paste and garam masala powder, add to fried masalas and allow to cook on 'sim' for 5-7 min.

6. Now add vegetables, continue to cook, adding ground almonds, kesar and a few raisins. Allow to cook some more time, till vegetables and masalas are well blended. Pour gravy into a bowl, garnish with fried almonds and raisins.

Serve hot with puris or parathas.

Kadai Vegetable

Ingredients

1 each potato and carrot
1 very small cauliflower
A handful of beans
¾-1 cup shelled peas
1 capsicum, chopped
3-4 medium tomatoes
1 cup paneer cubes
1-2 tbsp flour
15 cashew nuts, chopped
2 tbsp each, ghee and oil
1 tbsp chopped coriander leaves

Grind to paste
2 medium onions
5-6 cloves garlic
1" piece ginger
3-5 green chillies
Handful of coriander leaves

Powdered Masalas
½ tsp turmeric powder
1 tsp chilli powder
1 tsp garam masala
Salt to taste

Method

1. Peel and cut potato and carrot into cubes. Cut cauliflower into small florets. String and cut beans into ½" pieces. Steam cook all vegetables together with a little salt, set aside.

2. Boil tomatoes in water till soft. Discard water, peel skin and when cool, puree, set aside.

3. Grind to paste 8-10 of the cashew nuts with a little water or milk, set aside. Heat 1 tbsp ghee, fry the rest of the chopped nuts to a golden brown, remove from kadai, set aside for garnish.

4. Pour rest of the ghee into kadai, roll paneer cubes in flour, fry to a golden brown, set aside.

5. Add the oil to kadai, add ground paste and stir fry on low heat for 1-2 min. Add chopped capsicums. Fry till they turn soft.

6. Add tomato puree, keep frying adding dry masalas one by one including salt. Fry till oil surfaces.

7. Now add the vegetables, fry for a while. Add kaju paste (ground cashew nut), along with some water and half of the chopped coriander leaves. Cook till gravy is well blended.

Serve garnished with fried nuts and coriander leaves.

Dum Vegetables

Ingredients

1 each medium potato, carrot
$\frac{1}{2}$ small vegetable marrow
$\frac{1}{2}$ cup peas, shelled
1 dozen beans
$\frac{1}{2}$ small cauliflower
1 large onion, sliced
$1\frac{1}{2}$ tbsp ghee
2 tbsp chopped coriander leaves
$\frac{1}{2}$ tbsp chopped mint
1 cup curds (not sour)
A large pinch of saffron
$\frac{1}{2}$ cup hot milk
Salt to taste
2 tbsp wheat flour for paste

Grind to a fine paste
10-12 cashew nuts
2 tsp poppy seeds
6 cloves garlic
1" piece ginger
1 very small onion

Seasoning
3 cloves
2 large cardamoms
$2\frac{1}{2}$" stick cinnamon
2 green chillies
   cut into 2-3 pieces
1 tsp chilli powder
$\frac{1}{4}$ tsp turmeric powder

Method

1. Peel potato and vegetable marrow, scrape carrot. Cut all three into small cubes. String beans, cut into very small pieces. Break cauliflower into small florets, chopping the stem. All vegetables, when ready, should be 3 cups in all. Put these vegetables in a large sauce pan (a non-stick one, preferably with a tight fitting lid). Add chopped coriander leaves and mint.

2. Fry sliced onion in ghee to a golden brown colour, add to pan. Mix ground paste with kesar (soaked in milk), add to pan. Beat curds smooth, add salt and all the seasonings, mix thoroughly, pour into pan. Cover with lid. Allow to marinate for about 30-40 min.

3. Mix wheat flour with a little water to a smooth thick dough. Seal the cover of the pan with this, so that while cooking the steam does not escape (this type of cooking is called 'Dum' cooking). Place sauce pan on fire on low heat and cook for 30-40 min. by which time the vegetables will have become tender.

To Serve: when about to serve, break the seal by passing a knife through. Open and serve at once, preferably in the same pan at the table. A very delicious and nutritive preparation.

Serve with parathas or puris.

Vegetable Kachumber
(A mixed Vegetable Salad)

Ingredients

2 medium carrots

2 tomatoes (firm)

1 large onion

1 small cucumber

1-2 green chillies, minced

1 tbsp chopped coriander leaves

Juice of 1 lemon

Salt to taste

Method

1. Scrape carrots, peel cucumber. Chop onion, cucumber and tomatoes into very small pieces. Grate carrots. Mix all together, adding all the seasonings.

Serve chilled.

Note

If desired, a small piece of capsicum, 1 small radish may also be added.

Vegetable Biriyani

Ingredients

2 cups rice

1 small potato

1 small carrot

A dozen French beans

A few florets of cauliflower

$1/2$ cup shelled peas

1 large onion, sliced

2 green chillies, slit

$1/2$ tsp turmeric powder

$3/4$-1 cup ghee

2 bay leaves

6 cashew nuts (for garnish)

1 tbsp chopped coriander leaves

Salt to taste

For coconut milk

$1/2$ coconut, grated

1″ piece ginger, chopped

1 tbsp coriander seeds

For masala paste

1 medium onion

6 cloves garlic

A handful of coriander leaves

A few mint leaves

1 tsp aniseeds

1 tsp poppy seeds

3 cloves

1″ cinnamon

3 small cardamoms

Method

1. Lightly dry roast coriander seeds, add chopped ginger and grated coconut, add 1 cup hot water, allow to cool; pass through a liquidiser, squeeze gratings to get coconut 'milk'. Repeat process to get 4 cups in all. Discard gratings, mix the two 'milks', set aside.

2. Wash rice and allow to dry on a cloth.

3. Prepare vegetables by washing, peeling and cutting into pieces of desired size.

4. Heat half of the ghee in a cooker, add cashew nuts, fry until golden, remove. Add sliced onions, fry until crisp, remove and set aside.

5. Add bay leaves and fry. when done, add rice, fry 2-3 min., remove from cooker, set aside.

6. Add rest of the ghee, add chillies, fry for a while; add vegetables, fry until soft on low heat, covering cooker in- between frying.

7. Now add ground paste and turmeric powder, stir 3-4 min. or until ghee surfaces.

8. Put fried rice back into cooker, add salt, coconut milk and cook on 'sim' till done. If a pressure cooker is used, *do not* put the weight on. Take care that the rice is not over cooked.

9. Transfer rice onto a rice platter, garnish with chopped coriander leaves, fried nuts and onions.

Serve with curds and a salad.

Vegetable Kurma

The same ingredients as in Biriyani are to be used for kurma. Only *drop* rice and increase (about 1½-2 times) the quantity of vegetables.

As for the method, prepare coconut milk, vegetables and masalas as in Biriyani, *dropping* steps 2 and 5, continue from step 6. Work step 7, continue

8. When ghee surfaces, add salt, coconut milk, cover and cook on 'sim' till vegetables are tender and masalas have blended.

9. Pour kurma into a serving dish, garnish with chopped coriander leaves, fried nuts and raisin.

Serve with puris or parathas.

Vegetable Stew with Milk

Ingredients

1 each (large) carrot and
  potato
½ cauliflower
Small vegetable marrow
A handful of beans
½ cup shelled peas
1 medium onion
2 tbsp ghee
1½ tbsp flour
1½-2 cups milk
Salt to taste

Seasoning

3 green chillies
½" piece ginger
A little coriander leaves
3 cloves
2 big cardamoms
2 ½" piece cinnamon
½ tsp pepper corns
2 bay leaves

Method

1. Wash and prepare vegetables as follows: Peel potato, carrot and vegetable marrow. Cut potatoes and vegetable marrow into cubes, carrots into rounds. String beans and cut into 1″ long pieces. Break cauliflower into sprigs, slice onions, slit chillies, mince ginger.

2. Heat ghee, add spices, fry. When done, add chillies, ginger and onion, fry till onion turns light pink in colour – do not allow onion to become brown.

3. Add vegetables and fry for a while, keeping vessel covered in-between frying on 'sim'. The vegetables should become soft but not over cooked.

4. Blend flour with milk, add chopped coriander leaves and pour this into vegetables, simmer for a while till gravy is well blended.

Serve hot with puris or bread rolls. (A simple preparation. An ideal recipe for invalids and children.)

Aviyal

(Mixed vegetables in Curd Gravy)

Ingredients

1 small piece each
  ash gourd and pumpkin
Few cluster or French beans
1 medium potato and brinjal
1 small banana (raw)
½ piece snake gourd
  or vegetable marrow
2-3 drumsticks
2 sprigs curry leaves
A small pinch of suran (optional)
2 cups curds (not sour)
1 tbsp coconut oil
Salt to taste

Grind to paste

½ grated coconut
6-8 green chillies
1-1½ tsp cumin seeds
2 tsp rice flour

Method

1. Wash and peel vegetables. Cut each into 1″ long pieces, cut drumsticks into 3″ long pieces, break beans to 2-3 pieces each. Keep each separate.

2. In a large vessel boil some water, add salt and add vegetables one at a time (this is because different vegetables get tender at different levels of cooking). First put in beans, potato and drumsticks into the vessel – cook 3-4 min., then add banana (raw), ash gourd and vegetable marrow; then again, pumpkin and brinjal, add curry leaves, close vessel and allow to cook on 'sim' till all vegetables are tender but not mushy. Cook suran separate if you are using and add when vegetables are all done.

3. Add ground paste (mixed with a little water) to vegetables, cook till all the water has been absorbed.

4. When almost dry, add curds, simmer just once, remove from fire. Add coconut oil, mix thoroughly.

Serve with rice (a very common preparation in all regions of the South.)

Vegetable Kootu
(Mixed Vegetables and Dal Gravy)

Ingredients

½ small cabbage
1 each potato, carrot
A few French beans
½ cup shelled peas
½ cup moong dal
½ tsp turmeric powder
Salt to taste
1 tbsp chopped coriander leaves

Grind to paste
  4 tbsp grated coconut
  3-4 green chillies
  1 tsp cumin seeds

Seasoning
  2 tsp oil
  ½ tsp mustard seeds
  1 tsp urad dal
  2 sprigs curry leaves

Method

1. Boil dal with ¼ tsp turmeric powder, keep aside.
2. Wash and cut vegetables into small pieces, add salt, ¼ tsp turmeric powder; cook, till tender.
3. Mix together the cooked dal, vegetables, the ground masala, add some water if too thick; simmer for 3-4 min.
4. Season in oil the ingredients given, add to 'kootu'; sprinkle coriander leaves, mix, remove from fire.

Serve with rice or chapathis.

Note

A combination of 2, 3 or 4 vegetables can be used for this preparation. It can be vegetables like cauliflower, etc. as above or a combination of vegetables like ash gourd, brinjal, cluster beans, broad beans etc. This preparation again is common to all southern regions and is very popular.

Vegetable Navratan

(A combination of nine Vegetables-Salad Pickle)

Ingredients

1 small beet root
1 carrot
½ small cauliflower
1 small capsicum
3 cabbage leaves, small
6 very fresh green beans
½ cup very tender peas,
  shelled
Juice of 1 lemon
4 green chillies
A very small piece ginger
  (optional), minced
1 sprig curry leaves

Seasoning

2 tbsp sesame seed oil
½ tsp fenugreek seeds
½ tsp asafoetida
¼ tsp turmeric powder
½-1 tsp chilli powder
½ tsp mustard seeds
1-1½ tsp salt

Method

1. Wash and dry vegetables thoroughly before cutting. Cut beet root, carrot and capsicum into very fine pieces. Chop cabbage and beans. Cut chillies into 2-3 pieces each. Break cauliflower into very tiny florets. Put all the vegetables except chillies in a big stainless steel vessel.

2. In 1 tsp oil, fry fenugreek seeds and asafoetida, remove, powder, set aside.

3. Pour rest of the oil into kadai. Heat oil, add mustard seeds; when done, the chillies and curry leaves. Add chilli powder, turmeric powder, mix, pour into vessel.

4. Add salt, lemon juice, the fenugreek seed-asafoetida powder, mix well.

Note

This preparation will keep for only 2-3 days. It is more like a salad – spicy!

Serve this with curd rice and salad.

Abbreviations

tbsp	Table spoon
tsp	Tea spoon
cup	Referred to a standard tea cup
Dalda/Pakav/ Vanaspathi	Brand name for vegetable shortening
min.	Minute
'sim'	simmer

Measurment

(A standard teacup has been used in the book)

Liquid meassure	1 cup = 5 oz =150 c.c.
Solid measure	Flour = 4 oz
	Butter = 8 oz are level
	Sugar = 8 oz
Conversion	1 oz = 25 gms

Oven temperature

Moderate:	350-375°F (177-190°C)
Hot:	425-450°F (218-233°C)
Very Hot:	475-500°F (246-260°C)

Yam

Yam is cultivated for its giant size tubers. It is not very popular as many people are allergic to it. Has good amount of carbohydrate and some vitamin and protein. Here are given 5 ways of preparation of yam in five different regions.

Preparations

1. **Senai Roast** (Tamil Nadu)
2. **Senegedda Pulusu** (Andhra Pradesh)
3. **Senai Eriseri** (Kerala)
4. **Jamikhand Gravy** (Punjab)
5. **Suran Kabab** (Parsi)

Senai Roast
(Roasted Yam)

Ingredients

½ kg yam
3-4 tbsp oil
2 sprigs curry leaves

Grind to paste

1 large onion
4 red chillies
½ tsp turmeric powder
Salt to taste

Add

3 cloves garlic (optional)
½ tsp aniseeds (optional)

Method

1. Wash and cut yam into very thin slices. Smear ground paste on pieces, leave aside for an hour.
2. Heat oil, add curry leaves, the yam pieces, fry on low heat turning all the while. If required very crisp, add extra oil and fry. Remove when brown and crisp.

Serve with rice and sambar or 'morkuzhambu'.

Note

This can be made in a simple way by smearing the pieces with chilli, turmeric powders and salt and frying as in step 2.

Senegedda Pulusu
(Yam Gravy with Spinach)

Ingredients

½ kg yam
   (about 2 cups, cubed)
2 cups chopped spinach
1 lemon size ball of tamarind
Salt to taste
A pinch of turmeric powder
2 tsp oil
1 tbsp sesame seeds, broiled and
   powdered separately (optional)

Grind to paste

1 tsp mustard seeds
2 tsp rice
3-4 red chillies

Seasoning

¼ tsp methi seeds
½ tsp mustard seeds
1 red chilli, broken
2 sprigs curry leaves

Method

1. Cut yam into small cubes, add turmeric powder, salt and enough water to cook.

2. When yam is almost done, add chopped spinach. Cook both together till soft.

3. Extract tamarind pulp by soaking it in boiling water. Add this along with ground paste to yam, simmer all together for 3-5 min.

4. Season in oil ingredients given, pour into 'pulusu'. Add powdered sesame seeds, mix, remove from fire.

Senai Eriseri
(Yam with Coconut and Pepper)

Ingredients

¼ kg yam
½ tsp turmeric powder
2 tbsp coconut gratings
Salt to taste
½ tbsp oil
½ tsp mustard seeds
2 sprigs curry leaves

Grind to fine paste

6 tbsp coconut gratings
2 green chillies
½ tsp pepper corns

Method

1. Wash, peel and cut yam into small pieces. Add turmeric powder, salt and water, cook till yam is soft.

2. Add ground paste, cook further, adding some water if too thick.

3. Heat oil, add mustard seeds and when done, curry leaves and coconut; fry on low heat to a dark brown. Add to eriseri, mix thoroughly.

Note

Same kind of preparation can be made with banana (raw), pumpkin, etc. – a very popular dish in Kerala.

Jamikhand Gravy
(Yam with Curds and Masala)

Ingredients

¼ kg jamikhand
1 tomato, chopped
½ tsp turmeric powder
½-1 tsp chilli powder
½ cup curds
2 tbsp chopped coriander leaves
2 tbsp ghee/oil
Salt to taste

Grind to paste
1 large onion
5 cloves garlic
3 green chillies
1 tsp cumin powder
Mix 1 tbsp lemon juice
   or 2 tsp tamarind juice

Method

1. Cut jamikhand into cubes, add turmeric powder and salt, boil till soft.

2. Heat ghee/oil, fry ground paste, adding chopped tomatoes, continue to fry till oil surfaces.

3. Add cooked vegetable, chilli powder and stir fry till masalas are well coated with the pieces.

4. Beat curds (add a pinch of sugar, if desired), mix in half the coriander leaves, pour into kadai, simmer till gravy is thick. Remove from fire; garnish with the rest of the coriander leaves.

Serve with chapathis.

Suran Kabab
(Yam Cutlets)

Ingredients

¼ kg suran
1 tbsp minced coriander leaves
1 tsp minced mint leaves
1 slice bread, crumbled
2 tsp lemon juice
Little flour
Oil for frying

Grind to paste

1 medium onion
4 cloves garlic
½" piece ginger
1 tsp cumin powder
1 tsp poppy seeds
½ tsp chilli powder
Salt to taste

Method

1. Peel, cut, boil and mash suran.
2. Add all ingredients (except oil and flour) to form a soft dough.
3. Make balls, flatten into a cutlet, roll in flour and deep fry to golden brown.

Serve very hot with mint chutney.

A Vegetables Verse

Carrots dangled before donkeys
Drumsticks beating tattoo, tattoo
Brinjals purple in the face
Onions sneezing Aitchoo!

Potatoes in their muddy jackets
Green chillies full of bite
Peas, so alike, in their pods
All now, stiff with fright.

What a turmoil they are in!
Can't you hear the racket?
Poor things, they are being carted
Off to the **vegetable** market.

Arms flailing, feet kicking,
You can hear them crying hoarse –
They don't want to be **dressed** for dinner
Or prepared for a course!

Packed off now in baskets big
On a long, bone-rattling ride
Contemplating their unhappy fate
That determined **cooks** will decide.

Skinned and **peeled** and **grated**
Chopped, **minced** and **sliced**
Cooked or **fried to a turn**
They wait to be **peppered** or **spiced**.

Throw a prayer for them all
To set their spirits free
While we smack our lips
    And dig into
The delicious golden curry!

– Prema Ramakrishnan

Zucchini

This vegetable is very common in the U.S.A. and Western countries but not known in ours. The nearest substitute for it among our vegetables is the smooth variety of ridge gourd. Given here are two western recipes for zucchini which may be tried with smooth gourd.

Preparations

1. **Zucchini Carrot Casserole**
2. **Zucchini topping for Pizza**

Zucchini-Carrot Casserole

Ingredients

6 small zucchini

2 small carrots

1 medium onion, minced

2-3 cloves garlic, crushed

$\frac{1}{2}$ cup grated cheese

3 tbsp butter

1 tsp dried herbs

$\frac{1}{2}$-1 tsp pepper powder

Salt to taste

A little fresh parsley or dill

Method

1. Wash and cut carrots and zucchini into circles.

2. Melt butter, add onion and garlic, fry to a light brown, add carrots, fry 2-3 min.

3. Add zucchini, continue to fry till vegetable becomes soft.

4. Add seasonings (except parsley), sprinkle some water, simmer 5-7 min. or till done. Add cheese, mix.

5. Pour cooked vegetables into a casserole dish, garnish with chopped parsley.

Zucchini topping for Pizza

Ingredients

2 cups chopped zucchini
1 onion, chopped
2-3 cloves garlic, minced
1 capsicum, thinly sliced
2 nos. pizza base

1 cup grated cheese
1-1½ cups tomato sauce
½ tsp pepper powder
½ tsp oregano
2 tbsp butter
Salt to taste

Method

1. Melt butter, add garlic and onion, fry till pink; add capsicum, stir fry. Add zucchini, fry on low heat till soft.

2. Add seasonings and oregano, simmer 1-2 min. more.

3. Divide zucchini into 2 portions, spread one portion on one pizza base, cover with tomato sauce; cover sauce layer with half of the cheese. Make the second one in the same way

4. Bake in a moderate oven for 20 min. or till cheese melts.

Serve hot with a salad.

Glossary

English	Bengali	Gujarathi	Hindi	Kannada
Amaranth	Baropata nate	Tandaljo	Chawlai ka sag or Lal sag	Yele dantu
Aniseeds	Mowri	Saunf	Sounf	Sompu
Asafoetida	Hingh	Hingh	Hingh	Hingu
Ash Gourd	Chal kumra	–	Petha	Boodhkumblekai
Banana (Raw)	Kela	Kela	Kacha kela	Balekai
Bay leaf	Tejpatta	Tejpatta	Tejpatta	Biriyani ele
Beet root	Beet	Beet	Chuquandar	Beet
Bengal gram dal	Cholar dal	Channa	Channe ki dal	Kadale bele
Bitter Gourd	Karela	Karela	Karela	Hagalkai
Black gram dal	Kolai dal	Udad ni dal	Urad dal	Uddine bele
Bottle gourd	Lau	Doodhi	Lauki	Sorekai
Brinjal	Baigan	Ringan	Baigan	Badnekai
Broad Beans	Sem	Papadi	Badhisem	Chappradavarai
Buttermilk	Lossi	-	Lassi	Majjige
Cabbage	Band gobi	Kobich	Patha gobi	Kossu
Caraway seeds	-	-	Shajeera	-
Cardamom	Elaichi	Elaichi	Elaychi	Yelakki
Carrot	Gajar	Gajar	Gajar	Carrot
Cashew nut	Kaju	Kaju	Kaju	Godambi
Cauliflower	Phool gobi	Phule kobi	Phool gobi	Hookosu
Cinnamon	Dalchini	Dalchini	Dalchini	Chakke
Clarified butter	Ghee	Ghee	Ghee	Thuppa
Cloves	Labang	Lavang	Lavang	Lavanga
Cluster Beans	Sem	Gavar singh	Govar	Gori kai
Coconut	Narkol	Nariel	Nariel	Thenginkai
Colocasia	Arvi	Arvi-na-ganthi	Arvi	Samegedde
Coriander leaves	Dhanesag	Kothmer	Hara dania	Kothmiri soppu
Coriander seeds	Dhane	Dhana	Dhania	Kothambari beeja
Corn	Bhutta	Makka or Bhutta	Bhutta or Makka	Mushkinjola

Malayalam	Marathi	Tamil	Telugu	Oriya
Cheera	Math	Mulaikeerai	Thota kora	Khada saga
Perinjeerakam	Badishep	Perunjeeragam	Perinjeerakam	Paru kakharu
Kayam	Hing	Perungayam	Hinguva	-
Elavan	Kohela	Pushinikai	Budedagummidi	Ada
Vazhakka	Kachya kela	Vazhaikai	Aratikayi	Kadali
-	Tejpatta	Brinji ilai	Biriyani akku	Tej patta
Beet root	Beet	Manjal mullangi	Pechcha mullangi	Bita
Kadala paruppu	Hurbura	Kadalai paruppu	Sanage pappu	Buta
Kayppakka	Karli	Pagakkai	Kakara kaya	Bada kalara
Uzhunnu	Udad dal	Ulatham paruppu	Minappu	Biri
Churakkai	Dudhiya	Sorakkai	Surakaya	Lau
Vazhuthinga	Wangee	Katharikai	Vankayi	Baigana
Avarakka	Rund Gevada	Avarakai	Pedda chikkudu	Simba
Mor	-	Mor	Machige	-
Muttagos	Kobi	Muttakos	Goskura	Bandha kobi
-	-	-	-	-
Elathari	Velchi	Yelakkai	Elakkayi	Alaichi
Karat	Gajar	Carrot	Pechcha Mullangi	Gajara
Parangiyandi	Kaju	Mundhiri paruppu	Jeedi pappu	-
Kaliflower	Gobicheppal	Pookos	Kosu gadda	Phulkobi
Patta	Dalchini	Pattai	Lavanga patta	-
Nei	Ghee	Nei	Nei	-
Karambu	Lavang	Krambu	Endu lavangalu	Labang
Kothavara	Govari	Kottavarangai	Goruchekkadu kayalu	Guanra
Thenga	Nariel	Thengai	Gobbari kayi	Nadia
Chembu	Alukhanda gandhi	Cheppan-kizhangu	Chama dumpa	Saruwada
Kothamalli	Kothmir	Pachai kothamalli	Kotthimiri	Dhania
Kothamalli	Dhana	Kothamalli vidhai	Dhaniyalu	Dania
Cholam	Maka	Makkacholam	Mokka jonnalu	Kancha maka

English	Bengali	Gujarathi	Hindi	Kannada
Cottage cheese	Paneer	Paneer	Paneer	-
Cucumber	Sasha	Kakadi	Kakari	Southekai
Cumin seeds	Jeera	Jeera	Zira	Jeerage
Curds	Doi	Dahi	Dahi	Mosaru
Curry leaf	Bursunga	Mithe limbdo	Mita neem	Karibevina soppu
Drum stick	Sajanadanta	Sangveni Singh	Shinghphali	Nuggekai
Fenugreek leaves	Methi sag	Methi sag	Methi sag	Menthesoppu
Fenugreek seeds	Methi	Meethi	Methi	Menthya
Flat Beans	-	Wal papdi	Ghiyasem	Honagithe avarekai
French Beans	-	Fausi	Sem	Hurali kai
Garlic	Lasoon	Lasan	Lasoon	Bellulli
Ginger	Ade	Adhu	Adrak	Hasi sonti
Gram flour	Besun	Besan	Besan	Kadale hittu
Green chilli	Kamba launka	Lila mircha	Hari mirchi	Menesinekai
Green gram dal	Mug dal	Mug ni dal	Moong dal	Hesaru bele
Green peas	Mutter	Vatana	Mutter	Battani
Greens	Sag	-	Sag	Soppu
Ground nuts	Chana badam	Boi singh	Moongh falli	Kadalekai
Jack fruit	Kanthal	Phanas	Katahal	Halasinakai
Jaggery	Gur	Gur	Gur	Bella
Knol-khol	Nulkol	Mula	Khol rabi	knol-knol
Lady's finger	Bhendi	Bhendi	Bhindi	Bendekayi
Lemon	Nimbu	Limbu	Nimbu	Nimbe hannu
Mango powder	-	-	Amchoor	-
Mango (Raw)	Kaccha am	Keri	Keri	Mavinakai
Mint	Pudeena sag	Fudina	Pudina	Podeena soppy
Mustard seeds	Sharse	Rai	Rai	Sasve
Nutmeg	Jaiphal	-	Jaiphal	Jathikai
Onion	Pyaz	Dungli	Pyaj	Irulli
Onion seeds	Kalajeera	-	Kali jeera	-
Pepper corn	Gol mirch	Kali mari	Kali mirch	Karimensu

Malayalam	Marathi	Tamil	Telugu	Oriya
-	Paneer	-	-	-
Vellari	Kakadi	Vellarikai	Dosakaya	Kakudi
Jeerakam	Jhere	Jeeragam	Jeela kara	Jira
Thair	Teak	Thair	Machage	-
Kariveppila	Kadi limb	Kariveppilai	Karivepaku	Brusunga patra
Muringe kaya	Shevgyachya shenga	Murungaikai	Mulagakada	Sajane danta
-	Methi sag	Venthia keerai	Menthulu aka	Methi sag
Uluka	Methi	Venthayam	Menthulu	Methi
	Papadi	Mochakka	-	-
Seema avare	Pharasbi	Beans	Beans	Beans
Vella mulla	Lasoon	Ulli poondu	Vellulli	Rasuna
Inji	Ale	Inji	Allam	Ada
Kadale mavu	Besun	Kadali mavu	-	-
Pache milakai	-	Pacchai milagai	Pachimirapakayi	Kancha lauka
Cheru payaru	Mug dal	Payatham paruppu	Pesaru pappu	Mung dal
Pattani	-	Pattani	Pach pattani	Matara
Cheera	Bhajee	Keerai	Koora	Sag
Nelakadala	Shengh dana	Verkadalai	Verusanaga kayi	China badam
Chakka	Phanas	Palakkai	Panasa	Panasa katha
Sarakara	Gur	Vellam	Bellam	-
Nool-kol	Mula	Knol-knol	Knol-knol	Ul kobi
Vendakka	Bhendi	Vendakkai	Bendekayi	Bhendi
Cheru narenga	Limbu	Elumicham pazham	Nimma pandu	Lembu
-	-	-	-	-
Pacha manga	Amba kaccha	Mangai	Manvidi kayi	Kaccha amba
Mootha	Pudina	Pudeena	Pothina	Pudana patre
Kaduku	Moheri	Kadugu	Avalu	Sorisa
-	-	Jathikai		
Ulli	Khanda	Vengayam	Peddairulli	Piaja
-	-	Karunjeeragam	-	Kala jeera
Kurumolegu	Mire	Milagu	Hiriyalu	Gol marcha

English	Bengali	Gujarathi	Hindi	Kannada
Poppy seeds	Posto	Khus-khus	Khus-khus	Gas-gase
Potato	Aloo	Batata	Alu	Alugedde
Pumpkin	Kumda	Kolu	Kaddu	Seekumblekai
Radish	Mula	Mugari	Muli	Mullangi
Raisins	Kismis	Draksh	Kismis	Drakshee
Red chilli	Sukha lauki	Sukvele mircha	Lal mirchi	Vonamenasina kayi
Red gram	Musuri dol	Masoor dal	Masoor ki dal	Masur bele
Refined flour	Maida	Maida	Maida	Maida hittu
Ridge Gourd	Jhinga	Turiya padawal	Turai	Heera kai
Saffron	-	-	Kesar	-
Semolina	Sujj or rawa	Suji	Suji	Rave
Sesame seeds	Til	Til	Til	Ellu
Snake Gourd	Chuchinga	Padawal	-	Padaval kai
Spinach	Palak	Palak	Palak	Chegothene soppu
Tamarind	Tentul	Amli	Imli	Hunusehannu
Thymol	-	-	Ajwain	Omha
Tomato	Bilayathi baigan	Tamato	Vilayathi baigan	Tomato
Turmeric	Halud	Halad	Haldi	Arshana
Wheat flour	Atta	Atta	Gehu ka atta	Godhihittu
White beans	Barbatti	-	Chawlai (lobia)	Alasandhi
White chick pea	Chole	Chana	Kabuli chana	Kadalekallu
Yam	Ol	Suran	Jamikhand	Chooranagedde
Yellow lentils	Arahar dal	Tuvarni dal	Tur dal	Thogari bele

Note:

1. For popular usage, in some cases, English terms have been retained for the ethnic terms.
2. The main source of the Glossary is Home Science Text.

Malayalam	Marathi	Tamil	Telugu	Oriya
Khasa khasa	Khus-khus	Khasa-khasa	Gasa gasalu	-
Urula kizhangu	Batata	Urulai kizhangu	Urula gaddah	Alu
-	Lal bhopla	Parangikai	Gummudi kaya	Kakkaru
Mullangi	Mula	Mullangi	Mullangi	Mula
Unnaka munthringa	Manuka	Draksha pazham	Kisi misu	Kismis
Kappal mulaku	Mirchi lal	Milagai vattal	Endi miripikayi	Sukhila lauka
Masura payaru	-	Mysore paruppu	Misur pappu	Masura
Maida	Maida	Maida mavu	Maida	Maida
Peechinga	Shital or Dodera	Pirkangkai	Berakai	Janhi
-	-	Kunkuma poo	-	-
Rava	Rawe	Ravai	Rava	Soji
Ellu	Til	Ellu	Nuvvulu	-
Padvalanga	Palwal	Podalangai	Potlakayi	Chachindra
Vasala cheera	Palak	Seemai pasalai keerai	Dumba bucchale	Palanga saga
Puli	Chincha	Puli	Chintha pandu	Tentuli
-	Owa	Omam	-	-
Thakkali	Tomato	Thakkali	Seema Vanakayi	Bilati baigana
Manjal	Halad	Manjal	Pasupu	Haladi
-	Atta	Godumai mavu	-	-
Achinga payar	Kuleeth	Karamani	Alachandalu	Chani
Kadala	Hurbura	Punjabi kadalai (Kondai kadalai)	Sanagalu	Buta
Chena	Suran	Senai kizhangu	Kanda	Kambachu
Tuvaram paruppu	Tur chi dal	Tuvaram paruppu	Kandlu pappu	-

Index

A

Alu ka Tehri 259, 267
Alu Parathas 260, 268
Alu Tikkies 260, 273
Alu-Baigan Jhol 259, 266
Alu-Baigan Tharkari 259, 265
Amaranthus 1
Arvi Cutlet/Roast 117, 120
ASH GOURD 158
Avaraikai Paruppu Curry 17, 19
Aviyal 318, 337

B

Badanekai Gojju 43, 46
Baigan Burta 43, 53
Baigan Dali 44, 57
Baigan-Alu Charchari 44, 56
Baked Potatoes 260, 277
Banana (Raw) 7
Banana Flower Gravy 7, 10
Batata nu Shak 260, 269
Batata Vada 260, 270
Beans 17
Beans Ambat 18, 33
Beans Casserole 18, 30
Beans Curry 18, 28
Beans Soup 18, 29
Beans-Potato Stew 18, 28
Beet root 35
Beet root Aspic Salad 35, 42
Beet root Coconut Chutney 35, 39
Beet root Coconut Dry Curry 35, 36
Beet root Cutlets 35, 40
Beet root Halwa 35, 41
Beet root in Coconut Milk 35, 37
Beet root Parathas 35, 40
Beet root Salad (Boiled) 35, 38
Beet root Salad (Raw) 35, 38
Beet root Thair Pachadi 35, 36
Bendekai Gojju 219, 221
Bhagara Baigan 43, 52
Bhendi Fry 219, 222
Bhendi Masala Gravy 219, 223
BITTER GOURD 158

Boodhkumblekai Kootu 158, 162
BOTTLE GOURD 159
Bottle Gourd Stew in Milk 159, 169
Brinjal 43
Brinjal in Curds Gravy 44, 55
Brinjal Moilee 43, 50
Brinjals baked in Vegetable Sauce 44, 58
BROAD BEANS 17
Brown Onion Soup 232, 238
Bussar 192, 194

C

Cabbage 61
Cabbage Au-gratin 62, 73
Cabbage Banvade 61, 66
Cabbage Cutlet 61, 69
Cabbage Gashi 61, 65
Cabbage Koftas in Peas Gravy 61, 71
Cabbage Muthia 61, 67
Cabbage Pan Rolls 62, 75
Cabbage Rasedar 61, 68
Cabbage Sadam 61, 63
Cabbage Salad 62, 74
Cabbage Soup 61, 72
Cabbage Stew 61, 64
Cabbage Thoran 61, 64
Capsicum 77
Capsicum Besan - Dry or Gravy Curry 77, 81
Capsicum Gojju 77, 81
Capsicum in Coconut Milk 77, 80
Capsicum Salad/Raitha 77, 79
Capsicum Shahi Pulav 77, 78
Carrot 89
Carrot Cutlets 89, 95
Carrot Dhokla 90, 98
Carrot Kosamalli 90, 102
Carrot Poli 89, 92
Carrot Puris 89, 96
Carrot Raisin Loaf 89, 93
Carrot Rasam 90, 100
Carrot Rice 90, 99
Carrot Salad 89, 94
Carrot Soup 89, 94
Carrot Sundal 90, 101
Carrot-Cashew Payasam 89, 92

Cauliflower 103
Cauliflower & Noodles baked in Tomato Sauce 103, 116
Cauliflower Au-gratin (Indian Style) 103, 113
Cauliflower baked in Cheese Sauce 103, 114
Cauliflower Dry Curry 103, 105
Cauliflower Garam Masala Kootu 103, 106
Cauliflower Kheer 103, 112
Cauliflower Pakodas in Gravy 103, 111
Cauliflower Puris 103, 110
Cauliflower Rice 103, 104
Cauliflower Soup 103, 112
Cauliflower Sour Cream Salad 103, 115
Cauliflower Stew 103, 105
Cauliflower-Potato with Greens 103, 107
Chawlai ka sag 1, 5
CLUSTER BEANS 17
Colocasia 117
CORIANDER LEAVES 202
Coriander Rice 202, 203
Coriander-Coconut Chutney 202, 203
Cream of Vegetable Soup 317, 319
Cucumber 123
Cucumber Aspic Salad 123, 124
Cucumber Cold Soup 123, 124
Cucumber Cups - with Curds-Cheese Filling 123, 126
Cucumber Kosamalli 123, 127
Cucumber Salad 123, 125
Curry Leaf-Garlic Chutney Powder 202, 204
CURRY LEAVES 202

D

DILL 202
Dill-Potato Pancakes 202, 207
Doodhi Muthias 159, 171
DOUBLE BEANS 17
Double Beans Layered Rice 17, 23
Double Beans Masala Gravy 17, 24
Drumstick 131
Drumstick Flower Dry Curry 131, 132
Drumstick Fry 131, 135
Drumstick in Coconut Cream 131, 134
Drumstick Leaf Adai 131, 136
Drumstick Leaves with Sprouted Moong 131, 132
Drumstick Sambar 131, 133
Dum Arvi 117, 122
Dum Vegetables 318, 333

E

Egg plant Parmesan 44, 60
Ennai Katharikai 43, 47
Erulli Gojju 232, 234

F

Fenugreek Leaves 137
FIELD BEANS 18
FLAT BEANS 18
FRENCH BEANS 18
Fresh Tomato Sauce baked with Pasta/Eggs 300, 313
Fried Brinjal Slices 44, 56
Fried Karela - Plain or Spicy 158, 167

G

Gajar Masala 89, 97
Gajar-Badam Halwa 89, 91
GARLIC 148
Garlic Chutney 148, 150
Garlic Potatoes 259, 266
Garlic Rice 148, 149
Garlic Toast/Croutons 148, 151
Garlic, Ginger & Green Chillies 147
GINGER 148
Ginger Lemon 148, 152
Gourds 157
Green Bean Salad 18, 31
GREEN CHILLIES 148
Green Chillies Gojju (Chutney) 148, 154
Green Papaya and Green Gram Gravy 241, 242
Green Papaya Curry 241, 242
Green Papaya Paratha 241, 244
Green Peas in Coconut Gravy 245, 250
Green Peas Soup 245, 252
Green Potatoes - Parsi Style 260, 272
Greens 191
Greens Ambat 192, 197
Greens with Moong Dal 192, 196

H

Hagalkai Gojju 158, 165
Herbs 201

I

Idhukubele Sar 18, 26

Inji Pachadi 148, 152
Inji Rasam 148, 153

J

Jack fruit 209
Jack fruit Cutlet 209, 214
Jack fruit Seed Dry Curry 209, 212
Jamikhand Gravy 341, 344
Jhinga-Posto Charchari 159, 184

K

Kachi-Kerry-nu Shak 225, 229
Kadai Vegetable 318, 332
Kakadi Raitha 123, 126
Karbeva Sar 202, 205
Karela Nawabi 158, 168
Karuveppilai Kuzhambu 202, 205
Kashi Halwa 158, 163
Kathal Masala 209, 213
Katharikai Thair Pachadi and Baigan Raitha 43, 49
Keerai Kootu 1, 2
Keerai Kuzhambu 1, 2
Keerai Masiyal 1, 3
Keerai Pachadi 1, 4
Keerai Sadam 192, 193
Keerai Thoran 1, 4
Khandha Besan 232, 236
Knol-khol Coconut Dry Curry 215, 216
Knol-khol Tomato Gravy 215, 217
Knol-khol 215
Kothavarangai Paruppu Usli 17, 21
Kothavarangai Thoran 17, 22

L

Lady's Finger 219
Lauki Kheer 159, 173
Lauki Koftas in Tomato Gravy 159, 172
Lauki Parathas 159, 174
Lauki Raitha 159, 173
Lauki-Chana Dal in Coconut Milk 159, 170
Lettuce with Peas 192, 200
LIMA BEANS) 18
Lobia Gravy 18, 32

M

Mangai Pachadi 225, 226

Mangai Sadam 225, 226
Mango (Raw) 225
Mango Curry 225, 228
Mango Dal 225, 227
Mango-Coconut Chutney/Pachadi 225, 229
Mango-Mint Cooler 225, 230
Masala Arvi - Dry or Gravy 117, 121
Masala Bath 245, 249
Masoppu Sar 192, 195
Mathan Eriseri 159, 177
Mathan Puli Pachadi 159, 177
Methi-Alu 138, 143
Methi-Besan Dry Curry 138, 142
Methi-Gajar 138, 143
Methi-Moong Dal 138, 141
Methi-Muthias 138, 144
Mexican Rice 77, 86
MINT 202
Mirch-ke-salan 148, 155
Mochakka Sundal 18, 25
Moglai Vegetable 318, 331
Muli ka sag 192, 198
Muli Kadhi 279, 284
Muli Rotis 279, 283
Mullangi Kosamalli 279, 280
Mutter Ghanta 245, 251
Mutter Pulav 245, 246
Mutter-Paneer 245, 247

O

Onion 231
Onion Leaves with Potatoes 192, 199
Onion Pulav with Coconut Milk 232, 237
Onion-Potato/Egg Casserole 232, 239

P

Padavalkai Kootu 160, 186
Pagakkai Pitlai 158, 164
Palak Paneer 288
Palak-Chana 285, 287
Palak-Methi Parathas 285, 290
Palak-Methi Pulav 285, 286
Palak-Paneer 285, 288
Palakkai Curry 209, 210
Palakkai-Thengaipal Kootu 209, 211
Paneer Stuffed Brinjal 43, 54
Paneer Stuffed Cabbage Rolls 61, 70
Papaya 241

Papaya Parathas 241
Pappali Kootu 241, 243
Parangikai Palkootu 159, 175
Patrel 117, 118
Pattani Sundal 245, 251
Pavakkai Moilee 158, 165
Peas 245
Peas in Potato Cups 245, 253
Peerkangkai Chutney 159, 182
Peerkangkai Paruppu 159, 183
Phool Gobi-Alu Charchari 103, 108
Phool Gobi-Alu Rasedar 103, 109
Pickled Cucumber 123, 130
Pineapple 255
Pineapple Gojju 255, 257
Pineapple Rasam 255, 258
Pineapple-Coconut Milk Stew 255, 256
Poi sag with Garlic 192, 197
Poondu Rasam 148, 150
Potato 259
Potato Cold Salad 260, 278
Potato Croquette 260, 275
Potato Khorma - Moglai Style 260, 271
Potato Moilee 259, 263
Potato Pie 260, 276
Potato Podimas 259, 261
Potato Rabdi 260, 274
Potato Roast 259, 264
Potato Sagale 259, 262
Potato Soup 260, 275
Pudalangai Thair Pachadi 160, 185
Pudeena Chutney (North Indian Style) 202, 207
Pudeena Chutney (South Indian Style) 202, 207
Puli Inji 148, 154
PUMPKIN 159
Pumpkin - Sweet and Sour 159, 178
Pumpkin Halwa 159, 180
Pumpkin Khorma 159, 179
Pumpkin-Nut Pie 159, 181
Pushanikai Morkuzhambu 158, 161
Pyaj Kachumber/Raitha 232, 238

R

Radish 279
Radish Foogath 279, 281
Radish with Moong Dal 279, 282
Rasavanghi 43, 48
Raw Banana Koftas in Gravy 7, 14
Raw Banana Stuffed Parathas 7, 15

RIDGE GOURD 159

S

Sabbakki Amavadas 202, 206
Sarson ka sag 192, 199
Seekumblekai Gojju 159, 176
Sembu Elai Usli 117, 119
Senai Eriseri 341, 343
Senai Roast 341, 342
Senegedda Pulusu 341, 343
Shells baked in Capsicum Sauce 77, 85
Sindhi Palak 285, 289
SNAKE GOURD 160
Sorakkai Kootu 159, 169
Southekai Ambat 123, 128
Southekai Mosuru Gojju 123, 128
Spaghetti Spinach 285, 292
Spaghetti-Peas 245, 253
Spicy Beans Gravy 17, 20
Spicy Peas Parathas 245, 248
Spicy Spinach Soup 285, 290
Spinach 285
Spinach-Cheese Cutlets 285, 294
Spinach Cups 285, 293
Spinach Florentine 285, 291
Stuffed Bhendi 219, 224
Stuffed Capsicum 77, 82
    a) Chana Dal 77, 83
    b) Eggs-Cheese 77, 84
    c) Peas-Paneer 77, 84
    d) Rice-Peas 77, 85
Stuffed egg plant (Brinjals) 44, 59
Stuffed Karela 158, 166
Stuffed Padaval 160, 187
Stuffed Tomatoes 300
    – North Indian Style - Fried 300, 303
    – Western Style - Baked 300, 304
Suran Kabab 341, 345
Sukha/Surthi Papdi 18, 27
Sweet Potato 295
Sweet Potato Casserole 295, 298
Sweet Potato Paratha 295, 297
Sweet Potato with Garlic 295
Sweet Potato-Coconut Dry Curry 295

T

Theeyal 232, 235
Tomato 299

Tomato Aspic Salad 300, 314
Tomato Biriyani 300, 301
Tomato Flowers 300, 315
Tomato Kasaundi 300, 311
Tomato Khatta 300, 309
Tomato Kurma 300, 302
Tomato Kuzhhambu 300, 306
Tomato Pitla 300, 309
Tomato Raisin Chutney 300, 310
Tomato Raitha and Pachadi 300, 305
Tomato Rasam 300, 307
Tomato Soup with Coconut Milk Sauce 300, 312
Tomato Stew 300, 308
Turai Tomato 159, 183

V

Vangi Bath 43, 45
Vankai Pachadi 43, 51
Vazaikai Milaguttal 13
Vazhai thandu Dry Curry/Thair Pachadi 7, 8
Vazhaikai Eriseri 7, 11
Vazhaikai Kalan 7, 11
Vazhaikai Milaguttal 7, 13
Vazhaikai Podimas 7, 12
Vazhaikai Roast 7, 13
Vazhaippu Paruppu Usli 7, 9
Vegetable Au-gratin 317, 321
Vegetable Biriyani 318, 334
Vegetable Exotica 317, 320
Vegetable Gourmet 317, 324
Vegetable Kachumber 318, 334

Vegetable Kootu 318, 338
Vegetable Kurma 318, 335
VEGETABLE MARROW 160
Vegetable Marrow - Sweet and Sour 160, 188
Vegetable Marrow Puri 160, 189
Vegetable Marrow Soup 160, 188
Vegetable Medley 317, 322
Vegetable Navratan 318, 339
Vegetable Noodles 317, 325
Vegetable Pancakes 317, 327
Vegetable Rice 317, 329
Vegetable Stew with Milk 318, 336
Vegetable-Paneer Casserole 317, 330
Vegetables 317
Vegetables - Sweet and Sour 317, 326
Vellarikai Puli Kuzhambu 123, 129
Vendakkai Curry and Thair Pachadi 219, 220
Vendhia Keerai Masala Morkuzhambu 138, 145
Vendhia Keerai Paruppu 138, 140
Vendhia Keerai Sadam 138, 139
Vengaya Kara Kuzhambu 232, 233

Y

Yam 341

Z

Zucchini 347
Zucchini Carrot Casserole 347, 348
Zucchini topping for Pizza 347, 349